WITHD

ACRL PUBLICATIONS IN LIBRARIANSHIP NO. 69

Creating LEADERS:

An Examination of Academic and Research Library Leadership Institutes

Edited by
Irene M.H. Herold

Association of College and Research Libraries
A division of the American Library Association
Chicago, Illinois 2015

The paper used in this publication meets the minimum requirements of American National Standard for Information Sciences–Permanence of Paper for Printed Library Materials, ANSI Z39.48-1992. ∞

Library of Congress Cataloging-in-Publication Data

Creating leaders : an examination of academic and research library leadership institutes / edited by Irene M.H. Herold.
    pages cm
  Includes bibliographical references.
  ISBN 978-0-8389-8763-6 (pbk.) -- ISBN 978-0-8389-8765-0 (epub) -- ISBN 978-0-8389-8764-3 (pdf) -- ISBN 978-0-8389-8766-7 (Kindle) 1. Library institutes and workshops. 2. Library institutes and workshops--United States. 3. Librarians--In-service training. 4. Academic librarians--In-service training. 5. Library administrators--In-service training. 6. Library administration--Study and teaching (Continuing education) 7. Leadership--Study and teaching (Continuing education) I. Herold, Irene M. H.
  Z668.5.C72 2015
  020.71'55--dc23
                              2015029380

Printed in the United States of America.

19 18 17 16 15 5 4 3 2 1

Table of Contents

Foreword

Maureen Sullivan

IN THE FIRST chapter of *Leadership: Theory and Practice* (now in its sixth edition), author Peter Northouse makes the point that the word *leadership* has a variety of different definitions and a set of common components. From these components—"leadership is a process," "leadership involves influence," "leadership occurs in groups," and "leadership involves common goals"—Northouse crafted this definition of leadership: Leadership is a process whereby an individual influences a group of individuals to achieve a common goal. This definition describes how much of the work is accomplished in academic libraries today. Given that this work is done in a context of continuing transformational change and complexity, the need for effective, focused leadership is great and the means to ensure leadership development is essential.

In the past 30 years, the field has increasingly recognized the importance of targeted programs for this leadership development. The first of these were designed and offered by the Association of Research Libraries and evolved from their Management Skills Institutes. This book, *Creating Leaders: An Examination of Academic Library Leadership Institutes,* describes 18 programs that have been created to fulfill not only a need but also a growing demand for formal education and training programs. Managers and administrators in most academic libraries today recognize the importance of developing the leadership capabilities of their staff and are willing to invest in this effort. Individuals themselves also value education to improve their own leadership abilities. Many understand that leadership is both formal—appointed by virtue of the position held—and informal—assumed by an individual who sees an opportunity and takes the initiative to lead. Northouse describes these two forms of leadership as "assigned leadership and emergent leadership."

Both are found throughout academic libraries today.

Investment in the development of our leaders, both current and future, is critical to our success and the success of the students, faculty, and scholars we serve. As we continue to make the transition to a digital future, we need leaders with the knowledge, abilities, and drive to transform our organizations. Ron Heifetz calls for *the practice of adaptive leadership,* an approach in which we "continuously adapt to new realities." This approach requires that individuals "lead with the courage and skill to challenge the status quo, deploy themselves with agility, and mobilize others to step into the unknown." This practice requires a very different set of abilities than many first bring to their professional practice. The number and variety of leadership development programs that have been created in the past 25 years, including those described in this book, are an acknowledgment and strong response to this need.

The chapters in this book discuss within a common framework the major programs that now exist. It also accomplishes another more important purpose: It effectively illuminates what needs to be done to ensure we will have the leaders needed for future success and sustainability. This work includes finding a means to capture and publish evidence that participants have improved their skills and abilities; conducting research to determine if there is a correlation between participation and performance improvement and career progression; determining if the programs follow their stated objectives and if the participants learned what the objectives promised; developing a standard approach to program assessment that is consistently applied; defining a set of essential leadership competencies that might comprise the core curriculum for any program; and determining a set of best practices and principles for the design and execution of a program. It also includes a careful examination of the four most commonly referenced leadership theories or models: change management, transformative or transformational leadership, emotional intelligence, and being able to employ frame flipping. In the final chapter, the set of components found to be common across the programs is discussed.

This book is timely and essential for understanding how the field can ensure that academic and research libraries will have the necessary leadership and strong leaders to meet the challenges and to take advantage of the opportunities ahead. It is the foundation that library leaders, educators and practitioners need to understand and develop the programs and strategies that will be so critical to our success.

Introduction

Irene M.H. Herold

IN A LIBRARY career, there are many stages where individuals are asked to assume a leadership role or position. Helping develop individuals to meet these needs is a goal of many leadership development programs, whether aimed at new career, mid-career, or senior-career librarians. This work examines 18 leadership development programs that are either exclusively for academic and research librarians or include them in their participant groups. It does not purport to be an all-inclusive review of every academic and research librarian leadership development program; rather it is a sampling across a broad spectrum of programs. There are programs developed and managed by a single library, operated by a regional entity, or run by national organizations or associations.

Defining Leadership

Defining the concept of modern leadership may be traced back to James MacGregor Burns' 1978 definition of transformational leadership, linking leaders and followers and focusing on leaders who use the values and motives of followers to achieve goals.[1] John P. Kotter further defined leadership as establishing direction by creating a vision; aligning people to carry out that vision through communication and the creation of support coalitions; motivating and inspiring people to overcome barriers to change, whether political or resource-based; and then producing change, often to a dramatic degree.[2] This was compared to management, which Kotter characterized as planning, budgeting, organizing, staffing, controlling, and problem solving to produce a degree of predictability and stability in an organization.[3]

While some early leadership theories, such as trait theory, focused on skill sets that leaders held in common, leadership development theories now incorporate concepts of emotional intelligence, resonant leadership, and mindful leadership to describe the internal emotional growth of leaders as they develop.[4] Emotional intelligence (EI) was first popularized by Daniel Goleman, who characterized EI as the ability to manage the mood of an organization in two broad areas: personal and social competencies. Within these competencies are five components: self-awareness, self-regulation, motivation, empathy, and social skill.[5] According to Goleman, an EI leader understands the power of emotions in the workplace and uses this learned ability to be more effective than a leader who lacks EI. Followers perceive EI leaders as more caring and empathetic than other leaders, and therefore, the EI leader motivates followers to work beyond expectations.

Resonant leadership incorporates EI and adds renewal, or leader self-care, which is required to prevent burnout and sustain effectiveness.[6] Mindful leadership is an aspect of resonant leadership, which emphasizes the connection between the brain and leadership. It focuses on being in the moment and paying attention to the nurture and nature of intelligence when influencing others toward achievement, providing a compelling purpose, and guiding principles as opposed to using a universal prescription.[7] Mindful leaders lessen stress, promote community and communication, generate engagement, lower anxiety, provide access to information, encourage questioning of assumptions, and cultivate open minds. While EI, resonant leadership, and mindful leadership theories fit with Kotter's definition for motivating and inspiring followers, EI is focused less on external barriers and resources and more on self and others' emotional awareness. This awareness allows the leader to be successful.

The Essential Questions

How does a potential participant know if a leadership development program actually develops leadership? What does a leadership program develop—skills, abilities, self-reflection, knowledge? Or some combination? If asked by a chief academic officer to provide documentation that investing in sending librarians to a leadership program will result in leadership development, what proof could be provided? Unfortunately, there has been no study completed that could answer that question.

There have been overviews that list programs, such as the seminal article, "Learning to Lead: An Analysis of Current Training Programs for Library Leadership," in 2004 by Florence M. Mason and Louella V. Wetherbee.[8] An important new study, "Training the 21st Century Library Leader," by Katherine Skinner and Nick Krabbenhoeft, is a work-in-progress examining library leadership programs for all kinds of librarians.[9] Unlike this text, Skinner and Krabbenhoeft were unable to examine the curriculum of the programs included in their study. While there is some overlap between that study and this book due to the limited number of leadership programs, the two should be seen as complementary works. There are programs examined in this work that have not been included in the Skinner and Krabbenhoeft study and vice versa. However, no study to date has focused on examining whether the multiple programs that academic and research librarians participate in actually develop leadership.

Structure of the Chapters

This book surveys 18 library leadership programs, with chapter authors including information about the history of the program, what the program's curriculum contained, and a literature review of what has been written about the program. The contributing authors were all past participants of the programs they cover. They were encouraged to include a description of their personal experience attending the program and any evidence they had of personal leadership development as a result of the program. The authors were also asked to include any leadership theories or best practices espoused by the program and had the option to include a study of the program. They conclude with thoughts on how to improve the program or what was of enduring value. The chapters' contents are as varied as the programs and the individuals who participated.

Organization of the Book

This book is organized into five parts representing different program types: programs aimed generally at academic librarians; programs that focus on a specific type of library or position within libraries; and programs that include librarians but do not entirely comprise of librarians. Within each part, chapters are presented in alphabetical order according to the lead author's last name.

PART ONE: A PROGRAM FOR ALL TYPES OF ACADEMIC LIBRARIES

The first chapter discusses the Leadership Institute for Academic Librarians, a program that any academic librarian with leadership or management responsibilities may participate in. This program is sponsored by the Association of College and Research Libraries and the Harvard School of Graduate Education. Anne Marie Casey explores the program's content and provides a case study that reflects the application of the leadership frames learned during the program.

PART TWO: PROGRAMS FOR SPECIFIC TYPES OF ACADEMIC LIBRARIES

The second part focuses on programs for specific types of academic libraries. Leland R. Deeds and Miranda Bennett examine the American Theological Library Association's Creating the Leaders of Tomorrow program, which focuses on practical management skills within the context of leading change. This is followed by my look at the College Library Directors' Mentor Program, designed for new small college library directors. Monika Rhue writes about the Historically Black Colleges and Universities' (HBCU) Library Alliance Leadership Institute, which has an overall goal of ensuring success of HBCU libraries. Jeff Williams and Jennifer McKinnell present the final chapter in this part, examining the National Library of Medicine (NLM) and Association of Academic Health Sciences Libraries' (AAHS) Leadership Fellows Program. This program is highly selective and competitive with a focus on those in the health sciences field of librarianship.

PART THREE: PROGRAMS FOR ARL AND LARGE RESEARCH LIBRARIES

The third part focuses on Association of Research Libraries (ARL) and large research library programs. Jon E. Cawthorne and Teresa Y. Neely write about ARL's Leadership Career Development Program for Underrepresented Mid-Career Librarians. They include a review of leadership positions held by participants during the program and after the program concluded. Catherine Dixon and Karen B. Walfall provide their own personal descriptions and unofficial review of a past leadership development program at the Library of Congress. Ann Campion Riley examines her experience as a participant in ARL's Research Library Leadership Fellows program for mid-career librarians. The last chapter in this part, by Marianne Ryan, Kathleen DeLong, and Julie Garrison, reviews the UCLA Senior Fellows program, including a survey of past participants.

PART FOUR: PROGRAMS FOR MULTIPLE TYPES OF LIBRARIES

The fourth part includes programs offered to multiple types of libraries, such as academic, state, and public libraries. Rachel Besara describes The Sunshine State Library Leadership Institute, which focuses on developing leaders for Florida libraries from the ranks of librarians and paraprofessionals. The now-defunct Stanford Institute, a program for those aspiring to leadership positions, is the focus of Vicki D. Bloom's chapter. Trevor A. Dawes describes the Minnesota Institute for Early Career Librarians from Traditionally Underrepresented Groups, which is for librarians with five or fewer years in the profession. Melissa Jadlos reports on Accepting the Leadership Challenge: A Library Leadership Institute sponsored by the Rochester Regional Library Council and the Monroe County Library System. Like the Stanford Institute, the Rochester program ran only twice, but both were based upon leadership theories and made a lasting impression on the author participants. Shellie Jeffries also writes about a program no longer in existence, the Snowbird Library Leadership Institute. Founded in 1990, Snowbird ran until 2000 and focused on the premise that anyone can be a leader if he or she is aware of personal strengths and weaknesses. Jeffries includes a survey of past participants. This part closes with a review of the Texas Library Association's Texas Accelerated Library Leaders (TALL) program by Martha Rinn. TALL is for mid-career library professionals and paraprofessionals.

PART FIVE: PROGRAMS THAT INCLUDE LIBRARIANS AMONG THE PARTICIPANTS

The fifth part explores three programs in which librarians are an invited group, but not the only group of participants from higher education. Carolyn Carpan reflects on her experience with the Women's Leadership Institute. This program is coproduced by 15 different professional associations in higher education, including the Association of College and Research Libraries, and is limited to female participants in managerial positions. Adriene Lim, Vivian Lewis, and Neal Baker examine the Frye Leadership Institute, which ran between 2000 and 2012 for participants including IT professionals, faculty, and administrators in addition to librarians. While Frye has now been reborn as the Leading Change Institute, this chapter focuses only on Frye and includes a survey of the 2008 cohort. This part concludes with Lois K. Merry's chapter on the Higher Education Resource Services (HERS) management institute for academic women. Held in multiple locations and with different formats, this program is intended to increase the number of women administrators at colleges and universities and is limited to women participants. The program helps women explore higher position possibilities within the academe.

PART SIX: FINDINGS AND CONCLUSIONS

The book concludes with two chapters that consider the preceding program-specific chapters as if they were a single research study. The first comprises a review of program commonalities, an analysis of self-reported indications of leadership development provided by the chapter authors, a collation of leadership theories employed, and any research studies conducted. The last chapter provides an overview of next steps for research and how those creating or reviewing leadership development programs might use this text.

Ways to Read this Book

There are many approaches that may be taken in reading these chapters. Readers may accept the book's organization, start with Chapter 1 and read straight through to the end. That may not satisfy some readers who are looking for a different organizational approach. If readers want to read about programs specific to a particular point on a career trajectory, they may find table I to be helpful. Others may wish to read about programs focused on gender and/or diversity and would perhaps then just examine chapters 16 and 18 for gender-based programs and 4, 6, and 12 for diversity-based programs. If looking for programs sponsored by national associations, then chapters 1, 2, 5, 6, 8, and 16 may be of interest.

TABLE I. Chapters Arranged According to Career Trajectory			
Beginning	Mid-Career	Bridge between Mid- and Senior-Career	Senior-Career
12	2	11	1
1	6	16	3
	7	17	18
	13	8	9

TABLE I. Chapters Arranged According to Career Trajectory			
Beginning	Mid-Career	Bridge between Mid- and Senior-Career	Senior-Career
	18		
	4		
	15		
	5		

Another approach to reading this work would be to focus on a particular topic of interest in each chapter. Most chapters have a personal reflection. One could read the personal reflections and decide which programs appeal for further reading. If one's interest lies in the leadership theories underpinning library leadership programs, then a one could focus on this section in each chapter. If looking to create a leadership program, a scan of each chapter's conclusion may provide insight into what worked and where improvements can be made.

Whatever the approach to reading this volume, the variety of authors (26) who share their knowledge and experiences in 18 leadership development programs provides an engaging read. It was a pleasure to work with the contributing authors as each had a passion for his or her program. In its entirety, this is a revealing work on the history, structure, and perceived effectiveness of academic and research library leadership development programs.

Notes

1. Burns, *Leadership*.
2. Kotter, *A Force for Change*, 6.
3. Ibid.
4. Trait theory presumes there is a set of inheritable traits that leaders hold in common and that these can be predictive of a leader's success. Implicit in the concept is that traits produce a pattern of behavior that is the same across situations and that leaders' characteristics remain the same over time. Fleenor, "Trait Approach to Leadership," 830.
5. Goleman, *Emotional Intelligence*.
6. Boyatzis and McKee, *Resonant Leadership*.
7. Dickmann and Stanford-Blair, *Mindful Leadership*, 5.
8. Mason and Wetherbee, "Learning to Lead," 187–217.
9. Skinner and Krabbenhoeft, "Training the 21st Century Library Leader."

Bibliography

Boyatzis, Richard, and Annie McKee. Resonant Leadership: Renewing Yourself and Connecting with Others through Mindfulness, Hope, and Compassion. Boston, MA: Harvard Business School Press, 2007.

Burns, James MacGregor. Leadership. New York: Harper & Row, 1978.

Dickmann, Michael H., and Nancy Stanford-Blair. Mindful Leadership: A Brain-Based Framework. 2nd ed. Thousand Oaks, CA: Corwin Press, 2009.

Fleenor, John W. "Trait Approach to Leadership." In Encyclopedia of Industrial and Organizational Psychology," edited by Steven G. Rogelberg, 830. Thousand Oaks, CA: Sage Publications, 2006.

Goleman, Daniel. Emotional Intelligence. New York: Bantam Books, 1995.

Kotter, John P. A Force for Change: How Leadership Differs From Management. New York: The Free Press, 1990.

Mason, Florence M., and Louella V. Wetherbee. "Learning to Lead: An Analysis of Current Training Programs for Library Leadership," Library Trends 53, no. 1 (2004): 187–217.

Skinner, Katherine, and Nick Krabbenhoeft. "Training the 21st Century Library Leader: A Review of Library Leadership Training 1998–2013." Atlanta, GA: Educopia Institute, 2014. Accessed May 27, 2015. http://libraries.idaho.gov/files/Training_the_21st_Century_Library_Leader.pdf.

PART 1

A Program for All Types of Academic Libraries

CHAPTER 1

Leadership Institute for Academic Librarians

Anne Marie Casey

THE LEADERSHIP INSTITUTE for Academic Librarians (LIAL), which offered its first institute in 1999, is a collaboration of the Association of College and Research Libraries (ACRL) and the Harvard Institutes for Higher Education at the Harvard Graduate School of Education.[1] Intended to provide participants with the tools and insight needed to improve effectiveness and respond rapidly to a changing environment, LIAL is held each year for one week in August on the campus of Harvard University in Cambridge, Massachusetts.[2]

The need for leadership programs for librarians was recognized by John Collins, a librarian at Harvard University, who had lobbied for several years for an institute for librarians similar to those the university held for other academic administrators. In 1998, Harvard University invited ACRL to join with them in planning a leadership institute for academic librarians. The president of ACRL at the time, Maureen Sullivan, brought the proposal to the ACRL Board of Directors, which approved it. Sullivan shared in the initial curriculum development and has been a member of the LIAL faculty since the second institute in 2000.[3]

Academic library directors and assistant directors were the original target audience.[4] By 2013, the positions of those encouraged to apply had broadened to include college and university librarians with leadership and/or management responsibilities; library deans, directors, and those reporting to them in associate or assistant positions; and other campus administrators with responsibilities that routinely affect important library-related functions.[5] Typical cohorts come from all types and sizes of academic library organizations and generally number close to 100.

Curriculum

Participants are led in case-method discussions on a daily basis for a week in the summer by professors who are experts in various areas of leadership.[6] The textbook and background reading focus prominently on the concept of the four frames approach to leadership, first advanced by Lee G. Bolman and Terrence E. Deal in 1984 and later applied to academic leadership by Bolman and Joan V. Gallos.[7] The curriculum consists of lectures on leadership, particularly the four frames approach; case study discussions; and small group work. Each participant reads and discusses four to five case studies on leadership issues during the week and prepares in advance a mini-case related to an actual workplace issue, which he or she presents in a small group setting for peer feedback.[8] The program objectives focus on two key questions: How well positioned are the participants' organizations to meet current and future challenges, and how effective is the leadership of each participant?[9]

Joseph (Joe) Zolner, the senior director of the Harvard Institutes for Higher Education, has directed LIAL since the fourth institute in 2002. In a telephone conversation with me, Zolner stated that he audits the institute experience on a daily basis to ensure that the faculty are successful in fostering two types of learning: informational and transformational. Basing the instruction on the work of adult learning researcher and author Bob Kegan, a Harvard faculty member who taught in the LIAL program for several years, Zolner leads the faculty in a variety of techniques aimed at instilling both types of learning.[10]

In his description of informational learning, Zolner uses a metaphor of the mind as an open vessel that faculty and participants attempt to fill with new information. The LIAL faculty use lecture, assigned reading, and discussions to achieve informational learning. The aim of the program's informational portions is to make the unfamiliar more familiar.

Transformational learning, on the other hand, seeks to make the familiar less familiar in the interest of expanding a student's intellectual horizons. In this case, the metaphorical vessel of the mind changes shape and may be equipped to absorb more informational learning. The purpose of this method is to change the way a person actually thinks in order to open his or her mind up to absorb more information and consider different approaches to leadership. One of the exercises focusing on transformational learning helps identify for participants the incidents in their lives that may have contributed to an immunity to change.[11] Led through a series of steps related to a behavior they want to change helps the participants to recognize what lies at the root of their inability to make the desired change. This process often results in a deeper understanding of one's own thoughts and motivations and allows participants to move past an issue and develop new behaviors or practices.

Zolner emphasizes the importance of active engagement for adults to learn. He and the other faculty provide multiple ways for LIAL participants to engage with the concepts and with other participants. One example is the mini-case each participant is asked to share in an assigned small group. This pre-institute assignment, in which participants write a brief case describing a workplace challenge, allows them through the small group discussion to apply the techniques learned in the program to a real life situation. The discussion of the cases occurs in a daily session where group members help each other reflect the challenges from different perspectives and often suggest ways to resolve issues.

Leadership Approach

The leadership approach on which LIAL bases its instruction is Bolman and Deal's four frames approach to leadership.[12] Developed further in subsequent publications, this approach invites leaders to view their work through four different perspectives or frames, which provide them with a map to navigate through circumstances.[13] "A frame is a mental model—a set of ideas and assumptions—that you carry in your head to help you understand a particular territory. A good frame makes it easier to know what you are up against and, ultimately, what you can do about it."[14]

Bolman and Deal studied leadership theory and reviewed the many ideas about the ways in which organizations work. From this research they consolidated the major schools of organizational thought into "a comprehensive framework encompassing four perspectives."[15] Their goal was to provide a usable approach that enabled leaders to view a situation through one of four distinct frames: structural, human resources, political, and symbolic.[16]

Zolner states that the four frames set up the circumstances for transformational learning. Asking participants to look at the different ways they could respond to a situation, depending on the frame they view it through, encourages them to broaden their perspectives. Zolner believes that leaders who take a multifaceted approach to the issues that confront them are better at what they do than those who tackle issues in the same way all the time. He appreciates the four frames approach particularly because it encourages people to understand the context of their organizations, and he states, "Context matters!" He adds that the frames give leaders a roadmap that helps them take care of a situation within the context of the organization.

Literature Review

For several years, one or two LIAL alumni wrote synopses of their cohort experiences, most of which were published in *College & Research Libraries News*. These testimonials described themes from the curriculum, experiences, and faculty who taught that particular year in the Institute. They extolled the benefits of interactive learning and the positive difference the program made in their lives as well their enjoyment of the institute, which Larry Hardesty summed up as, "We worked hard and we had fun." [17]

While similar in their descriptions of the institutes, each alum focused on a different strength or experience of the program. Laverna Saunders wrote about the first program, which took place in the summer of 1999.[18] Her article contained a brief history, details of the format, and information on the faculty. One facet she emphasized was that the ground rules empowered both the introverts and the extroverts to participate. Three other alumni of the first institute, David Bilyeau, Marianne Gaunt, and Maryruth Glogowski, authored an article that focused on the particular takeaways they experienced. These included increasing the use of the four frames approach to leadership challenges, creating opportunities to think, and learning to pay attention to the context.[19]

Hardesty's report on the second institute in 2000 focused on the strengths of the faculty and the goal each participant left with: to do something different based on what they had learned.[20] Linda Marie Golian and Rebecca Donlan, who wrote about their experiences in 2001, the third year, discussed the shift in perspective that many participants observed.[21] The description of the fourth institute in 2002 highlighted the amount of time the planners built in for socialization and disengagement from the world of work and home.[22] The account that Ed Garten wrote about the fifth program in 2003 brings out the fact that peer-to-peer learning is as valuable as the curriculum.[23]

Two articles explored year six. Linda Masselink and Kelly Jacobsma described the program in 2004 with particular emphasis on the value of the case study method, especially the library case discussion led by Maureen Sullivan.[24] Another 2004 alumna, Sally Kalin, wrote an article several years after her experience in which she described the program, faculty, and readings in detail. She also stated that LIAL was the best leadership program she had experienced.[25] The final summary covered the seventh institute in 2005. Deborah B. Dancik wrote glowingly about the important contributions her colleagues made to build a collective understanding of leadership and the importance of their continued connection after they all went home.[26]

THE FOUR FRAMES APPROACH TO LEADERSHIP IN LIBRARIES

A substantial amount of research has been conducted on the four frames approach to leadership since Bolman and Deal first published in 1984.[27] A number of them are highlighted by Bolman on his website.[28] Few publications, however, deal with this approach in libraries. Among them is the dissertation research conducted by Zhixian Yi, in which he explored how academic library directors deal with change based on the guidelines of Bolman and Deal.[29] Subsequent articles based on the research of Bolman and Deal explored the ways directors conduct meetings and set goals.[30] Other dissertation research includes that of Vinaya L. Tripuraneni, who used Bolman and Deal's Leadership Orientations instrument to investigate the leadership approach considered ideal for academic library leaders by their colleagues.[31]

A small number of additional publications reference the four frames approach as applied to libraries. Irene M.H. Herold, in her dissertation study of the College Library Directors' Mentor Program, suggests that the concept may provide a basis for a reenvisioned version of the program.[32] Felix T. Chu explores the idea of approaching a reference encounter through the lenses of the four frames, while Mott Linn urges new library leaders to embrace this approach as they are learning about their organizations.[33]

My Experience

I attended the Harvard LIAL program in 2012. Much of the week-long session was interesting. Various lectures and specific discussions in the small groups and the larger setting built on leadership principles I had learned in my doctoral program (managerial leadership in the information professions at Simmons College in Boston, Massachusetts) and in workshops at library conferences. After completing the program, I read books and articles recommended by faculty and fellow participants, which contributed to enhancing my communication style.

Two sessions, in particular, resonated very strongly with me. The first was the immunity to change exercise presented by Lisa Lahey. At the beginning of the session, she asked us to partner up with one student and write down a behavior we wished to change. I decided to explore my hesitation to attend social gatherings at work and, when forced to participate, my tendency to socialize only with the secretaries. During this exercise, I investigated the foundation of my discomfort with operating in the political frame, particularly networking and building alliances with the upper levels of the university organization, and discovered the underlying beliefs that often held me back. Related to my upbringing, the root cause had nothing to do with my abilities, but with beliefs and assumptions I had carried from childhood. Realizing this freed me to feel more comfortable in political situations.

The other session that was very helpful to me was the discussion of my mini-case in the small group setting. It dealt with an issue that kept recurring in some interactions with supervisors and subordinates in the three years I had held my position as a library director. After describing it to my small group colleagues, I was surprised to receive meaningful feedback immediately. Through their guidance, I discovered that I had been trying to impose the collaborative, shared governance culture of my former institution on my current workplace, which is hierarchical. Realizing this has helped me to work more effectively within the context of my organization and to stop trying to transform it into the culture I was used to.

THE FOUR FRAMES APPROACH TO LEADERSHIP

Much of the LIAL program focuses on the four frames approach to academic leadership. In 2012, Bolman was a primary lecturer and discussion leader.[34] While all the frames were covered, the faculty continuously drew our attention to the importance of the political frame. They pointed out that this is the view most often missed by those who do not succeed in leadership positions. One particular lecture included a video demonstrating Ronald Reagan's ability to operate in the political frame and Jimmy Carter's seeming dismissal of the importance of building political alliances. After viewing the clip, we discussed the relative success of both presidents and how much depended on one's ability and the other's ignorance of the importance of political alliances. I realized that I avoided working in the political frame wherever I could and saw myself in the depiction of Jimmy Carter. This caused me to reflect on the fact that my behavior was probably detrimental to my effectiveness as a leader, just as his appeared to be.

Of the four frames, structural, human resources, political, and symbolic, my natural tendency had been to rely heavily on the human resources frame. I recalled many incidents in the past where I had reacted like a mother hen protecting her chicks when I experienced what I considered to be attacks on them. I also had some strengths in the structural frame and considered the symbolic view often enough, but I tended to avoid conflict, negotiation, and developing alliances.

The case study (see Appendix 1.1) explores the application of the four frames through the description of a challenge experienced by my library. Many of the events occurred before I attended LIAL and reflect the way I approached problems then, by flipping among the structural, human resources, and symbolic frames, while I pushed a subordinate to handle the networking and coalition building that we needed. Other events occurred after LIAL and showed how the personal changes inspired by the institute have benefited my leadership abilities and my organization.

Conclusion

Changes that occur in the thinking and behavior of participants in a leadership institute may be dramatic enough that they fully realize they are going home a changed person. In my case, the changes from my week at LIAL seem to have been subtle and organic, so that they went unnoticed by me initially. Yes, I had enjoyed the lectures and exercises, the social events, and making new friends. I was particularly happy to be attending Harvard for a week and walking the streets of Cambridge. But, when I hopped on the T to head home, I was not convinced I had learned much. Like most professional development opportunities, LIAL seemed at first to have been a nice time away from work to think and talk to colleagues.

But then, I told the story of the lost floor (see Appendix 1.1) as a way to inform my management team about reframing and realized that although I operated effectively in three of the frames, I often shied away from the political frame, the one emphasized by the LIAL faculty. As I reflected on this, I discovered that I no longer felt the need to avoid the political frame. The immunity to change exercise had altered my way of thinking, and all of the information I received at LIAL on the importance of navigating the political shoals of academia made perfect sense. By embracing every opportunity to network and discuss the value of the library to the university's mission, we are experiencing a more positive interaction with university administration.

The Hunt Library at Embry-Riddle Aeronautical University is a more engaged part of the university in 2013. The building now houses a print collection that is better-used and more focused on the university curriculum, while the new furniture and reconfiguration of service areas has attracted more students on a regular basis than in the preceding three years. When the Office of Undergraduate Research had its grand opening in January 2013, I cut the ribbon with the chief academic officer and the university president, which made me and the library staff feel exceedingly proud.

Borrowing Zolner's metaphor, the vessel of my mind was transformed. The new shape is open to more information and greater experiences. Telling the story revealed this to me in a profound way. I am not sure I would have come to this realization if I filled out a survey or evaluation of the program. Perhaps an area of further research on the effect of LIAL on the leadership growth of its alumni is to ask participants to write the story of the important events in their lives after the program. After all, the case study method is the primary tool of instruction in this program. It may also be valuable as a tool of its evaluation.

LIAL is the only formal leadership institute I have participated in. Many of the lectures, readings, and group work contained familiar content or processes. The case study approach as the primary method of instruction was new to me, and I found it to be effective because I absorb new concepts and ideas more readily through the medium of story than any other. In addition, the immunity to change exercise was transformational for me. It may not have been for others in the same institute. It is difficult to conclude that LIAL would have the same effect on every participant, but it clearly has on many, judging from the enthusiastic articles written by past participants.

In the end, the teaching methods and curriculum of leadership institutes are probably more or less effective, depending on the learning styles and level of participation of the individual participants. The LIAL program was the perfect one for me at this time in my life. As I look back and recognize the significant changes in my leadership and personal interactions with others as a result of that week in August in Cambridge, I was in the perfect program for me at the right time. Perhaps that is the best result we can expect from a leadership program.

Appendix 1.1. Case Study and Analysis Using the Four Frames: The Story of the Lost Floor

Embry-Riddle Aeronautical University (ERAU), dedicated to instruction and research in aviation science and aeronautical engineering, offers degrees ranging from associates to PhD. ERAU has residential campuses in Florida and Arizona and over 20,000 distance learning students taking classes at 150 centers around the world or online. In 2012, the university undertook an ambitious five-year plan to enhance its global reputation for research. A major initiative of this plan was the establishment of three centers dedicated to the expansion of undergraduate research and assessment, with the primary center located at the headquarters campus in Daytona Beach, Florida.

One of two ERAU libraries, the Hunt Library, serves the residential campus and university administration in Daytona Beach as well as the distance learning programs. The library staff consists of 20 librarians, 16 library technicians, and several student assistants. The organization is relatively flat, with the majority of staff reporting to three of four associate directors or the director. The four associate directors have responsibility for reference, budget and planning, access services, and electronic and technical Services. The director and associate directors work together as a management team to lead the library.

Opened in 1985, the Hunt Library building contains 42,000 square feet on three floors. The first floor is much larger than the second and third floors, making the building resemble a tiered wedding cake from a distance. An atrium in the middle of the three-storied section of the building provides most of the natural light to that part of the building and is the home to a working glider suspended from the ceiling, one of the most-visited attractions on campus.

In 2007–2008, the university administration, struggling with space constraints brought on by the growth of the university and the loss of some buildings to a tornado in 2006, relocated offices and a coffee shop to the first floor of the Hunt Library building. Although concerned about the loss of student seating, the library management team generally negotiated for cosmetic upgrades and new furniture that made the environment more pleasant. They also consolidated staff offices to open new public areas and mitigate the loss of seating.

Shortly after the current director started in 2009, the chief academic officer (CAO) required more space on the first floor for an administrative office. The director encouraged her managers and staff to accept this change without complaint, for the good of the university, but worried about the ongoing loss of library space. She had recently taken a class on leading in the political environment and understood that she should develop a plan to demonstrate the value of the library to university administrators. She just didn't know how to go about it. Speaking to her superiors outside of routine meetings caused her a great deal of anxiety, so she tended to avoid social functions or university events where she may have had some opportunities to network with the power players on campus. She worried that the administration did not consider the library a vital part of the university and knew it was her responsibility to strengthen the role of the library at the university, but did nothing. She hoped the library space would remain intact, but it did not!

In December 2011, the CAO informed the director that the university administration planned to locate two new departments, Educational Technology (EdTech) and the Office of Undergraduate Research (OUR) to the third floor of the library in the summer of 2012. The third floor at that time housed one-third of the book collection and four group study rooms. These two departments, which were integral to the university's research initiative, needed space in the center of campus, and there was no place else to locate them. The CAO showed the director the plans, which called for filling in the atrium with new flooring on the second and third floors.

How Do We Tell the Others?

Later that afternoon, the director called an emergency management team meeting. She gave the news about the third floor to the associate directors. Team members expressed frustration at the seeming lack of concern for the students who filled the building every day. Where else would they go to study? How would the faculty react to the library eliminating one third of the print collection? What would the building be like once the atrium with its natural light, comfortable seating area, and magnificent glider disappeared? After an hour of this conversation, they decided to hold a staff meeting to explain the circumstances.

The following Monday, the director sent out an e-mail message requiring all staff to attend a special meeting late that morning. The normal joking and conversation that precedes staff meetings at Hunt Library was absent that day. Unexpected staff meetings are not the norm, so everyone seemed to know something was up. As the director began to address the group, the calm she had maintained since first hearing the news about losing the third floor dissolved. Her voice cracked, and she blinked back tears as she recapped the meeting with the CAO. She then invited everyone to ask questions and express their feelings. She assured them that they were in a safe zone and that the management team wanted them to vent.

Shock, anger, and sadness reverberated through the room as one after another, staff members expressed their frustration at an administration that did not seem to recognize the importance of the library space to the students. People spoke about the strong culture of customer service shared by everyone in the library and the praise they regularly received from students and faculty. Many suggested ways to fight back. They thought the library should encourage students to protest the loss of space, or they should refuse to give up the floor.

When the director spoke again, she explained that it would be politically unwise to fight this change. The associate director of reference reminded everyone that the building did not belong to the library staff but to the university. She went on to say that what do belong to the staff did are their customer service ethic and the dedication to students that had been the hallmark of the organization from day one. "The university administration can do what they want with the building," she said, "but no one could take away our dedication to great customer service."

The meeting ended with a discussion of next steps. The management team would develop a document containing their questions and concerns to share with the director of facilities. The managers stressed the importance of staff input and requested feedback by the end of the first week of January. The director also invited anyone to talk to her or one of the associate directors any time they needed to vent. After the meeting, one librarian approached the director and said, "This is a bad situation, but we are in it together, and we can get through anything as long as we stay together."

The Library Takes Action

Armed with their list of questions and concerns, the management team met with the director of facilities and the project architect in late January. As the group walked around the second and third floors, the librarians asked about the construction project and pointed out some details that had not arisen in earlier planning, such as reinforcing the infill on the second floor to withstand the weight of the books. By the end of this meeting, the architect and director of facilities admitted that they had not considered several of the issues raised by the library administrators and agreed to redraw the plans.

In early February, the director sent a funding proposal to the CAO. In order to ameliorate the reduction of seats and print collections, the management team proposed reconfiguring the reference desk area to create more open seating on the first floor, placing a moratorium on the purchase of print books until after the move from the third floor was completed, and using book money to buy new furniture. The proposal also requested the CAO to match the funds the library was spending, so that the last of the old 1980s furniture could be refreshed. His immediate response was that there was no money at the time. The director interpreted his response to mean there might be some money at another time, so she put the proposal away for a couple of months.

Simultaneously, the associate director for reference, a longtime Hunt Library employee and former interim library director, offered to start working her contacts, especially the director of the OUR. The director, who served on a committee with the EdTech director, then said she would contact him to discuss collaborative planning. The library leaders shared the construction questions with the other two directors and requested the three groups join together to work with facilities on the reconstruction of the building so that the needs of the students would be the highest priority.

The director of EdTech did not respond to the invitation to collaborate, but the director of OUR expressed a strong interest in working together. He invited the library director to his next meeting with the facilities department and shared his plans with her prior to the meeting. Following this meeting, the directors of the OUR and the library met regularly to discuss ongoing plans and construction timelines. They participated in all construction meetings together.

What Do We Do with All of These Books?

In mid-February, the library embarked on an aggressive weeding project. Already on the library's strategic plan for that year, a preliminary weeding procedure had been drafted. The associate director for access services expanded the procedures into a project plan that included participation from everyone in the library. Most staff jumped into this project because they recognized that the reconstruction gave the library an opportunity to prioritize the long-overdue removal of books that were old and rarely, if ever, used.

The staff areas of the library very quickly became crowded with boxes of books destined for new homes. The library reserved a small number of the books removed from the collection to sell at the semiannual book sale. Some of the proceeds went to partially fund food and soft drinks for students studying in the library during finals. The majority of the books were sent to Better World Books to be resold or recycled. A small share of the proceeds from the sales was donated to the county literacy council.

The initial weeding goal was to weed 15,000 books by the last week of April. One of the staff created a thermometer to measure the weeding progress. Each time a threshold of 5,000 books was pulled out of the catalog, the library threw a party. At one party, dozens of mini-cupcakes were served. At another threshold, the staff had a "make your own sundae" party. During each of these occasions, new information on the weeding process was shared, and the staff joked and showed pictures of the progress.

What Did They Just Say?

In late March, at a planning meeting, the facilities department informed the directors of the library and the OUR that the amount of time and money needed to infill the atrium and reinforce the new floors was not cost-effective. They learned that the administration had found a new home for the EdTech department and the OUR would have the third floor to itself. Construction would be minimal and would take place beginning the second week of May, as soon as finals ended.

The overwhelming response on the library side was relief at not losing the atrium and in gaining a group of people who wanted to work closely with them to provide the best possible resources to students and faculty. Immediately the director of the OUR and the library management team consulted on the best third floor configuration and new, comfortable furniture that would be placed throughout the building. The library director took the funding proposal back to the CAO, and this time he agreed to pay one-third of the cost of replacing outdated furniture.

Although the new plan was welcomed, it created another challenge. By not infilling the second floor, the library had to recalculate the number of books to weed in order to consolidate the collections into a smaller space. The new number was 25,000, and just over a month before finals, staff redoubled their weeding efforts, reaching their goal a few days ahead of the deadline. They celebrated their achievement with a big meal catered by a local restaurant and laughed at the funny stories and pictures they shared about the big weed.

Viewing the Case through the Four Frames

STRUCTURAL

The structural view of academic leadership casts those in charge as architects, analysts, and systems designers. The basic leadership task is to divide the work and coordinate the pieces.[35] The structural frame deals with planning. It is often the first approach leaders take when faced with the prospect of change.

The structural frame is apparent throughout the case. At the beginning of each new phase and relationship, the management team developed plans, procedures, and processes to move the organization along to the end that the CAO required of them. They sought input and created plans related to moving the collections, weeding, restructuring open space, seeking additional funding, and forming partnerships.

The library leaders used the initial plans as their roadmap through the process and adjusted them as necessary. When the university changed course on the extent of the construction, library leaders adjusted their roadmap to meet the alterations. In addition, as they worked more closely with the director of the OUR and received funding from the CAO for new furniture, they altered earlier strategies to meet the new situation. Throughout the process, each new change initiated a return to the structural frame to tweak the roadmaps.

HUMAN RESOURCES

The human resources view of academic leadership sees the organization as an extended family and the leader as a servant, catalyst, or coach. The basic leadership task of this frame is to facilitate the alignment between organizational and individual needs.[36] In this frame, the leader's thoughts turn to the people in the organization and focus on ways to take care of them.

Evidence of the human resources frame arises early in the case. When the management team met with staff, they encouraged them to share their emotions and ideas. They validated these by incorporating staff feedback into the planning documents. The library leaders also communicated with their subordinates in a positive and supportive way.

The management team encouraged everyone in the library to play a role in the projects needed to consolidate the collections onto the first two floors of the building. They participated by weeding, pulling books, and helping at the book sale. They also fed the staff while encouraging questions and feedback and laughter when they met to discuss and celebrate their progress. From the beginning, the library leadership maintained a positive attitude in all their communication with staff. This engendered camaraderie in the library, and everyone felt like they were in it together. They were an extended family.

POLITICAL

A jungle is the metaphor for the organization in the political view of academic leadership. The basic leadership tasks in this frame are bargaining, negotiating, building coalitions, setting agendas, and managing conflict. The emphasis of the political frame is the allocation of power and scarce resources.[37] In this case, the crux of the situation is the lack of an important resource, sufficient space on the Daytona Beach campus. Additionally, one of the players in a potential conflict over the space, the OUR, is empowered by the administration because it is the primary engine of the university's current highest priority.

The library director understood immediately from the CAO that the library power in this situation was limited as she discovered plans had been developed for library space with no input from her. In consultation with her management team, one of her first moves was to set an agenda in which the management team could offer input. They met with the architects and builders to ask questions and provide facts about the building that contributed to a change in the construction plan, which benefited the library.

The management team understood that the library would be moved off the third floor, regardless of any action they might take to prevent this happening. They also acknowledged the importance of the OUR to current university priorities and the fact that the building held a print collection that was old and, in many cases, unused. So they used the situation to their advantage by developing a relationship with a powerful colleague, making progress toward a requirement from the administration, and negotiating for additional resources to make the library a better place for students.

SYMBOLIC

In the symbolic frame, the institution is viewed as a temple or theater. The leadership tasks are to see possibilities; create common vision; manage meaning; and infuse passion, creativity, and soul into the work of the organization. Leaders working in this frame use ceremonies, rituals, stories, and vision to motivate and celebrate success.[38]

There are several times in the case where the management team operated in the symbolic frame. The most pronounced of these appear in the weeding process. They threw parties to congratulate themselves on their progress. They also created a large thermometer that they kept in a staff area and updated as the weeding progressed. At each of the parties, they shared pictures and funny stories about flagging the books or packing them up to ship them out of the building. In addition, each of the management team members led by example. They participated in some aspect of the weeding or deaccessioning process. The director determined that no one could complain about the assignments they received in this process because she was up in the stacks every week weeding her assigned areas, which were larger than many of the others.

Other evidence of the symbolic frame occur in the first staff meeting where the director allowed herself to show some emotion as she explained the circumstances and in the story of the strong customer service ethic that the associate director for reference related, reminding everyone what their highest priority and strengths are. In addition, the symbolic view is apparent in the disposal of the books that were weeded. They went to an organization that supports sustainability, or they were sold to raise money to buy food for students while they study for finals in the library.

The Rest of the Story: After the Dust Cleared

In August 2012 the library director participated in LIAL. The experience was profoundly positive. When she returned to work, she set aside an hour to describe the benefits of the program. As she thought about the best way to explain reframing to the associate directors, she retold the story of the lost floor, pointing out to them the many times they successfully navigated the challenges by viewing situations through different frames. As she reflected on the experience of the last several months, she realized the number of times she had avoided the political view or expected the associate director for reference to handle the political aspects of the situation. She thought about how much the political frame had been emphasized in the LIAL program and realized that it was her job to operate from this viewpoint rather than to abdicate this responsibility to a subordinate.

In the fall of 2013, capitalizing on the relationship she had forged with the director of the Office of Undergraduate Research (OUR), she enlisted him as an ally in the library's goal to secure funding and support for the establishment of an institutional repository (IR). Together, they convinced the chief information officer (CIO) of the benefits to ERAU of an IR and arranged for vendors to demonstrate IR products to administrators and faculty.

She also started attending social events and ceremonies in other departments. She made a point of speaking to the president, vice presidents, deans, and faculty at each of these occasions. She emphasized the positive aspects of locating the OUR in the library building and spoke passionately about the benefits of providing open access to ERAU research through the establishment of the IR, assuring all who had doubts because of anticipated workload increases that the library would manage it. Before long, she started receiving requests to attend meetings to explain how the library would advance university priorities by establishing and maintaining an IR. In late December, the university signed a contract with a leading provider of IR platforms, and she led the steering committee that is overseeing the implementation.

Notes

1. For more information about all of the Harvard Institutes for Higher Education, see http://www.gse.harvard.edu/ppe/programs/higher-education/.
2. Association of College and Research Libraries, "ACRL Harvard Leadership Institute."
3. Saunders, "ACRL Harvard Leadership Institute."
4. Mason and Wetherbee, "Learning to Lead."
5. Harvard University, "Leadership Institute for Academic Librarians."
6. Gjelten and Fishel, "Developing Leaders and Transforming Libraries."
7. Bolman and Deal, *Modern Approaches*; Bolman and Gallos, *Reframing Academic Leadership*.

8.   Sullivan, "Case Studies Method," 115.
9.   Harvard University, "Leadership Institute for Academic Librarians."
10. Information on Kegan's research areas and publications is available at http://www.gse.harvard.edu/directory/faculty/faculty-detail/?fc=318&flt=k&sub=all.
11. In 2012, this session was conducted by Lisa Lahey and based on the book by Kegan and Lahey, *Immunity to Change*.
12. Bolman and Deal, *Modern Approaches*.
13. Bolman and Deal, *Reframing Organizations*.
14. Ibid., 11.
15. Ibid., 14.
16. The frames are covered in some detail in the case analysis in the Appendix.
17. Hardesty, "ACRL/Harvard Leadership Institute," 805.
18. Saunders, "ACRL Harvard Leadership Institute," 647.
19. Bilyeu, Gaunt, and Glogowski, "ACRL Harvard Leadership Institute."
20. Hardesty, "ACRL/Harvard Leadership Institute."
21. Golian and Donlan, "ACRL Harvard Leadership Institute."
22. Gilreath, "ACRL Harvard Leadership Institute."
23. Garten, "ACRL Harvard Leadership Institute."
24. Masselink and Jacobsma, "Reframing our Viewpoint."
25. Kalin, "Reframing Leadership," 261–70.
26. Dancik, "Borrowing from the Balcony."
27. Bolman and Deal, *Modern Approaches*.
28. Bolman, "Research Using or Influenced."
29. Yi, "The Management of Change."
30. Yi, "Conducting Meetings"; Yi, "Setting Goals."
31. Tripuraneni, "Leader or Manager."
32. Herold, "An Examination of the Leadership Program."
33. Chu, "Framing Reference Encounters"; Linn, "Perspectives on Managing a Library."
34. Bolman and Gallos, *Reframing Academic Leadership*.
35. Bolman and Gallos, *Reframing Academic Leadership*, 50.
36. Ibid., 93.
37. Ibid., 72.
38. Ibid., 110.

Bibliography

Association of College and Research Libraries. "ACRL Harvard leadership Institute for Academic Librarians." Accessed February 7, 2013. http://www.ala.

org/conferencesevents/acrl-harvard-leadership-institute-academic-librarians.

Bilyeu, David, Marianne Gaunt, and Maryruth Glogowski. "ACRL Harvard Leadership Institute: Three Participants Share Their Rewarding Experiences." *College & Research Libraries News* 61, no. 2 (2000): 106–20.

Bolman, Lee G. "Research Using or Influenced by Bolman & Deal's Four Frames." Last modified July 2011. Accessed February 9, 2013. http://www.leebolman.com/four_frame_research.htm.

Bolman, Lee G., and Terrence E. Deal. *Modern Approaches to Managing and Understanding Organizations.* San Francisco: Jossey-Bass, 1984.

———. *Reframing Organizations: Artistry, Choice, and Leadership.* 4th ed. San Francisco: Jossey-Bass, 2008.

Bolman, Lee G., and Joan V. Gallos. *Reframing Academic Leadership.* San Francisco: Jossey-Bass, 2011.

Chu, Felix T. "Framing Reference Encounters." *RQ* 36, no. 1 (1996): 93–101.

Dancik, Deborah B. "Borrowing from the Balcony." *College & Research Libraries News* 67, no. 3 (2006): 166–67, 176.

Garten, Ed. "ACRL Harvard Leadership Institute: A Five-Year Old Spreads Its Wings." *College & Research Libraries News* 65, no. 2 (2004): 81–83.

Gilreath, Charles. "ACRL Harvard Leadership Institute: Highlights form the Fourth Annual Institute." *College & Research Libraries News* 64, no. 2 (2003): 90–91.

Gjelten, Dan, and Teresa Fishel. "Developing Leaders and Transforming Libraries: Leadership Institutes for Librarians." *College & Research Libraries News* 67, no. 7 (2006): 409–12.

Golian, Linda Marie, and Rebecca Donlan. "ACRL Harvard Leadership Institute: Highlights form the Third Annual Institute." *College & Research Libraries News* 62, no. 11 (2001): 1069–72.

Hardesty, Larry. "ACRL/Harvard Leadership Institute: Still Receiving Winning Reviews in Its Second Year." *College & Research Libraries News* 61, no. 9 (2000): 805–07.

Harvard University. Graduate School of Education. "Leadership Institute for Academic Librarians: Program Objectives." Accessed February 8, 2013. http://www.gse.harvard.edu/ppe/programs/higher-education/portfolio/leadership-academic-librarians.html.

———. "Leadership Institute for Academic Librarians: Who Should Attend." Accessed February 8, 2013. http://www.gse.harvard.edu/ppe/programs/higher-education/portfolio/leadership-academic-librarians.html.

Herold, Irene M. H. "An Examination of the Leadership Program for College Library Directors Associated with ACRL's College Libraries Section." PhD diss., Simmons College, 2012. ProQuest (ATT 3515783).

Kalin, Sally W. "Reframing leadership: The ACRL/Harvard Leadership Institute for Academic Librarians," *Journal of Business & Finance Librarianship* 13, no. 3 (2008): 261–70. doi:10.1080/08963560802183047.

Kegan, Robert, and Lisa Laskow Lahey. *Immunity to Change: How to Overcome It and Unlock the Potential in Yourself and Your Organization.* Boston: Harvard Business Press, 2009.

Linn, Mott. "Perspectives on Managing a Library." *The Bottom Line: Managing Library Finances* 21, no. 4 (2008): 124–28. doi: 10.1108/08880450810929107.

Mason, Florence M., and Louella V. Wetherbee. "Learning to Lead: An Analysis of Current Training Programs for Library Leadership." *Library Trends* 53, no. 1 (2004): 187–217.

Masselink, Linda, and Kelly Jacobsma. "Reframing our Viewpoint: The 6th ACRL Harvard Leadership Institute." *College & Research Libraries News* 66, no. 2 (2005): 99–101.

Saunders, Laverna. "ACRL Harvard Leadership Institute: Professional Development at Its Best." *College & Research Libraries News* 60, no. 8 (1999): 645–47.

Sullivan, Maureen. "Case Studies Method: An Overview." In *Shaping the Future: Advancing the Understanding of Leadership*, edited by Peter Hernon, 115–17. Santa Barbara, CA: Libraries Unlimited, 2010.

Tripuraneni, Vinaya L. "Leader or Manager: Academic Library Leader's Leadership Orientation Considered Ideal by Faculty, Administrators, and Librarians at Private, Nonprofit Doctoral Universities in Southern California." PhD diss., University of LaVerne, 2010. ProQuest (ATT 3430266).

Yi, Zhixian. "Conducting Meetings in the Change Process: Approaches of Academic Library Directors in the United States." *Library Management* 33, no. 1 (2012): 22–35. doi: 10.1108/01435121211203293.

———. "The Management of Change in the Information Age: Approaches of Academic Library Directors in the United States." PhD diss., Texas Woman's University, 2010. ProQuest (ATT 3414408).

———. "Setting Goals for Change in the Information Age: Approaches of Academic Library Directors in the USA." *Library Management* 34, no. 1/2: 5–19. doi: 10.1108/01435121311298234.

Programs for Specific Types of Academic Libraries

CHAPTER 2

The American Theological Library Association's Creating the Leaders of Tomorrow Program

Leland R. Deeds and Miranda Bennett

THE CREATING THE Leaders of Tomorrow Program (CLTP) is a yearlong leadership development program developed and sponsored by the American Theological Library Association (ATLA), "a professional association providing support of theological and religious studies libraries and librarians."[1] The program began in 2012 with a cohort of nine librarians. ATLA's program seeks to give librarians with a possible interest in library leadership—in particular, library director positions at seminaries or other theological libraries—an opportunity for extended conversations about and reflections on both the theoretical and the practical aspects of leadership.

In planning and implementing the curriculum for the CLTP, ATLA staff worked with a management consultant, Mick Weltman of Weltman Consulting. Weltman interviewed several ATLA members known to have an interest in leadership development, including us, the authors of this chapter. The purpose was to create a program well suited to the particular needs of potential theological library leaders.

The Curriculum

Among the most significant features of the CLTP is its length. Unlike intensive, multiday leadership institutes or short workshops, the ATLA program is yearlong. The inaugural cohort worked together from January to December 2012, participating in a variety of activities.

The backbone of the program is a series of monthly webinars featuring presenters from within and outside theological librarianship. The webinar schedule is formed by the program organizers and made available to participants at the start of the year. ATLA used Microsoft Lync to host the webinars, and during the 2012 program, participants and presenters experienced only occasional and minor technological glitches.

Webinar presenters, who ranged from theological library directors to the executive director of ATLA to finance professionals, covered a broad spectrum of topics. The 2012 program began with two sessions focused on definitions of leadership and understanding ourselves as leaders, including a lively discussion of the perennial question of "leadership versus management." Readings for these sessions included an excerpt from *Leading Change* by John P. Kotter, whose emphasis on leadership as "coping with change" seemed to resonate with many program participants, and Daniel Goleman's "What Makes a Leader?," the classic *Harvard Business Review* article presenting the role of emotional intelligence in leadership.[2]

These sessions were followed by an extended section of the curriculum devoted to the topic of managing financial resources. Consisting of three webinars, this part of the program introduced participants to the basic vocabulary and activities of budgeting and organizational financial planning, including a detailed examination of the budget process in a particular theological library. Following the in-person workshop in June, the program offered two webinars addressing personnel management issues, including staff recruitment, training, and conflict management. The final sessions presented the basics of strategic and operational planning and managing library and campus politics. The program concluded with a wrap-up webinar featuring each participant sharing how his or her leadership knowledge and skills had developed over the course of the year.

In between the monthly webinars, CLTP participants spoke by phone with an assigned mentor. The 2012 mentors were current theological library directors, many of who had a history of leadership within ATLA. For some topics, the program organizers provided participants with suggested questions to focus the mentoring conversations; in other cases, participants and mentors were invited to discuss the content of the month's webinar or reading. Comments from participants throughout the program and in the final wrap-up webinar indicated that the mentoring relationship was the most consistently valuable aspect of the program.

One of the most exciting and enjoyable parts of the CLTP was its one in-person gathering, a daylong workshop at the annual meeting of ATLA. Because the initial cohort began the program in January, but the ATLA annual meeting was not until June, participants were eager to spend time in the same physical space with people we had come to know virtually over the course of the previous six months. The workshop consisted of facilitated conversations about the effect of the program thus far on our professional aspirations, topical presentations by two of the mentors (one on the increasing expectation that theological library directors will also fulfill non-library roles in their institutions and the other on developing good communication skills), lunch with mentors and ATLA leaders, and group presentations by participants. These group presentations were based on projects, such as surveying theological librarians about leadership and management issues or developing case studies exploring leadership scenarios in theological libraries, enabling cohort members to work together to investigate a leadership topic of interest.

The program's final webinar, held in December 2012, offered all participants the opportunity to share with the group the most important lessons they learned from the program and an outline of their professional development plan. Several participants spoke highly of particular aspects of the program, especially working with their mentors, and most participants noted that they felt they had a clearer understanding of the role of theological library directors. In a few cases, this understanding led to a reconsideration of career plans, but some members of the cohort still planned to pursue formal leadership positions within theological librarianship.

Program Leadership Theories

The CLTP opened with the second chapter of *Leading Change*, laying out Kotter's eight-stage process of creating major change, establishing definitions for and distinctions between management and leadership and contextualizing Kotter's view of the struggle within organizations to foster leadership over the past several decades.[3] Management, according to Kotter, is "a set of processes that can keep a complicated system …running smoothly. The most important aspects …include planning, budgeting, organizing, staffing, controlling, and problem solving."[4] All of these areas are familiar and important topics for a would-be theological library director, and several were the thematic topic of a CLTP webinar. Kotter summarizes management further, saying it "is about coping with complexity."[5] How coping with complexity is distinct from leadership and why is the distinction important was answered by Kotter's work on change and the growing organizational need for individuals who can lead change. "At the beginning, those who attempt to create major change with simple, linear, analytical processes almost always fail."[6] According to Kotter, the reason for this is that the organization has moved beyond the need for incremental improvement because of environmental pressures. The pace of change and the business cycle dictate more radical measures. "Yet for historical reasons, many organizations today don't have much leadership. And almost everyone thinks about the problem here as one of *managing* change."[7] For this changing context, Kotter says, organizations need individuals skilled at leadership, which he describes as "a set of processes that creates organizations in the first place or adapts them to significantly changing circumstances. Leadership defines what the future should look like, aligns people with that vision, and inspires them to make it happen despite the obstacles."[8] Leadership, then, is "about coping with change."[9]

The CLTP's opening sessions also used Goleman's concept of emotional intelligence to expand what the attributes or abilities of a leader would look like within Kotter's broader definition and model of change management. Effective leaders, Goleman claims, "are alike in one crucial way: They all have a high degree of what has come to be known as emotional intelligence."[10] Emotional intelligence was defined by psychologists John Mayer and Peter Salovey in the 1990s as "the ability to perceive emotions, to access and generate emotions so as to assist thought, to understand emotions and emotional knowledge, and to reflectively regulate emotions so as to promote emotional and intellectual growth."[11] The four stages of emotional intelligence identified by Mayer and Salovey included recognizing one's own emotions as well as the emotions of others, applying emotion appropriately to facilitate reasoning, understanding complex emotions and their influence on succeeding emotional states, and having the ability to manage one's emotions as well as those of others.[12] Goleman described these stages of emotional intelligence as self-awareness, self-regulation, motivation, empathy, and social skills.[13] These were the traits Goleman's "superb leader" would need to facilitate Kotter's process. The eight steps to creating change are (1) establishing a sense of urgency, (2) creating the guiding coalition, (3) developing a vision and strategy, (4) communicating the change vision, (5) empowering broad-based action, (6) generating short-term wins, (7) consolidating gains and producing more change, and (8) anchoring new approaches in the culture.[14] All of these steps are crucial, if messy, and cannot be skipped or made more efficient, even when a large initiative is truly many smaller projects within a project and all at different places on the scale because only "leadership can blast through the many sources of corporate inertia."[15]

Experience with the Program

BENNETT

The CLTP first caught my interest because of two features I had not found in other leadership development programs: its focus on theological librarianship and its yearlong timeframe. I have participated in many leadership and management training programs, including the American Library Association's Emerging Leaders, the Texas Library Association's Texas Accelerated Library Leaders, and the Triangle Research Libraries Network's Management Academy, but these are all designed for a relatively broad cross-section of librarians and take place over a shorter time period.[16]

Because I was already well versed in leadership and management issues, I found the most opportunity for professional growth came from the two features mentioned above. As a program intentionally designed to address the needs and interests of potential future theological library directors, the CLTP provides opportunities to discuss matters of special relevance to that role. I learned a great deal about the challenges of leading small seminary libraries and the new expectations being placed on library directors in such institutions. As these institutions struggle to adapt to financial hardship, changing demographics, and an evolving religious landscape, they are beginning to ask library directors to take on broader responsibilities, such as classroom instruction and high-level administrative assignments. I welcomed the chance to think through and discuss what library leadership means in such a context. As a librarian who earned a doctorate prior to attending library school, I was intrigued by the possibility of a library position that offers opportunities to serve the institution outside of the library, but I could also see the danger of devoting too much of a library director's time and energy to non-library concerns. Additionally, the willingness of an institution to ask a library director to serve simultaneously, for instance, as the coordinator of institutional assessment suggests that an institution may not consider library leadership a full-time job.

A second example of a specific issue the CLTP brought to the fore in a way I had not previously experienced in a leadership development program was in the identification of educational qualifications for library leadership. Specifically, whether having a PhD is a reasonable requirement for a theological library director. Because our conversations focused on a small niche within librarianship, we were able to talk in specific, substantive terms about what academic degrees mean in our profession. We considered the role of the standards of the Association of Theological Schools, the accrediting body for most schools affiliated with ATLA, which included the expectation that the chief library administrator or theological librarian "should ordinarily be a voting member of the faculty."[17] This may imply in some contexts that the director would need educational credentials beyond the MLS or equivalent. Additionally, as theological schools look to library directors to take on additional roles, such as teaching credit-bearing courses, the need for directors to have degrees appropriate to those roles becomes more important. Many in the 2012 cohort, however, strongly objected to the requirement of a doctorate for library directors, since the work of library leadership differs markedly from that of teaching faculty. The issue remains unresolved within theological librarianship, but CLTP participants have begun to discuss their concerns with the leadership of ATLA.

The yearlong duration of the CLTP program also contributed to its impact on my leadership knowledge and skills. Because I had a full year to learn more about leadership topics, while actively engaged in my work as a department head at a large academic library, I was routinely able to see connections between CLTP webinars, assigned readings, and conversations with my mentor and my life on the job. For instance, the CLTP presentation and discussion about strategic planning helped me think more clearly and critically about my performance as cochair of my library's strategic directions initiative.

My experience with the CLTP also included many benefits, such as new friendships and an expanded professional network, an eye-opening reading or two, plenty of commiseration with a group of sympathetic colleagues, and nuggets of leadership wisdom you can return to again and again throughout your career. In the case of the CLTP, the idea I found most provocative and which has had a significant impact on my thinking about leadership involved the application of family systems theory to leadership. This model was presented in the webinar on "office politics" as well as via a book recommended by another cohort member, Edwin H. Friedman's *A Failure of Nerve: Leadership in the Age of the Quick Fix.*[18] Friedman, a pioneer in family systems theory, describes the model as "shift[ing] the unity of observation from a person to a network, and …focus[ing] on the network principles that were universal rather than specific to culture." This leads to his understanding of leadership as "essentially an *emotional* process rather than a *cognitive* phenomenon," a perspective that has served me well in practical workplace situations and given me a great deal of productive food for thought.[19]

DEEDS

Similarly to my coauthor, when the ATLA director of membership originally mentioned the launch of the CLTP, the three key features that intrigued me were its pragmatic focus, its intentional target (individuals seriously considering moving to directorship positions within theological libraries), and its yearlong duration. Prior to the CLTP, I had been fortunate to participate in multiple leadership workshops and initiatives while serving as a librarian within the University of Virginia Libraries. These varied from single-afternoon workshops to multiple-session programs stretched out across a two-week period. All of these sessions were significantly limited in the depth that they could cover any topic because of their duration. The sessions were also limited in the topics addressed because participants were pulled from the entirety of the university's divisions, making topics somewhat generic, such as working with various personality types, offering feedback, or developing emotional intelligence.

Three areas that were key for my learning during the CLTP were related to workflow or viewing my work within the library in the greater context of my institution and other institutional departments. The first was the reminder of how important it is, organizationally, to assign tasks to the lowest level within the organization that can successfully complete it—no matter whether completion could be done faster or better by someone else. This helps prevent a "bottleneck" effect, free up my time for assignments that only I can do, and ideally maximize how all staff are utilized. Though this topic did arise during our sessions on managing people, it was a repeated point of conversation during my talks with my mentor, where we discussed reviewing both my own work and constructively reviewing library-wide workflow issues.

An example of how I have put this into practice is delegating to key staff more formal responsibilities for the decisions related to selecting optional feature implementations during upgrades to our automation systems. Prior to this, the departmental culture relied heavily on the systems librarian, who made all key decisions and acted as a buffer for the staff, even unit heads, from having to participate in systems planning. Another example is my formal request for dedicated student employee hours with standing areas of responsibility. During the fiscal restraint of the past several years, my unit was "borrowing" student employees on a project-to-project basis from other units, but this significantly drove up the time expended on management of the projects because of the associated training time required per student employee per project, while also lowering overall productivity during a project because of my increased direct involvement.

My second key learning moment involved viewing library or departmental priorities within the broader institutional context, leaning toward Kotter's view of leadership opposed to management.[20] The need to focus on the library's institutional context cropped up repeatedly in sections on finance, budgeting, human resources, and, of course, workplace politics. I learned that our perspective of our own priorities is affected if viewed within their institutional context. This also helps keep the library's mid-to-long term planning in sync with institutional planning. Has the percentage of the overall educational budget represented by the library stayed steady? Climbed? Declined? Are major upcoming needs of the library tied to fundraising and program planning within other key units in the institution? Is the institution launching new programs or closing older programs? All of these would impact the type of services and collections the library needs to offer. One example of applying this in-house is our library's current efforts to adjust our collection strategy and shift monograph purchasing toward e-books, which can be readily accessed by both our campuses and our distance students.

The final insight learned involved the organizational reality of the current status of many support-service departments in a theological institution and the pace of improvement or change that can be expected. Every library is dependent in various ways on other support services, such as campus IT, the registrar, the physical plant department, or a business office, for infrastructure or information sharing. Every institution has some unique mix of issues and challenges as it tries to keep its internal workflows coordinated and efficient. Program sessions on finance and politics covered aspects of this topic as did the corresponding monthly mentoring conversations. While this insight is a version of the broader institutional awareness previously mentioned, it is more narrowly focused on forming an assessment of functional needs across campus that impact the library and determining a timeline for improvement or resolution. With this topic in mind, I worked with our circulation unit to resolve a long-standing institutional problem concerning sharing student data updates. On our campus, such data resides in three discrete locations: the library, the alumni office, and with the registrar. Each office needs their data to be current, but do not share a common data pool. The library reached out directly to stakeholders within our campus's advancement and registrar offices to try to improve the workflow for and quality of these updates across our departments.

Best Practices or Lessons Learned

The CLTP, in its totality, tried to achieve three ends: to give a pragmatic approach on a set of key managerial skills necessary for success within a library director's role; to contextualize these managerial functions within Kotter's focus on the dynamics of change and leading an organization through change; and lastly, to create within the mentoring pairs a conversation space where cohort members could discuss both topics as well as how they play out in practice.

What the program leaders considered practical management skills, based on Kotter, made up the heart of the yearlong roster of monthly webinars in the CLTP: finance, human resources, budgeting, institutional politics, and planning being only a few of the examples. Throughout these webinars and their accompanying mentoring sessions, each topic was presented to participants as learned skills with established practices and additional resources. Local institutional examples were frequently given or discussed to illustrate each area and make them immediately interpretable in a local context as part of the library director's work world.

Some skills were cross-topic in nature, such as communication and data analysis. Communication played a central part in many of these conversations on management, whether as essential to managing staff within the library, advocating for the library as part of campus leadership, or in shaping the relationship of the library with its blended community of the immediate campus, alumni, and local friends. Not a great deal of time was spent on the practice of "shaping" communication other than when it came to the crossroads of planning and advocacy for the library to institutional leaders and trustees. Simple best practices were discussed as well as the danger of no purposeful communication.

Data analysis was emphasized as essential to working successfully at a director level within theological libraries. Analysis was discussed across the spectrum from the simple, such as monitoring of institutional financial health in annual reports (and how to read them) or trends in departmental costs over time (using basic tools like Microsoft Excel) to the complex, such as peer comparisons using publicly available data from the Association of Theological Schools (ATS).

The management focus areas of the program were framed within a discussion of leadership and change and included discussions on finance and planning. These two topics particularly placed the library within the context of the ATS-level trends concerning endowment performance and stability, enrollment trends, and changes in institutional accreditation. Discussions were threaded throughout the program related to the role a theological library director can play as an institutional leader to proactively meet challenges to the institution caused by current economic and enrollment trends. One topic that may be somewhat unique to theological library directors and ATS institutions and that drew a significant amount of debate among cohort members was what the long-term impact might be for libraries of the current trend to merge the library director and lead institutional accreditation officer roles.

Recommendations for the Future

The CLTP built into its initial cohort year three mechanisms for feedback, outside the standing monthly "check-in" that opened each web-based meeting. The CLTP mentors were asked for input on their experience with the program directly from the CLTP leader by e-mail and in a follow-up phone conversation with Weltman. Those evaluations have not been shared with the cohort members to date, though known areas discussed by some mentor-participants surrounded issues of sharing webinar topics and assigned material with mentors in a timely fashion and a discussion of what represented a reasonable time allotment for mentors in their monthly phone meetings with cohort members. The latter is known to have varied widely across CLTP participants and over the course of the program's year.

The cohort members were surveyed by the association's Professional Development Committee, which sponsored the program during the spring of 2013. Members were also offered an opportunity to share feedback with the program leader, Weltman. This opportunity came as part of the final meeting of the cohort participants and the program leader in December 2012. As discussed above, the final webinar was designed to allow each individual time to comment on how they envisioned their own career goals moving forward and how the CLTP experience had changed those goals as well as to offer concrete suggestions for the program's improvement.

Seven of the suggested improvements by CLTP participants shared during this final webinar were

1. Change the program's 12-month calendar to run from June to June, rather than from January to December, in order to begin and end during an ATLA annual conference, which would open the program with face-to-face meetings between cohort members as well as members and their mentors instead of this opportunity coming mid-program.

2. Provide opportunities for different cohorts to interact with each other as the program continues (e.g., hold an event for current and past participants during the annual conference).

3. Improve the technological support for communication and community building among participants during the time between the monthly webinars.

4. Provide clear expectations for cohort member participation in each webinar (e.g., invite each person to offer a two-minute response to a question provided ahead of time).

5. Produce a resource bibliography or resource site around the program's webinar topics that cohorts could access and contribute to over time.

6. Provide a members-only forum within the association's Microsoft SharePoint site for current and past cohort members, similar to an existing "Directors Space" forum.
7. Improve the process used for selecting program mentors and for matching mentors to cohort members.

A final point, while the mentoring conversations were a highlight of the program for the 2012 cohort, other between-meeting activities were less successful. Despite the efforts of a number of participants to facilitate online, asynchronous discussions about assigned or recommended readings or leadership issues they encountered in their work, these conversations never gained traction. The lack of a satisfactory platform for online discussions—the group tried Microsoft SharePoint, Google Groups, and a private Facebook group—presented a significant barrier, but the CTLP could certainly be enriched by robust engagement among participants outside of the webinars as well as during them.

The CLTP tried to complement practical sessions on key areas of managerial competency, such as budget and planning, within the broader context of the issues challenging theological institutions such as market pressures, requiring both more radical change within theological institutions and theological library directors who are prepared to facilitate Kotter's process of leading change.

Notes

1. American Theological Library Association homepage.
2. Kotter, *Leading Change*; Kotter, "What Leaders Really Do;" Goleman, "What Makes a Leader?"
3. Kotter, *Leading Change*, 21.
4. Ibid., 25.
5. Kotter, "What Leaders Really Do," 38.
6. Kotter, *Leading Change*, 25.
7. Ibid., 26–27.
8. Ibid., 25.
9. Kotter, "What Leaders Really Do," 38.
10. Goleman, "What Makes a Leader?," 93.
11. *Encyclopædia Britannica Online Library Edition*, s.v. "intelligence, human."
12. Ibid.
13. Goleman, "What Makes a Leader?," 93.
14. Kotter, *Leading Change*, 21.

15. Ibid., 30.
16. American Library Association, "Emerging Leaders Program;" Texas Library Association, "Texas Accelerated Library Leaders;" Triangle Research Libraries Network, "Management Academy 2013."
17. Association of Theological Schools, Standard 4.4, "General Institutional Standards."
18. Friedman, *A Failure of Nerve.*
19. Ibid., 195, 13.
20. Kotter, "What Leaders Really Do," 38.

Bibliography

American Library Association. "Emerging Leaders Program." American Library Association. Accessed November 13, 2013. http://www.ala.org/education-careers/leadership/emergingleaders.

American Theological Library Association. Homepage. Accessed April 1, 2013. https://www.atla.com/Pages/default.aspx.

Association of Theological Schools. "General Institutional Standards." Accessed April 1, 2013. http://www.ats.edu/Accrediting/Documents/GeneralInstitutionalStandards.pdf.

Friedman, Edwin H. *A Failure of Nerve: Leadership in the Age of the Quick Fix.* New York: Seabury Books, 2007.

Goleman, Daniel. "What Makes a Leader?" *Harvard Business Review* 76, no. 6 (1998): 93–102.

Kotter, John P. *Leading Change.* Boston: Harvard Business School Press, 1996.

———. "What Leaders Really Do." In *HBR's 10 Must Reads on Leadership*, 37–55. Boston: Harvard Business Review Press, 2011.

Texas Library Association. "Texas Accelerated Library Leaders." Accessed November 13, 2013. http://www.txla.org/texas-accelerated-library-leaders.

Triangle Research Libraries Network. "Management Academy 2013." Accessed November 13, 2013. http://www.trln.org/academy2013/.

CHAPTER 3

Help for New College Library Directors:
College Library Directors' Mentor Program

Irene M.H. Herold

THE COLLEGE LIBRARY Directors' Mentor Program (CLDMP) grew out of the Association of College and Research Libraries' (ACRL) College Library Section's (CLS) Leadership Committee's identification of a need to support new college library directors.[1] The program was founded in the early 1990s with the assistance of Council on Library Resources (CLR) grant funding; and the enthusiasm of its directors, Larry Hardesty, Mignon Adams, and Evan Farber.[2] The history of the program, CLS, and the Leadership Committee has been thoroughly documented in my dissertation, "An Examination of the Leadership Program for College Library Directors Associated with ACRL's College Libraries Section."[3] In brief, CLS identified a need for leadership development for its members. It then formed the Leadership Committee to identify options, the first of which was the CLDMP, specifically designed to help new college library directors in their first year. Finding they could not secure grant funding easily under the ALA-ACRL umbrella, the program founders formed what they termed a loosely aegis relationship under CLS and later their own nonprofit organization to run the CLDMP. After 20 years, the two remaining founding directors, Hardesty and Adams along with Tom Kirk (who came onboard after Evan Farber), passed on the directorship of the program to me for a year with a new board of directors. After a year, I changed jobs, moving to an ARL institution, and Melissa Jadlos and Susan Barnes Whyte assumed codirectorship.

Program Structure

The CLDMP has three parts:

1. Mentoring: Each new director is paired with an experienced director for site visits and direct mentoring.
2. Seminar: Mid-year new directors meet with the program directors for a three-day face-to-face seminar.
3. Listserv: New directors are enrolled in a private listserv of current and past new directors and mentors.

In its 22 years, there have been only slight variations in the program's structure, such as the listserv, which was added after the first year and is hosted by ALA; a tour of a local academic library; and adjustment of the seminar's timing. New directors and mentors are expected to visit each other's libraries at least once with the program reimbursing mileage and meals. New directors' institutions are expected to provide program fees, which range from $500–$750 annually, depending upon subsidies during grant-supported years. Additionally, a sliding scale helps those at financially struggling institutions to further reduce the program fee. For the seminar, new directors' institutions are expected to pay travel and housing costs, while almost all of the meals are covered by the program fee.

Seminar Curriculum

The seminar is composed of guest speakers from a local college, typically a chief academic officer, faculty member, and other administrators who talk about how to work effectively with the library; some exercises, such as a modified personal style inventory or a Native American-based leadership style exercise; and discussion of topics identified by that year's cohort as issues of immediate importance. The seminar ends with a panel of not-so-new directors, who are in their fifth or more year as a director and who are former CLDMP participants; they speak about their experiences and growth from that first year.

Table 3.1 presents the outline of the seminar from the 2012–2013 cohort year. Every year the content is slightly different, depending on the program directors; whether the seminar is held on a college campus or a local hotel; the availability of speakers; the college library to tour; and what the participants identify as their burning issues or hot topics for discussion. An overview of the burning issues, for the first two decades of the program are administrative relationships, assessment, budget, communication, collection management, curriculum, documentation, fundraising, facilities planning, personnel management, professional development, role of the director, strategic planning, and technology.[4] In cohort year 2012–2013, the seminar faculty decided to use the book *Strengths Based Leadership* by Tom Rath and Barry Conchie for their leadership style exercise.[5] The seminar was held in a hotel.

TABLE 3.1. 2012–2013 Seminar Outline		
Date	Action	Outcome
Tuesday	Dinner and ice breaker activity	Meet and start process of becoming a cohort.
Wednesday	*Strengths Based Leadership*	Participants will recognize their own leadership strengths and understand that a variety of different strengths can deepen an organization's effectiveness.
	Learning about Your Institution	Participants will be able to analyze a scenario with an understanding of management and leadership issues.
	Lunch with discussion topic, What have you learned from participating in the program so far?	Participants will be able to share experiences with mentors and using the listserv.
	Session with local college provost	Participants will gain strategies for working more effectively with their chief academic officers.
	Small group discussions about working effectively with CAOs	Participants will begin to plan how to implement lessons heard during the session.
	Budgeting	Participants will gain a better understanding of budgets and learn to use their budgets strategically.

TABLE 3.1. 2012–2013 Seminar Outline		
Date	Action	Outcome
	Discussion of assignment for Thursday and adjournment into small groups to work on assignment Dinner on own, but encouraged to dine with group	Participants will get to know each other better to foster cohort cohesion.
Thursday	Group presentations	Participants will apply knowledge learned from *Strengths Based Leadership* and other seminar content. Participants will learn the value of finding and using peer relationships.
	Education Advisory Board Report *Redefining the Academic Library* (2011)	Participants will consider the future of the college library and how to talk about it internally and externally.
	Small group discussions about burning issues and the opportunity during lunch to discuss other burning issues	Participants will experience that they are not alone in dealing with issues and learn from peers.
	Building capacity for demonstrating the value of academic libraries	Participants will gain strategies for communicating the value of the library to their campuses.
	Recap of the past two days and what's missing. In other words, what have we not talked about yet that you really think we need to before we all leave tomorrow or have as a topic for a spring webinar conversation?	Participants will take ownership of their learning and feel valued.

TABLE 3.1. **2012–2013 Seminar Outline**		
Date	Action	Outcome
	Tour of local college library	Participants will be exposed to new ideas from a physical building and organizational structure that is not their own.
Friday (half day)	ACRL Standards for Libraries in Higher Education	Participants will be able to apply the new standards and the values document to library assessment on their campuses.
	Not-so-new directors panel	Participants will hear lessons learned by those who went through the program at least five years before.
	Evaluation and wrap-up	Participants will provide feedback to help improve the seminar for the future.
Note: Adapted from the 2012–2013 cohort seminar schedule, which was handed out during the seminar.		

From 2007 until 2012, seminar participants were given a chapter on library directors' views on leadership to read prior to the seminar. Over the years, participants generated a list of readings they found valuable. The most commonly cited authors were Aaron Wildavsky, Daniel Goleman, and Michael Gorman and Walt Crawford. Subjects clustered around library science, leadership, technology, and management.

The seminars ended with an exchange of business cards. Starting in 2012, an optional spring virtual meeting was added, but the participants were asked to set it up and run the agenda. From fall 2012 to today, webinars prior to the seminar were added to help the cohort bond earlier in the program year and to address topics and generate thinking helpful for the new directors as they commenced their first year of directorship.

Literature Review

There are four publications that either studied the CLDMP or used former participants as research subjects. The most recent is "Mindful Leadership Defined and Explained," a chapter in *Management and Leadership Innovations in Advances in Librarianship*.[6] The CLDMP is presented as a case study, analyzed through the mindful leadership lens.[7] As previously mentioned, the CLDMP was the subject of my 2012 dissertation, which included a review of program evaluations and mentor and participant end-of-year reports, with the conclusion that there were hints but not evidence of leadership development as a result of participation in the program.[8] Hardesty, Kirk, and Adams wrote about how chief academic officers and new library directors can create a productive working relationship with each other.[9] They interviewed over 300 college librarians and chief academic officers at predominantly smaller institutions via discussions, reports, and e-mails, with a majority being former participants in the CLDMP. The interviewees mentioned the CLDMP as a resource for mentorship and professional development. Julie O'Keeffe surveyed 189 midwestern college library directors from institutions with student enrollments under 2,000, and she questioned the 15 participants of the 1995–1996 CLDMP cohort about what they saw as essential skills for their positions.

Several articles about the program have been written by the former program directors, participants, and mentors. Some served the purpose of describing the program and promoting it to potential participants; many just reference the program, while others have been enthusiastic testimonials of the program. Writing in the first few years of the program's existence, Hardesty described the formation and history of the program, which, he pointed out, was intended to "enhance the leadership capabilities of newly appointed college library directors."[10] He maintained that participants displayed leadership beyond their employment by being elected to office in organizations and that the receipt of awards was further acknowledgment of their leadership. For the tenth anniversary of the CLDMP, Hardesty (2001) published a promotional piece on the program in the online newsletter *Info Career Trends*.[11] When the founding program directors officially announced their retirement, handing off the program to new leaders and a new board to oversee the program, Hardesty, Kirk, and Adams authored "New Leadership for College Library Directors' Mentor Program."[12]

Many publications reference the program. Loriene Roy mentioned the CLDMP in her chapter on mentoring students of color as an example of an existing mentoring program.[13] Steven Bell reflected on his experiences with mentors, including the CLDMP, in "The Next Generation May Not Want Your Mentoring: Leading From the Library."[14] As the article title suggests, Bell concluded that in his experience, after two years of being mentored and mentoring, the relationships lost relevance. Jessica Olin listed a quotation about the CLDMP as advice she received about what a new director should do when starting in a leadership position.[15] She then followed up with a blog post a year later, referencing the application of something she learned via the program for work-life balance.[16]

An advanced Google search for "college library directors' mentor program" returned over 4,900 items. The results fell into two major categories: listing the program as a resource and listing the program as something the individual participated in, such as on a CV or in an announcement of a new hire. Examples of listing the program as a resource included The Medical Library Association and an article by Elizabeth M. Doolittle and others.[17]

Testimonials about the program were written by new directors and mentors. Susan Stroyan , Janis Bandelin and others, and Charles M. Getchell each described their experiences as new directors participating in the program.[18] Stroyan stated that the program created a "leadership network."[19] Oakley Coburn wrote from the perspective of a mentor, and he referred to managing change.[20]

More recent *CLS Newsletter* articles commemorated the program during certain years, noted significant events, or just mentioned it. The 15th anniversary of the program was noted in Kudos to Participants in the College Library Directors Mentor Program.[21] The article stated the purpose of the program "is to enhance the leadership capabilities of the new directors and to help them meet the challenges involved in directing small college libraries."[22] Christopher Millson-Martula mentioned the CLDMP in his CLS chair column as something the section supports to "enhance organizational effectiveness and strengthen the programs of library services that a college or small university library typically offers."[23] The transition to new leadership was noted in 2012 with the announcement of the retirement of the program's founders.[24]

Planting Seeds: A Personal Reflection on Participation

I participated in CLDMP's 1998–1999. The seminar was held in Philadelphia, Pennsylvania before the January ALA Midwinter Meeting. We did a modified personal style type inventory during the session, but because I had done one five years before it did not reveal anything unknown, as I was aware I was extroverted, intuitive, thinking, and quick to form judgments. I enjoyed meeting the other new directors in my cohort and the intense discussions. I noted at the end of the year,

> At first I thought the mentor, site visits, listserv, and networking with the other new directors were the most valuable components of the program. I saw little value, except for the [personal style type inventory] exercise, which I did with my staff as a [lead] into evaluation in February, in the actual seminar sessions. As time has passed, I've come to realize that the value for me did not lie in the actual content of the sessions, but in how the group interacted and responded to the sessions. The role-playing over the various "problems" still lasts in my memory while the other sessions fade, not because of the content of the solutions. It lasts first because it was illuminating to see how other decision-makers make decisions. (pers. comm.)

Rereading my end-of-year report from 1999, my comments parallel those of other participants throughout the years of the program.[25] I made some important connections and friends from my cohort, which made a difference in my career path. Understanding that there is more than one kind of route to decision making was an invaluable lesson to learn early in my leadership role.

Also my time with my mentor while useful—though when she visited my library and spoke with my staff about what is an academic library, at least one person commented to me later that my mentor was saying things I had said—did not change my work in an immediate sense. When I visited my mentor's site, she gave me John P. Kotter's book, *Leading Change*. I did not read it for three years, until I started my next director's position. She and I had only minimal contact over the years, but I always felt like I could contact her with a question and sometimes did. In my 1998–1999 reports after our exchange of visits, I did note that I had the opportunity to brainstorm with her in a safe environment on a personnel situation. Since isolation of college library directors is noted as one of the reasons the CLDMP is needed, my experience was that the program helped to overcome that separation via my mentor and provided a confidential and experienced person to bounce ideas off.

The effects of the program, which included modeling national leadership and providing mentorship, became apparent with the passage of time. Two from my cohort went on to serve as ACRL presidents. Two served as CLS chair. One appointed me to a CLS committee, which started me on the path to eventual CLS chair and now ACRL board director-at-large. The former program directors enthusiastically nominated me to serve on an editorial board. They tapped me to research and write a report for a grant project on the CLDMP. The CLDMP became a focal point of my dissertation work and continuing scholarship. The book my mentor gave me, Leading Change, became the framework for strategic planning in my applied practice and a presentation I gave at an ALA conference, and later I used Kotter's continuing work in my dissertation.[26] I was so inspired and believed in the value of the program that I applied to become the program's director when the founding directors announced their retirement. The CLDMP has been an important part of my leadership development.

Leadership Theories

There were no explicitly utilized leadership theories underlying the framework of the CLDMP. In fact, one of the program founders noted the CLDMP was not a "course in management theory, but a practical introduction to the responsibilities, duties, and tribulations of a college library director" (Mignon Adams, pers. comm.). In my dissertation, I identified in CLDMP's content hints of leadership and potential application of leadership theories, such as transformational leadership. I also identified emotional intelligence and resonant leadership as part of mindful leadership, which explains why participants and mentors identify what happens in CLDMP as leadership development.[27]

Since 2012, the CLDMP seminar content has intentionally included a focus on leadership in addition to management. The seminar curriculum for January 2013 included learning outcomes, which were previously unstated for the program. The use of *Strengths Based Leadership* was intended to launch a leadership-focused discussion during the seminar.[28] There was also a new director webinar in the fall on the topic of leadership versus management.

Conclusion

While no new study of leadership development evidence has been conducted since my dissertation, the cumulative, self-reported perceptions of participants and mentors in the program indicate feelings of high value associated with the program. This comes through feeling supported; valued for their experience; and in having safe spaces, such as the listserv and mentoring relationships, for expressing concerns. During a period of transition, such as undertaking a first directorship at a college, the creation of an environment such as the CLDMP may assist in a leader's development; however, this is an area that needs further study.

Recently, the CLDMP evaluation has attempted to obtain self-reported evidence of change in the participants due to participation in the program. For example, a question was added to the post-seminar evaluation asking what new directors would do differently based on something that they learned during the seminar. Responses varied from adjusting attitudes, which could be counted as emotional intelligence, to the concrete actions of creating a new policy or procedure, which could be counted as transformational leadership if applied to create change. Self-reported evaluations do not provide enough evidence to state that leadership development occurred due to participation in this program. A focused case study of several new directors over a period of two years, capturing observed pre-, during, and post-program participation would perhaps provide clearer documentation of leadership actions leading to change demonstrating development. This would not provide information about the effectiveness of the leadership actions but could help in understanding the effect of programs such as the CLDMP.

The CLDMP is the only program specifically for new college library directors at small institutions. It provides an affordable niche for a cohort that still demonstrates a need for the program. High satisfaction with their experience reported by participants and mentors indicate it is meeting expectations for support of new college library directors. The program has had multiple inquiries over the years by others seeking to emulate or broaden the program's focus to include other types of academic libraries, such as community colleges and larger-sized colleges, but the program directors have resisted straying far from its originally defined purpose, recognizing that its specialized focus contributes to the enduring nature of the program.

Notes

1. The CLS maintains information about the program at http://www.ala.org/acrl/about/sections/cls/collprogdisc/collegelibrary.
2. For information about CLR, now called Council on Library and Information Resources (CLIR), see http://www.clir.org/.
3. Herold, "An Examination of the Leadership Program." See Chapter 1 for a review of CLS's history and the Leadership Committee's formation. See Chapter 3 for a review of CLS leadership activities and the CLDMP's development.
4. Herold, "E-Mentoring."
5. Rath and Conchie, *Strengths Based Leadership*. The book has a unique access code that allows you to take a leadership version of Gallup's StrengthsFinder assessment.
6. Beverage et al., "Mindful Leadership Defined and Explained."
7. Ibid., 31–34.
8. Herold, "An Examination of the Leadership Program."
9. Hardesty, Kirk, and Adams, "Off to a Good Start."
10. Hardesty, "Who You Goin' a Call?"; "College Library Mentor Program," 7; "College Library Directors Mentor Program, 284"
11. Hardesty, "College Library Directors' Mentor Program."
12. Hardesty, Kirk, and Adams, "New Leadership."
13. Roy, "Creating Opportunities and Opening Doors," 131–32.
14. Bell, "The Next Generation."
15. Olin, "Leading Change."
16. Olin, "What a Difference a Year Makes."
17. Medical Library Association, "Selected Web Resources"; Doolittle et al., "Creating a Culture."
18. Stroyan, "New Director Praises Mentor Program"; Bandelin et al., "Mentor Program"; Getchell, "Mentor Program Praised."
19. Stroyan, "New Director Praises Mentor Program," 9.
20. Coburn, "Mentors Are Mentored Too."
21. College Libraries Section, Kudos to Participants.
22. Ibid., 3.
23. Millson-Martula, "CLS—What Can It Do For You?"
24. College Libraries Section, Kudos.
25. In Herold, "An Examination of the Leadership Program," Chapter 5, 178–81. Seminar evaluations asking what was liked best and least were analyzed. Themes of value included meeting with peers in a similar situation, networking during the seminar, availability of the network after the seminar, access to seminar leaders and guest expertise, new ideas, and how the experience

provided an affirmation that they were either on the right track or at least not unique or alone in their work. Areas needing improvement focused on seminar arrangements, desire for more pre-readings, sessions on budget and personnel issues, and seminar length (too short for some, too long for others).

26. Kotter, *Leading Change.*
27. Herold, "An Examination of the Leadership Program"; Beverage et al., "Mindful Leadership Defined and Explained." Transformational leadership was a concept first introduced by Burns in his book *Leadership* and refers to leaders who inspire and mobilize change by helping people in their organization reach their fullest potential. Goleman, in *Emotional Intelligence*, coined *emotional intelligence*, and in a later work, *Primal Leadership*, Goleman, Boyatzis, and McKee defined it as referring to four areas of self-awareness, self-management, social awareness, and relationship management. Resonant leadership is defined in Boyatzis and McKee's book *Resonant Leadership*: Resonant leaders read individuals and groups accurately, build a sense of community, create an environment where things can be accomplished, move in positive directions, and manage of their emotions to avoid burnout (p. 22).
28. Rath and Conchie, *Strengths Based Leadership.*

Bibliography

Bandelin, Janis, Daria Bossman, Kate Hickey, Steven McKinzie, and Patricia Payne.. "Mentor Program 'Class of '97' Bonds at Seminar." *CLS Newsletter* 13, no. 1 (1997). http://www.ala.org/acrl/sites/ala.org.acrl/files/content/aboutacrl/directoryofleadership/sections/cls/clswebsite/newsletters/1997%20Spring%20CLS%20News.pdf.

Bell, Steven. "The Next Generation May Not Want Your Mentoring: Leading from the Library." *Library Journal*, April 24, 2013. http://lj.libraryjournal.com/2013/04/opinion/leading-from-the-library/the-next-generation-may-not-want-your-mentoring-leading-from-the-library/#_.

Beverage Stephanie, Kathleen DeLong, Irene M.H. Herold, and Kenley Neufeld. "Mindful Leadership Defined and Explained." In *Management and Leadership Innovations Advances in Librarianship*, Vol. 38, edited by Anne Woodsworth and W. David Penniman, 21–35. United Kingdom: Emerald Publishing Limited, 2014.

Boyatzis, Richard, and Annie McKee. *Resonant Leadership: Renewing Yourself and Connecting with Others through Mindfulness, Hope, and Compassion.* Boston: Harvard Business School Press, 2007.

Burns, James MacGregor. *Leadership.* New York: Harper & Row, 1978.

Coburn, Oakley. "Mentors are Mentored Too in Program for New Directors." *CLS Newsletter* 12, no. 1 (1996). http://www.ala.org/acrl/sites/ala.org.acrl/files/content/aboutacrl/directoryofleadership/sections/cls/clswebsite/newsletters/1996%20Spring%20CLS%20News.pdf.

College Libraries Section. Kudos to Participants of College Library Directors Mentor Program. *CLS Newsletter* 22, no. 2 (2006): 3. http://www.ala.org/acrl/sites/ala.org.acrl/files/content/aboutacrl/directoryofleadership/sections/cls/clswebsite/newsletters/CLSFall2006.pdf.

College Libraries Section. Kudos. *CLS Newsletter* 28, no. 2 (2012): 2. http://www.ala.org/acrl/sites/ala.org.acrl/files/content/aboutacrl/directoryofleadership/sections/cls/clswebsite/newsletters/cls_fall2012.pdf.

Doolittle, Elizabeth M., John-Bauer Graham, Alyssa Martin, Hal Mendelsohn, and Kent Snowden. "Creating a Culture of Mentoring @ Your Library." *The Southeastern Librarian* 57, no. 1 (2009): 38. http://digitalcommons.kennesaw.edu/seln/vol57/iss1/7.

Galloway, Ann-Christie. "Grants and Acquisitions." *College and Research Libraries News* 7, no. 8 (2010): 448–49.

Getchell, Charles M. "Mentor Program Praised by Member of 'Class of '96.'" *CLS Newsletter* 13, no. 1 (1997). http://www.ala.org/acrl/sites/ala.org.acrl/files/content/aboutacrl/directoryofleadership/sections/cls/clswebsite/newsletters/1997%20Spring%20CLS%20News.pdf.

Goleman, Daniel. *Emotional Intelligence: Why It Can Matter More than IQ*. New York: Bantam Books, 1995.

Goleman, Daniel, Richard E. Boyatzis, and Annie McKee. *Primal Leadership: Realizing the Power of Emotional Intelligence*. Boston: Harvard Business School Press, 2002.

Hardesty, Larry. "Who You Goin' a Call? The College Library Director Mentor Program." *CLS Newsletter,* 9, no. 1 (1993): 2–3. http://www.ala.org/acrl/sites/ala.org.acrl/files/content/aboutacrl/directoryofleadership/sections/cls/clswebsite/newsletters/clsfall1993.pdf.

———. "College Library Mentor Program." *College & Research Libraries News* 55 (1994): 7.

———. "College Library Directors Mentor Program: 'Passing It On:' A Personal Reflection." *Journal of Academic Librarianship* 23, no. 4 (1997): 281–90.

———. "College Library Directors' Mentor Program Enters Tenth Year." *Info Career Trends: LISjobs.com's Career Development Newsletter* (2001). Accessed August 10, 2014. http://www.lisjobs.com/career_trends/?p=130.

Hardesty, Larry, Tom Kirk, and Mignon Adams. "Off to a Good Start: Foundations for Strong CAO–Library Director Relationships." *Library Issues:*

Briefings for Faculty and Administrators 28, no. 1 (2007): 1–4. http://www.libraryissues.com/sub/LI280001.asp.

———. "New Leadership for College Library Directors' Mentor Program." *College and Research Libraries News* 73, no. 10 (2012): 579.

Herold, Irene M.H. "E-Mentoring: An Analysis of Listserv Content for Leadership." Unpublished manuscript, last modified 2009. Microsoft Word file.

———. "An Examination of the Leadership Program for College Library Directors Associated with ACRL's College Libraries Section." PhD diss., Simmons College, 2012. ProQuest (ATT 3515783).

Kotter, John P.. *Leading Change*. Boston: Harvard Business School Press, 1996.

Medical Library Association. "Selected Web Resources for Librarian Mentors." *Resources for Mentors*, accessed June 13, 2013. http://blueline.mlanet.org/mentor/mentor_resources.html.

Millson-Martula, Christopher. "CLS—What Can It Do For You?" *CLS Newsletter* 27, no. 1 (2011): 1. http://www.ala.org/acrl/sites/ala.org.acrl/files/content/aboutacrl/directoryofleadership/sections/cls/clswebsite/newsletters/cls-spr11.pdf.

Olin, Jessica R. "Leading Change as a Library Administrator." *EDUCAUSE Review Online* (June 3, 2013). http://www.educause.edu/ero/article/leading-change-library-administrator.

———. "What a Difference a Year Makes: My First Year as a Library Director." *Letters to a Young Librarian* (blog). February 4, 2014. http://letterstoayounglibrarian.blogspot.com/2014/02/what-difference-year-makes-my-first.html.

Rath, Tom, and Barry Conchie. *Strengths Based Leadership: Great Leaders, Teams, and Why People Follow*. New York: Gallup Press, 2008.

Roy, Loriene. "Creating Opportunities and Opening Doors: Recruiting and Mentoring Students of Color." In *Unfinished Business: Race, Equity, and Diversity in Library and Information Science Education*, edited by Maurice B. Wheeler. 131–48. Lanham, MD: Scarecrow Press, 2005.

Stroyan, Susan. "New Director Praises Mentor Program." *CLS Newsletter* 9, no. 2 (1994): 8–9. http://www.ala.org/acrl/sites/ala.org.acrl/files/content/aboutacrl/directoryofleadership/sections/cls/clswebsite/newsletters/1994%20Spring%20CLS%20News.pdf.

CHAPTER 4

HBCU Library Alliance Leadership Institute

Monika Rhue

HISTORICALLY BLACK COLLEGES and universities (HBCUs) were the only place African Americans could go to pursue a higher education. After the Civil War, slavery, Jim Crow, and the Civil Rights Movement, there were rarely any other options for higher education for African Americans. Out of this need to educate African Americans came a rich culture and legacy of HBCUs. HBCUs are defined as private and public colleges founded prior to 1964 for the education of freed slaves.[1]

Establishment of the HBCU Library Alliance

The HBCU Library Alliance was established as a 501(c)(3) nonprofit corporation on October 29, 2002 in Atlanta, Georgia. Its purpose is to provide an array of resources to strengthen HBCUs and their constituents. The HBCU Library Alliance is governed by a board of directors, which is composed of directors and deans from several HBCUs founded before 1964.[2]

The HBCU Library Alliance acts a consortium that supports collaboration among HBCUs to ensure excellence in library services, program development, preservation, and leadership for its members. The primary purpose of the HBCU Library Alliance is to ensure the overall success of HBCU libraries.[3]

LEADERSHIP PROGRAM OVERVIEW

The Andrew W. Mellon Foundation provided support to the HBCU Library Alliance members during 2003–2004 to address challenges facing HBCUs and to develop a needs assessment. The assessment identified three core areas that were of major concern to HBCU libraries: growth of leadership, fiscal constraints, and keeping abreast of technology. The HBCU Library Alliance partnered with the Southeastern Library Network (SOLINET) to implement the first Leadership Institute from 2005–2006, funded by the Mellon Foundation.[4] This pilot leadership institute had five components, two-session leadership institutes, site visits, scholarships for daylong workshops on specific topics, and an exchange program for librarians from HBCUs. A mentorship program was also implemented after analyzing the results from the pilot leadership institute. The first leadership institute also provided scholarships for HBCU library staff to attend training in strategic planning, fund-raising, disaster preparedness, and team management. Funding was provided in this phase of the institute for a pilot exchange program that allowed five HBCU librarians to spend two weeks at an Association of Southeastern Research Libraries' (ASERL) institute. The goal of the exchange program was to have the HBCU librarians develop a strategic plan for their libraries and foster a stronger relationship between HBCU libraries and ASERL libraries and librarians (Sandra Phoenix, pers. comm.).

The HBCU Library Alliance concluded its first leadership institute with 48 participants from 24 HBCUs (Sandy Nyberg, pers. comm.). The Mellon Foundation funded the second leadership institute in 2007–2008. The second institute had a series of workshops targeted towards leadership development and focused on future directions and critical leadership issues.[5] I participated in the second institute.

The Curriculum

The second HBCU Library Alliance Leadership Institute was held August 10–15, 2007, at the Aberdeen Woods Conference Center in Peachtree City, Georgia. The lead instructor was Dr. Karyn Trader-Leigh, president of KTA Global Partners, with guest instructors Marsha Hughes-Rease, organizational development consultant with Dannemiller Tyson Associates, and Cleave Clarke, executive vice president of Comprehensive Integrated Solutions.

"Redefining Leadership for 21st Century Librarians" was the theme. The content for the institute centered on innovating knowledge, adapting new strategies and competencies, and building coalitions and part-nerships.[6] With these themes came excitement, uncertainty, and hope for those directors, deans, and staff charged with strengthening or cultivating their leadership skills. Each participant received a binder with articles, ac-tivities, and reflection note pages. The first page included an introduction by Trader-Leigh, which stated,

> We are in a new century of library leadership… The li-brary landscape has changed dramatically… Today's li-brary leaders cannot operate in insular environments … we must develop library leaders who think and act dif-ferently, who are capable of working across boundaries and understanding the issues, who are willing to develop themselves and their organizations and who are willing to facilitate culture change and lead the transformation in HBCU libraries… To do this we must focus on leadership issues and develop the necessary capabilities and compe-tencies in HBCU librarians.[7]

Trader-Leigh's words were inspiring to participants, and she estab-lished the tone for the curriculum materials. The binder was divided into four chapters: "Building the Strategy-Focused Organization," "Aligning Performance with Strategy," "New Leadership," and "Transforming Orga-nizations and Leading Change." Each chapter had a series of articles, ex-amples, and reflections.

BUILDING THE STRATEGY-FOCUSED ORGANIZATION
This chapter laid the foundation in strategic thinking, planning, conduct-ing an environmental scan, creating your mission and vision statement, and identifying stakeholders. It also shared information on how to develop a strategic management plan.[8]

ALIGNING PERFORMANCE WITH STRATEGY
This chapter focused on crafting the elements of a strategic plan by looking at the consumer. It included reviewing a video on how to put the consumer

first and practice exercises that placed an emphasis on creating "customer value" through innovation and strategy. The concept for this chapter was to learn how to use "strategy to make decisions about innovations and deliver innovative services to the consumer."[9]

NEW LEADERSHIP

These materials were all about understanding one's leadership type and personality. This section was individually focused because it was all about evaluating yourself. The components of this section helped me to identify my leadership type. It allowed me to review and reflect on three leadership styles: visionary, transformative, and principled leadership.[10] The use of the Myers-Briggs Type Indicator helped me understand my preferred personality type and how to use this tool to understand the people I would lead as a new library director. I was also introduced to the concept of "emotional intelligence to leadership."[11] Learning about this concept gave me the opportunity to evaluate my emotional triggers and to learn about the emotional triggers of others.[12]

TRANSFORMING ORGANIZATIONS AND LEADING CHANGE

The work in this chapter provided several guidelines for how to help organizations through transformation and transitions, how to use reframing experiences to discover new possibilities, and how to gain a greater understanding of leading systems.[13] The reframing organizations materials were based on Lee G. Bolman and Terrence E. Deal's Four Frameworks Approach.[14] Highlights from this section also included reviewing scenarios for managing transformation. Several strategies were shared for looking at the institution's change history, managing transitions, managing resistance to change, and implementing change.[15] The change model in this section was based on strategies and examples from *Beyond Change Management: Advanced Strategies for Today's Transformation Leaders*.[16]

The core contents for the HBCU Library Alliance Leadership Institute addressed practical solutions for HBCUs moving towards becoming 21st-century library leaders. The week-long program gave a foundation and examples for implementing Promoting Active Library Services (PALS), which was my new initiative as the library director.

Literature Review

The HBCU Library Alliance disseminated the plans, announcements, and results of the HBCU Library Alliance Leadership Institute in several publications. The publications established the foundation for the leadership institute by reporting on the purpose and need for such a program centered on a potential crisis projected to affect library leadership at HBCUs because of a large pool of deans and directors near retirement.[17] The late Lillian Lewis, who served as the HBCU Library Alliance program officer, provided a statement in *Diverse: Issues in Education* on how the institute was implemented. It started with a few HBCU deans and directors coming together in 2003 to discuss the potential retirement of HBCUs' leaders and to plan the core content for the leadership institute, which included strategies for advocating "total integration into campus programs for teaching and learning" among librarians.[18] The planning project was funded by Mellon Foundation. The planning grant allowed members of the HBCU Library Alliance and SOLINET to identify and analyze obstacles that impeded HBCUs library leaders from being a part of their universities' decision-making process when it came to budgeting, being a part of the teaching and learning environment, and managing rapidly changing technology.[19]

The result of the planning generated the pilot institute funded by a $500,000 Mellon Foundation grant. During 2005–2006, the institute created the training schedule and ran the pilot institute. The pilot tested the methodology and case studies of leadership styles, developed the mentoring program, and established the exchange program through a collaborative partnership with the ASERL. [20]

In 2007, the HBCU Library Alliance was awarded funding for the second phase of the institute. *The Southeastern Librarian* published a series of announcements on the funding received by the HBCU Library Alliance to continue the leadership institute and mentorship program.[21] A *College & Research Libraries News* announcement highlighted the institute lead instructor, Trader-Leigh, and acknowledged presentations by Kate Nevins, executive director of SOLINET (now LYRASIS), and Charles Greene of the White House Initiative on HBCUs.[22]

Two articles shared some of the outcomes of the leadership program and the exchange program. "Each One Teach One" appeared in the February 2007 edition of *American Libraries*.[23] This article included several quotes from participants on the success of the exchange program between ASERL and the HBCU Library Alliance. It described how associate-level HBCU librarians spent two weeks with an ASERL partner institution. The ASERL director traveled to an HBCU to learn about the librarians' working environment. The exchange program provided learning opportunities in the areas of information literacy, merging of the information technology and library department into one unit, budgeting, and building relationships on campus and in the community. The exchange librarians and the ASERL partners commented on how the program fostered a reciprocal learning experience and showed potential for future collaborations.[24] The article concluded with comments by Loretta Parham, director and CEO of the Robert W. Woodruff Library, "It is clear that these exchanges will lead to new and exciting partnerships between HBCU and ASERL libraries. And most importantly, these exchanges will promote the values of diversity and collaboration at each of the institutions involved."[25]

The second article, "The HBCU Library Alliance: Developing Leadership," published in *Virginia Libraries*, provided an in-depth look at the HBCU Library Alliance Leadership Institute.[26] A brief history of the HBCU Library Alliance was provided with an overview on how the leadership institute was planned and the institute's five components. The article highlighted feedback from the participants on how they benefited from the leadership program. Cultivating strong leadership skills, which is important to the future of HBCUs' libraries, was one of the noted priorities.[27] The article also stated that the leadership program came at a critical moment in the history of HBCU libraries. With the anticipated retirement of many deans and directors in librarianship, the founding members of the HBCU Library Alliance recognized that unless there is a cadre of trained leaders, armed with the knowledge and skills needed to deal with the constant change and complexity of the library and information profession, there was going to be a shortage of potential library directors, which would be devastating to HBCU institutions.[28] The article reported that three out of four librarians who participated in the leadership program were now serving as a library director.[29]

Ana Guthrie, reference and instruction librarian at Florida Memorial University, contributed her personal experiences about the HBCU Library Alliance in *Solutions,* a LYRASIS publication, entitled "The HBCU Library Alliance 'Gets Me.'"[30] Guthrie shared her new librarian anxieties when working for the first time at an HBCU. Guthrie told how the HBCU Library Alliance Leadership Institute helped her to discover her leadership style, gain an understanding of the cause of her public speaking nervousness, and provided her with the tools to manage conflict. At the conclusion of her leadership experience Guthrie knew that she belonged at Florida Memorial University.[31] Guthrie stated,

> I was groomed to stand firm as an information profession-
> al who knew what she was doing. It was drilled into me
> that I am a working woman who could finally stop con-
> centrating on whether she'd fall on her face when present-
> ing, answering reference questions, or dealing with intelli-
> gentsia. The HBCU Library Alliance Leadership Institute,
> in essence, trained me to take seriously my responsibili-
> ty as an information professional at a vital, ever-relevant
> HBCU institution.[32]

The leadership institute continued with the backing of the Mellon Foundation. Phase IV of the leadership institute was announced in the October 2011 issue of *College & Research Libraries News*.[33] The announcement shared the new features of the program: "mentoring, coaching, and face-to-face and Web-based classes, for a new group of HBCU librarians …effective assessment strategies, programs for current library deans and directors, and plans for post-grant sustainability of the Leadership Program."[34]

The HBCU Library Leadership Institute concluded in 2012 with 54 institutions participating in one or more of the five leadership programs. There were a total of 112 librarians who participated in HBCU Library Leadership Institute (Sandy Nyberg, pers. comm.). As a participant, I had the freedom to state my challenges and receive guidance from seasoned and knowledgeable librarians in the profession.

Personal Experience in the Program

I had never dreamed of becoming a library director. I had pored my passion and love into rebuilding the Inez Moore Parker Archives at Johnson C. Smith University (JCSU). I was happy being tucked away with old and fragile records dating back to 1876. In the archival profession, most archivists mange the operation of their archives single-handedly, which was my experience. I directed processing collections, managed the archives budget, and supervised student interns. I performed community outreach, wrote grant writing, managed grants, and ran promotions of the archives. Little did I know that these skills would contribute to my becoming a library director.

In 2007, I was invited by the director of library services at JCSU to attend the HBCU Library Alliance Leadership Institute. I was surprise by this invitation. Nonetheless, I accepted the opportunity to learn how I could further my leadership skills as the archival services librarian. The first day was orientation, getting to know one another and allowing the directors to share why they selected us (junior librarians) to attend the leadership institute. My director shared how she witnessed my management of the archives with little supervision and how I was able to turn the JCSU archives program around. The group sharing and the binder of leadership styles and strategies set the tone for the institute. Later that night, over dinner my director informed me that she had accepted another director position and wanted to recommend me as the interim library director at JCSU. I could not answer immediately for I was in shock. I had never thought about being a library director.

The HBCU Library Alliance Leadership Institute changed the course of my professional career. For the first time I had the opportunity to learn about my leadership style. I learned about my emotional triggers and how to identify the emotional triggers of others. I learned strategies for managing my emotions when leading others. The most enriching experience was being introduced to the strength, weakness, opportunities, and threat (SWOT) assessment. This assessment proved to be very useful. The year I was promoted to interim director of library services, JCSU also hired a new president. The president requested a SWOT from each department. I was not intimidated by this request; I was prepared and had solid examples of how to fulfill this request from the leadership institute.

Being promoted from within, where you are no longer looked upon as a colleague but as the director, had its own unique challenges. I am so thankful that as a participant of the HBCU Library Alliance Leadership Institute that I was assigned a mentor. My mentor, Joan Williams, library director at Bennett College, was instrumental in helping me to deal with personnel issues. In conjunction with receiving a mentor, I also received communication exercises on how to listen and not be defensive. I reread these materials several times when working with library staff. The section on how to implement change was very useful. Learning how to get buy-in from library staff and administrators, plus understanding how change brings about anxieties, allowed me to carefully introduce new initiatives and projects.

The "Thrill of the Grill" team-building exercise was a fun day at the institute.[35] It takes a lot of teamwork and collaboration to deliver a meal that is presented well and tasteful. Team members had to select a head chef, agree upon a dish, and then coordinate workstations. Every team was given the same foods to cook and one hour to complete the meal. The meal was judged. My team received the "Thrill of the Grill" medal. The lesson I learned from this exercise was to make meetings engaging. Before each library staff meeting I engage the staff with a game, door prizes, or a team-building exercise. I introduced the Library Family Feud game. This game was filled with questions that recapped the library activities for that year instead of reading a summary.

My participation in the HBCU Library Alliance Leadership Institute was memorable. It shaped my leadership style. I still connect with the deans, directors, and librarians I met through the institute. I continue to use the resource binder. The discussions and resources were crafted to address the issues relevant to HBCUs. I participated in the HBCU Library Leadership Institute as the university archivist. Many of my colleagues in the profession have often shared that this was an unusual journey. The leadership institute helped me transform this unusual journey of being the university archivist into a success story: becoming the director of library services in 2008.

Conclusion

The HBCU Library Alliance Leadership Institute had a long-term impact in helping shape leadership among HBCUs. The institute cultivated a unique environment that allowed deans, directors, and librarians to learn, grow, and expound upon issues directly related to HBCUs. As a new director, participating in the HBCU Library Alliance Leadership Institute gave me the freedom to state my challenges and receive guidance from seasoned and knowledgeable librarians in the profession. I continue to use the resources, aiding me with my growth and development as a leader.

Further research needs to be done to determine how the resources were used by other participants. The literature review provided general feedback and benefits of the institute. Specific data is needed to determine how the curriculum, the mentorship program, and the exchange program were used or how they were useful to participants after the institute. For instance, it is unknown how many participants implemented the emotional intelligence model or developed a SWOT analysis for their library. Analysis of the results of such implementation or the implementation of the reframing an organization concept need further study. Examples of how this reorganization was done in an HBCU library environment may be helpful to other HBCUs. The HBCU Library Alliance Leadership Institute goal was to provide an environment to assist HBCU librarians to "articulate and advance a vision for the library as a valued partner in the teaching and learning; manage change that will transform the library into a 'learning commons;' build partnerships with faculty and administrators and with the broader HBCU community; and create a culture of leadership within the library staff."[36] Writing about the accomplishments of the leadership institute as it relates to the goals and outcomes of the program could provide additional research avenues specifically from the HBCU community. Publishing the final outcome on how this leadership program helped HBCU deans, directors, and librarians apply the concepts of emotional intelligence and reframing organizations could be useful information to others seeking a leadership institute model.

During August 3–8, 2008, I participated in Harvard's Leadership Institute for Academic Librarians. *Reframing Leadership, Diagnosing Organization*, based on Lee G. Bolman and Terrence E. Deal's *Reframing Organization,* was one of the required readings.[37] The Leadership Institute for Academic Librarians reinforced what I learned at the HBCU Library Alliance Leadership Institute. The Leadership Institute for Academic Librarians used mini-case studies and group discussions to provided participants with examples of how institutions and companies used the "four frames" model for leadership and change.[38] The mini-case studies were instrumental in helping to understand how the four frames may be applied in an academic library.

Both leadership institutes provided me with a foundation of resources for evaluating my leadership type and capabilities. The leadership institutes taught me how to shape and mold my leadership style from various lenses when it comes to dealing with the complexities of personalities, implementing change, and receiving buy-in from employees to administrators during the implementation of new initiatives. I keep both programs' binders of resources in my office. I am approaching seven years as the library director. Leadership is a revolving door; these institutes provided me with the tools I needed to be successful as a leader.

Notes

1. Brooks and Starks, *Historically Black Colleges and Universities*, xv–xvi.
2. HBCU Library Alliance, HBCU Library Alliance about Us page.
3. Ibid.
4. The Southeastern Library Network (SOLINET) served as a membership network of libraries and information organizations supporting libraries in the southeastern United States as well as Puerto Rico and the US Virgin Islands. In 2008, SOLINET became a part of the merger between PALINET (Mid-Atlantic region) and NELINET (New England region) to create the largest membership organization, LYRASIS, serving libraries and information professionals (Anderson, "LYRASIS").
5. Ibid.
6. Trader-Leigh, "Leadership Institute," iv.
7. Ibid., iv.
8. Ibid., 3–34.
9. Ibid., 49–50.
10. Ibid., 80–81.
11. Goleman, Boyatzis, and McKee, *Primal Leadership*.
12. Trader-Leigh, 95–96.
13. Ibid., 117.
14. Bolman and Deal, *Reframing Organizations*.
15. Trader-Leigh, 118–24.
16. Anderson and Ackerman, *Beyond Change Management,* 129–36.
17. Pluviose, "HBCU Library Alliance."
18. Ibid.
19. Hart et al., "The HBCU Library Alliance."
20. Ibid., 17.
21. Davis, "HBCU News," (2005); "HBCU News," (2007).
22. Orphan, "Mellon Foundation."
23. Burger and Lewis, "Each One Teach One."
24. Ibid.
25. Ibid., 36.

26. Hart et al., "The HBCU Library Alliance."
27. Ibid., 16.
28. Ibid.,16–17.
29. Ibid., 20.
30. Guthrie, "LYRASIS: The HBCU Library Alliance."
31. Ibid., 1
32. Ibid., 2.
33. Galloway, "LYRASIS and the HBCU."
34. Ibid.
35. "Thrill of the Grill" team-building exercise was a part of The New Leadership section from the materials provided by Trader-Leigh, *Leadership Institute.*
36. Lewis, *The HBCU Library.*
37. Bolman and Deal, *Reframing Organizations.*
38. Ibid.

Bibliography

Anderson, Dean, and Linda Anderson Ackerman. *Beyond Change Management: Advanced Strategies for Today's Transformational Leaders.* San Francisco: Jossey-Bass, 2002.

Anderson, Kathy. "LYRASIS: A Collaborative Success Story." *Collaborative Librarianship* 2, no. 2 (2010): 105–08.

Bolman, Lee G., and Terrence E. Deal. *Reframing Organizations: Artistry, Choice, and Leadership.* San Francisco: Jossey-Bass, 1997.

Brooks, F. Erik, and Glenn L. Starks. *Historically Black Colleges and Universities: an Encyclopedia.* Santa Barbara, CA: Greenwood, 2011.

Burger, John, and Lewis, Lillian. "Each One Teach One." American Libraries 38, no. 2 (2007): 34.

Davis, Rose. "HBCU News." *The Southeastern Librarian* 53, no. 2 (2005). http://www.selaonline.org/SoutheasternLibrarian/SELnSummer05.pdf.

———. "HBCU News." *The Southeastern Librarian* 55, no. 4 (2007). http://www.selaonline.org/SoutheasternLibrarian/Winter2008.pdf.

Galloway, Ann-Christe. "LYRASIS and the HBCU Library Alliance." *College & Research Libraries News* 72 (2011), no. 9: 550.

Goleman, Daniel, Richard Boyatzis, and Annie McKee. *Primal Leadership: Realizing the Power of Emotional Intelligence.* Boston: Harvard Business School Press, 2002.

Guthrie, Ana "LYRASIS: The HBCU Library Alliance 'Gets Me.'" In *Library Alliance Leadership Program Phase 3 Final Report*, by Sandra Phoenix, September 16, 2011.

Hart, Carolyn, Lillian Lewis, Elizabeth McClenney, V. Tessa Perry, Iyanna Sims, and Adrienne Webber, "The HBCU Library Alliance: Developing Leadership." *Virginia Libraries* 53, no. 4 (2007): 16–20.

HBCU Library Alliance. "HBCU Library Alliance about Us." HBCU Library Alliance. Accessed March 9, 2013. http://www.hbculibraries.org/.

Lewis, Lillian. *The HBCU Library Leadership Program, 2005–2006: A Final Report to The Andrew W. Mellon Foundation*. Unpublished manuscript. Microsoft Word file.

Orphan, Stephanie. "Mellon Foundation Increases Funding for HBCU Leadership Program." *College & Research Libraries News* 68, no. 7 (2007): 417.

Pluviose, David. "HBCU Library Alliance Hosts Panel Discussion on Leadership." *Diverse: Issues in Higher Education*, April 1, 2007. http://diverseeducation.com/article/7170.

Trader-Leigh, Karyn. *Leadership Institute: Redefining Leadership for 21st-Century Librarians Participants Guidebook*. Atlanta, GA: HBCU Library Alliance, 2007.

CHAPTER 5

Investing in the Future:
Examining the NLM/AAHSL Leadership Fellows Program

Jeff Williams and Jennifer McKinnell

NOT UNLIKE OTHER areas of librarianship, health sciences librarianship faces ongoing demographic challenges. Experienced leaders are rapidly retiring or leaving the profession, resulting in a tremendous loss of knowledge and expertise. For several years, academic health sciences library leaders have expressed a sense of urgency regarding recruiting and educating the next generation of library leaders.[1]

In response to these concerns, the Association of Academic Health Sciences Libraries (AAHSL) undertook the Future Leadership Initiative.[2] Specifically, this initiative was designed to focus on issues of recruitment, education, training, mentoring, and research for the purpose of developing first-class leaders in academic health sciences libraries. As part of the initiative, data were collected on the timeline of future retirements by current directors, demographics of professional staff working in academic libraries, and readiness and interest of professional librarians to pursue directorship positions. Analysis of this data highlighted the need to identify and cultivate new leaders.

As a result of this work, the National Library of Medicine (NLM) and AAHSL collaboratively launched the NLM/AAHSL Leadership Fellows

Program (LFP) in 2002. This chapter provides a detailed overview of the LFP elements, including its strengths and weaknesses. In addition, we will include reflections on our personal learning experiences, the merit of implementing individual learning plans, and mentor support as a means of developing leadership knowledge and skill.

The Program

Initial program funding was provided by the NLM for a three-year period. The financial support provided for the development of a well-designed, multifaceted program and allowed participants to engage in face-to-face and online learning opportunities. Today, the NLM continues its financial commitment. Additional AAHSL funds also support the program. A portion of these funds pays for participant travel expenses, making this program accessible to all involved, regardless of the funding available through their home institutions.

Participants include fellows (individuals expressing an interest in academic health sciences leadership) and mentors (academic health sciences library directors willing to embrace the spirit of the program and share from their own experiences). Admission to the program is competitive and requires both potential fellows and mentors to include statements outlining personal goals for participating and professional relevance. Only five fellows and five mentors are selected each year.

The goals of the one-year LFP include providing instruction on leadership theories focused on implementing change within organizations, improving performance using practical tools, discussing issues facing academic health sciences libraries, and developing professional relationships between fellows and mentors to provide access to career guidance and support. Two one-week site visits to the mentor's university give each fellow the chance to learn about another academic health sciences library and the mentor's approach to leadership. The program was specifically designed to create a cohort of leaders who will draw upon each other for support during the program as well as throughout their careers. Finally, the program is intended to promote diversity as it relates to gender, ethnicity, geography, library background, and expertise in leadership within academic health sciences libraries. In combination, program content and components are designed to balance leadership development, practical experience, and significant interaction between fellows, mentors, and program faculty.

The Year in Review

The program commences with a day-long orientation in conjunction with attendance at the Association of Academic Medical Colleges (AAMC) Annual Meeting. Attendance at this meeting is included to encourage exposure to issues and members of the academic medicine community. This initial event marks the first face-to-face encounter between fellows, mentors, and program faculty. The orientation incorporates an overview of the curriculum; provides a chance for faculty, fellows, and mentors to state their expectations; and serves as a first opportunity for fellows to get to know each other and outline their selected areas of professional interest.

Prior to the orientation session, the community of learners is connected electronically through the program's virtual learning community. Between face-to-face meetings, this online learning space encourages an exchange of information about program components and discussions of issues and ideas that surface throughout the year. Webinars are facilitated by experienced faculty and mentors with expertise in the curriculum content. Fellows are required to undertake activities and participate in discussions.

Also prior to orientation, participants complete two leadership instruments, the Myers-Briggs Type Indicator (MBTI) and the FIRO-B (Fundamental Interpersonal Relations Orientation-Behavior). These instruments help fellows and mentors identify strengths and preferences and form a basis for developing personal learning goals. Program faculty administer the instruments and guide each fellow through the development of a leadership profile and its application to the program components.

Approximately midway through the year, a half-day leadership institute is scheduled in conjunction with the Medical Library Association (MLA) Annual Meeting. This second in-person event serves as another opportunity to engage the cohort as a whole and allows faculty to follow up with fellows and mentors midway through the program, promoting open and timely communication.

Both the orientation and the leadership institute include the presentation and discussion of leadership issues affecting academic health sciences libraries and the larger professional community. All of this is set against the backdrop of individual career goals and aspirations. Faculty experienced with the program and having expertise in leadership and career development instruction, carefully design and facilitate both events so as to best meet the participants' learning needs.

The mentor site visits are a crucial element of the program as they provide the fellows with first-hand experience under the tutelage of their committed and knowledgeable mentors. Each mentor works together with his or her fellow to design and schedule two one-week or one two-week site visit to the mentor's home library. Activities are coordinated to best meet mentor and fellow expectations and fulfill the program's goal of exposing fellows to diverse leadership styles and organizational developments that future leaders will need to be aware of.

The cohort of fellows and mentors culminates at the capstone event held in Washington, DC. This event brings together program participants, faculty, and national leaders in the library and academic health professions. The curriculum focuses on environmental forces helping to shape academic health sciences libraries and provides the opportunity to meet with leaders in AAHSL and NLM and their partner organizations. Discussions related to issues such as federal information policy, the changing role of the national libraries, scholarly communication, the role of the library in informatics development, and inter-professional education and team-based care help to weave together the various concepts raised throughout the year. The concluding ceremony recognizes participants' completion of the program and allows them one last opportunity to spend time together as a group. The capstone not only reinforces the strength of the cohort of fellows and mentors, but also serves as a powerful networking experience for future academic health sciences library leaders.

Mentor Relationship

The relationship fellows have with their mentors is the thread that ties the program pieces together. Fellows are paired with mentors based on the fellow's expressed professional development areas and the mentor's fields of interest, areas of expertise, and characteristics of the mentor's institution. Fellow and mentor pairs establish mutual expectations for their newly developed working relationship. They are expected to communicate on a regular and frequent basis to discuss topics of their choosing, such as challenges faced by the fellow and issues in his or her home library and the profession. During this time, fellows and mentors build relationships, with mentors supporting fellows as they consider their next career decisions.

Literature Review

The NLM/AAHSL LFP has been reviewed and evaluated throughout the years of its existence. In 2009, the 2003–2004 cohort published in the *Journal of Library Administration* a description of the progression of their activities and learning experiences.[3] Their work emphasized the evolution of their personal understanding of a library director's role and concepts related to leadership over the course of the year. The authors described the importance of the support they provided to each other throughout the year and highlighted the value of their close relationship that continues today. Finally, the authors provided an overview of their learning and reflected on the overall value of the program for emerging leaders in academic health sciences libraries.

Also in 2009, a publication provided an in-depth description of the history and design of the LFP.[4] This article presented demographic information that served as the inspiration for the establishment of the Association of Academic Health Sciences Libraries' Future Leadership for Academic Health Sciences Libraries Task Force. Charged with developing and recommending an action plan to address challenges in recruitment, leadership development, and mentoring, the task force compiled the documentation that ultimately became the foundation for the LFP. The launch and ongoing development of the program and the establishment of the partnership with the National Library of Medicine are described in detail. In their description of the selection process for both fellows and mentors, Lipscomb and others highlight the emphasis placed on matching fellows with mentors who can support their professional development goals and offer exposure to institutions that complement the fellows' experience related to characteristics like public or private status, institution size, and geographic factors. Finally, diversity of the cohort is taken into consideration.

In 2012, a poster presented at the annual meeting of the MLA described the development of the program as well as provided quantitative and qualitative assessment of the program's impact.[5] The poster reported that as of 2012, 19, or 42 percent, of the fellows who completed the program were now in director positions. Qualitative evaluations derived from former fellows' focus groups identified positive outcomes of the program such as enhanced leadership skills and credibility as director candidates as well as gaining a cohort of peers who share career aspirations.

Curriculum Content

Each year, program content is determined based on a number of factors, including the actual and perceived needs of the academic health sciences library community, feedback from previous cohorts of mentors and fellows, input from program planners, and the personal interests of the incoming cohort of mentors. The 2011–2012 curriculum focused on several areas, including budget strategies, workforce issues, e-science, revenue generation, organizational culture, diversity and inclusion, and power and influence. Each curriculum area was presented by one of the mentors or program faculty during one of the leadership institutes or bimonthly webinar discussions.

BUDGET STRATEGIES

The first online session focused on budget strategies. The mentor assigned to lead our discussion presented this topic using a scenario-based approach—laying out a set of assumptions that include the type of library, reporting structure, and instructions for the fellows to imagine themselves as acting deputy director while the director is out on extended medical leave. With this background established, the scenario was distributed on consecutive days as a sequential set of events that progressed from a routine "budget call" to a call for a significant budget reduction and then finally an "emergency" event with a larger budget reduction and a new finances distribution approach that could potentially be detrimental to the library. During the webinar, each fellow described how he or she would react to each of the situations as the events became more challenging.

WORKFORCE ISSUES

Workforce issues centered on the opportunities and challenges of different generations working together. The workforce characteristics and supervisorial preferences of traditionalists (born before 1945), baby boomers (born 1946–1964), generation X (born 1965–1978), and millennials (born 1979–present) were explored. Activities included reviewing data about demographic and workforce characteristics, reading Neil Howe and William Strauss's work on generational differences in the workforce, and completing a number of additional preparatory assignments.[6] The preparatory assignments included identifying the generations of our supervisor and coworkers while reflecting on the challenges caused by the differences in work styles and supervisorial approach.

E-SCIENCE

The e-science topic included a case review, required reading from a paper presented at the 2009 American Geophysical Union meeting, and a website evaluation.[7] The topic facilitator also suggested that fellows interview a local researcher on his or her data storage practice and needs. The case centered on a large-scale, personalized medicine research program and the steps needed to position the library to play a role in areas of data curation for this new program. Beyond reading articles and reviewing websites focused on data curation and e-science, the fellows reviewed a webinar and were given questions to guide the online discussion.

REVENUE GENERATION

The goals for our work around the topic of revenue generation were to

- understand concepts and processes around revenue generation in academic health sciences libraries,
- recognize the environmental aspects and challenges as a result of where academic health sciences libraries organizationally reside,
- assess our own attitudes and skills around revenue generation, and
- understand the typical roles and expectations for library directors.

Based on these goals, the fellows were asked to perform an inventory of revenue-generating activities underway at both their library and their mentor's library and to interview someone responsible for library fundraising at their institution as well as their director. Fellows were also asked to assess their own experience, attitudes, and skills in revenue generation and to reflect on what was learned during the inventory and interview activities.

ORGANIZATIONAL CULTURE

The topic of organizational culture was introduced through a proposed definition and other background information. The fellows were asked to think about their library and its parent organization's culture and how they would describe their organization to an outsider. Following this, they were asked to try and describe, from their point of view, how the culture of their organization has changed over time. This topic was also investigated by considering how different types of change initiatives fared in the organization and to what extent acknowledged and unacknowledged aspects of the organizational culture affected the outcomes. Finally, the fellows asked the same questions of others about their respective libraries so as to compare perceptions of their organizational culture and how it affects attempts at change.

DIVERSITY AND INCLUSION

The fellows prepared for the topic of diversity and inclusion as it related to gender, ethnicity, geography, background, and leadership expertise by investigating whether the fellows' home institution had a diversity and inclusion plan, and if so, restating the plan's guiding philosophy and strategy for implementation. Fellows who worked at an institution without a formal plan assessed the "informal" messages the institution provided on diversity and inclusion. As a final exercise, the fellows described their library's role in achieving these objectives, including the existence of formal plans and specific ways their library supported and benefited from these efforts. All of this formed the basis of an in-depth discussion of the topic facilitated by program faculty members with strong experience in this area.

POWER AND INFLUENCE

Power and influence was the final curricular topic addressed by the cohort. As with many of the topic areas, there was an assignment designed to draw upon several readings, including chapters from Harvard Business Essentials' *Power, Influence, and Persuasion* and Robert P. Vecchio's *Leadership: Understanding the Dynamics of Power and Influence in Organizations*.[8] The assignment required each fellow to write a one- to two-page description of a recent situation they experienced where power, leadership, and influence had a role in the outcome. The fellows were instructed to select a situation that was challenging to them to illustrate leadership challenges when navigating institutional politics and the unique characteristics of their home institution. For each participant, the depth of learning for the various curricular topics depended upon on personal learning style, workplace and research interests, and articulated learning goals.

The Fellowship Year in Review: Two Personal Experiences

LEARNING GOALS

Williams

As part of the program, each fellow developed his or her own learning plan, outlining personal goals for the program and strategies for achieving them. For me, primary personal learning goals focused on establishing and maintaining strong relationships with administrators in the schools and departments served by the library. My interest in learning about this came from watching my former institution struggle over a number of years with unprecedented and permanent budget reductions. During this time, I realized how critical strong relationships and consistent communication with campus administrators are for academic health sciences libraries. I also came to understand that changes in the overall structure of the university libraries had weakened relationships between the director of my library and the leaders of schools and departments the library served. As the budget situation worsened, my library struggled, fending off disproportionate budget cuts because the value and impact of library services and resources was not apparent to these critical stakeholders. The library was viewed by many campus administrators as a costly study hall with a bunch of books that nobody used in the age of Google.

McKinnell

For me, completing the NLM/AAHSL LFP application required reflection on areas of professional success and personal weakness. Using the tools provided by program faculty and building on advice from my mentor, I used this reflection to design a personal learning plan that focused on three specific goals: (1) taking time to reflect and learn more about new and continuing roles for the academic health sciences libraries, (2) exploring new directions in medical education, and (3) learning about change management theory. I worked in an innovative and creative environment and wanted to continue making a positive contribution. I believed that taking time to reflect on and think critically about library service delivery was an essential element of my professional future, and one especially needed for future leadership opportunities. Understanding change management was directly related to my desire to explore different professional roles in the library. Finally, my interest in focusing on medical education connected directly to what I perceived to be a personal knowledge gap.

MENTOR PAIRING

Williams

My mentor had served as the director of an academic health sciences library for over 20 years. In 2011, he was also appointed associate vice president for the health sciences at his university. I learned that my mentor was highly regarded for his ability to develop and maintain partnerships with the schools and departments served by his library. During the two site visits to my mentor's campus, I was impressed by the high degree of respect my mentor enjoyed from health sciences leaders at the university, and this seemed critical in positioning libraries for success.

As the fellowship year progressed, my mentor conscientiously provided input and assistance with the elements of the program. We arranged biweekly phone conversations as well as frequent e-mail conversations. Through these calls and e-mails, we discussed the various curricular topics to contrast how these issues played out at our respective universities. This was useful to me as I saw how much variation there can be in budgeting, opportunities for revenue generation, and organizational culture. My mentor paid particular attention to ensuring that the activities planned for both site visits were closely aligned with my learning goals. Although our relationship was arranged as part of the program, over time it became a true mentor-mentee relationship, and our relationship has continued after the completion of the fellowship year.

McKinnell

My mentor had held leadership positions in health science libraries for over 20 years. In her most recent position, my mentor focused on re-visioning her library's strategic direction. Specifically, her work focused on redefining librarian and staff roles, creating better alignment of library services with faculty priorities, and reimagining library space to address the learning needs of students, faculty, and clinical staff. Given my personal interests and learning goals, I felt the pairing was ideal.

LEADERSHIP INSTRUMENTS

A personal leadership profile was developed for each mentor and fellow using the familiar MBTI and somewhat less familiar FIRO-B instruments.[9] The FIRO-B instrument assesses how individuals behave and interpret individual and group behaviors in interpersonal situations. In addition to a written report, individuals had one-on-one discussions with a program faculty member. The purpose of the discussion was to provide more detailed information about the individual profile documents.

Williams

I had taken the MBTI instrument a number of times before with consistent results. This was the first time I had taken the FIRO-B instrument, so it was unfortunate that there was a problem with how the instrument compiled my responses. In consultation with one of the program's faculty members, it was agreed that a subset of results was reliable. Even with these drawbacks, the combination of these two instruments gave me new information on my personality characteristics and preferences for working in group settings.

McKinnell

The discussion of my leadership profile forced me to reflect on my own leadership characteristics, managerial style, and group participation preferences. As my work environment was extremely busy, I had limited time to critically evaluate my leadership profile results. The required discussion with the program faculty member forced me to slow down, reflect, and appreciate the value in the exercise. Combined, the report, supporting documents, and discussion gave me a strong foundation upon which to build future learning goals. Although the profile document did not reveal any major surprises for me about my personality preferences, I found it was valuable to place these preferences into a formal leadership context. Specifically, the profile helped me understand why I expressed herself differently in different situations and how I dealt with conflict in the workplace. The report highlighted the importance I placed on honest (although sometimes painful) communication and made it easier for me to understand why I became frustrated when others did not communicate freely. One element of the report that was particularly enlightening for me was the MBTI profile identifying me as an introvert. Although I found this initially confusing, especially because I believed I was perceived otherwise by my peers, the supporting documentation and discussion helped me to understand that introverts do not necessarily shy away from social settings, but they do require time alone to "recharge." This small insight was valuable to me both personally and professionally. Overall, I felt the profile gave me a good set of tools to identify and manage my leadership strengths and weaknesses.

ORIENTATION

The orientation was an important opportunity for the cohort of fellows and mentors to meet with program faculty to set the schedule for the upcoming year and to describe the expectations for fellow-mentor interaction and communication during the program. The orientation also allowed the fellows and mentors to begin in-depth discussions of the fellows' learning goals and develop plans for the site visits supporting these goals. Both of us felt the orientation's large and small group discussions were valuable for helping the cohort coalesce as a cohesive and mutually supportive group, while allowing the program faculty to set the stage for the months ahead.

BUDGET STRATEGIES

Budget strategies was the first topic delivered via the virtual learning community. Group members were new to the process, so this activity helped establish group norms and expectations. The topic established that academic health sciences library directors often face fast-moving, challenging issues. A consistent theme that emerged during the discussion of this topic was how few library directors had formal training or significant experience in budget planning and management.

Williams

For me, the scenarios around budgeting helped me understand the importance of the issues I would face if I later became a director and strongly resonated with my personal learning goals around relationship building. The scenarios exemplified why I believed libraries need to cultivate strong relationships and library champions at all levels of the organization. Because of unique aspects of the roles of libraries play in academic institutions, I had seen situations where libraries were lumped into odd groupings within organizations. The budget scenarios the cohort discussed emphasized how critical it is to educate administrators and faculty about the value libraries bring in supporting research, educational, and clinical activities across the institution.

McKinnell

Prior to the discussion, I spent a great deal of time preparing in an attempt to demonstrate that I was both ready for and appreciative of the learning opportunity. As part of this preparation, I worked closely with my library director reviewing the materials and working through the accompanying assignment. I quickly learned that in my workplace, the narrative surrounding the budget often held as much weight, if not more, than the actual dollar amounts. Clear messaging about the library's priorities and a well-articulated rationale for how and why expenditures are planned (or unplanned) were an essential part of the budgeting process. I learned to never make assumptions about the group charged with listening to the library's strategies. "Educate your audience as you go" seemed to be the underlying theme for successful budget presentations.

In addition to learning about the specific budgeting process at the fellows' home institutions, the activities helped me establish a tone for learning that continues today. Sitting down with my director and working through the assignment allowed us to discuss how library directors make choices, address competing demands, and respond when resources are limited. The conversation provided a context in which they both continued to discuss broader theoretical concepts within our shared work environment. Because this unit was delivered in stages, I was able to slow down, reflect, and tie the content to my workplace. I was then able to identify the role I could play in my library's budgeting process. Although I had always participated on the library management committee, prior to this assignment, I rarely took the time to critically evaluate the influence I had on budget planning and implementation.

WORKFORCE ISSUES

Like most work settings, health sciences libraries have a range of generations working together.

Williams

I found the discussion of different generations working together valuable in transitioning to a new position providing leadership for an intergenerational group of library faculty. My new position also entailed serving on the library's leadership team, and this is where I experienced a different aspect of "workforce issues" that in hindsight I wished had been addressed during the program. Namely, the dramatic challenges health sciences libraries are facing because of the accelerating changes in the nature of library work. For me, my library was quickly becoming less about transactional operations like checking out books, cataloging new titles, or managing a large physical collection and more about providing in-depth information assistance within research, education, and clinical teams. This change in focus was having a profound impact on the range of skills needed across the professional and nonprofessional staff and the required size of the library's workforce.

McKinnell

Compared to budget strategies, the workforce issues unit had a lesser effect on my overall learning. I felt the readings and assignment were traditional in their delivery, having already been exposed to similar content in other ways such as through conferences, articles, and listserv discussions. I also felt the assignment did not encourage dialogue with my director or peers. The content, focused on generational characteristics and how these might influence workplace culture and expectations, did not reflect my experiences in the workplace. On the surface, it seemed that factors other than generational (i.e., education, job responsibility, gender, years of service) provided a better gauge for understanding where and why workplace issues might arise. It was only in my reflection *after* the online discussion that I began to see the value in the exercise. After hearing about the issues facing others in their work environments, I was able to see how library service models might be tweaked to better suit the needs of younger generational users while recognizing that such changes might cause stress for staff represented by other generations. Further reflection, prompted by my mentor, allowed me to see that I had the capacity to recognize that in my own work environment, there were individuals with different personal histories and values that might be influencing how they set their job priorities.

E-SCIENCE

Williams

A cross-country move and being in-between jobs and institutions during the fellowship year prevented me from fully engaging with the e-science topic. Nevertheless, I did participate in the discussion between the fellows and mentors, sharing my perspective based on a recent task force experience. This task force examined the rationale for my former library to support data curation and preservation as part of campus-wide e-science efforts. I shared that at my former institution a common challenge was helping researchers and information technology professionals understand there was more to data curation and preservation than simply backing up the data. Further, I shared the experience that my library gained buy-in from information technology professionals by bringing skills in content and domain expertise, metadata and ontology experience, and process management that they found valuable.

McKinnell

Like the budgeting exercises, for me the e-science unit required that I go beyond simply reading and reflecting. As part of the activity, I met with two researchers, one with a background in social sciences data collection and another who conducted lab research. Working through the required readings, interviewing the researchers, writing up and sharing my thoughts, reviewing other participant submissions, and then engaging in a discussion on the topic was time consuming, but it provided a significant learning opportunity. The diversity of participant experiences helped broaden my understanding of the topic. I struggled with my own perceptions of where and how health sciences libraries should contribute to data management and curation. Speaking to researchers about data management needs was not something my library actively engaged in, and yet the feedback from the researchers suggested that starting this discussion was essential. Issues related to infrastructure requirements, opportunities for collaborative storage, privacy, data ownership, funding agency requirements, and data maintenance were in the forefront of the various research units' planning initiatives.

REVENUE GENERATION

Williams

I had a number of informative discussions with my mentor and his director regarding revenue generation in academic health sciences libraries. I learned that the libraries on my mentor's campus were not permitted to have a direct role in development; rather, the university's office of development coordinated all campus fund-raising. My mentor did have a limited ability to work with the development office on ideas and goals. My mentor shared that his library did have some endowed book funds and generated some revenue through interlibrary loan and indirect cost recovery for grants.

I also learned that my director had recently worked with a development office to create a "storefront," or menu of development possibilities, for the library. He shared a story similar to my mentor's story regarding limited opportunities for significant revenue generation. In talking about some of the difficulties libraries have in fund-raising, we discussed the fact that libraries do not have alumni so development opportunities are reduced. I also spoke with the development director responsible for coordinating fundraising on behalf of the library. During this discussion, the development director stressed that success in fundraising usually comes as a result of a partnership between development staff and knowledgeable institution staff because donors often do not have specific ideas on what they would like to support—rather, they have a general idea like, "I'd like to help the library." In a situation like this, the development office needs to work closely with the library to develop ideas that resonate with the donor. He also shared his view that donors are motivated to donate toward a vision or an idea that excites them.

I came to this learning topic somewhat jaded about the prospects of revenue generation and libraries. I had experienced putting a lot of effort into soliciting donors as part of a major renovation and expansion of the library facility where I had worked previously. Although there were some small successes, a large-scale facility-naming type of donation never materialized. It was difficult for me not to notice the constant construction all around the library of large-scale, multimillion dollar named buildings. This gave the impression that it was hard for the library to compete with the cancer hospitals and cutting-edge research institutes. After the discussion of this topic, I was more optimistic that by increasing communication and demonstrating the value libraries bring to academic medical centers, academic health sciences libraries may be better prepared to create visions that excite donors.

McKinnell

Similar to the previous unit, the revenue generation unit incorporated readings, a requirement to initiate discussions with relevant campus partners, assignment preparation, and group discussion. The content presented was perhaps the least relevant for me as the funding structure for academic institutions in Canada varies significantly from the United States. The culture of working with alumni organizations, private foundations, and industry donors is also dissimilar. Despite these differences, I found value in the group discussion. The variability in the descriptions of revenue-generation initiatives at individual participants' home intuitions was remarkable. What resonated with me was the notion that the library is just one of several faculty units vying for the opportunity to work more closely with donors.

For me, the greatest benefit to completing the revenue generation assignment was that it forced me to return to my director's office for another discussion about budget planning. In addition to exploring current and future cost recovery services, we worked with our faculty development officer, who was trialing a new method for identifying projects that could be presented to potential donors. Through this process, we wrote up a learning space improvement proposal that was approved, and renovations were scheduled to begin the same year.

My work on this topic also led me to the office of the central campus library development officer. Together, we discussed current and past practice as well as future plans for revenue generation on campus.

ORGANIZATIONAL CULTURE

Content related to organizational culture was delivered through a series of readings, worksheets, and a face-to-face discussion held at the Seattle MLA meeting in the spring of 2012. By this time, program participants were a cohesive group, and everyone had experienced at least one site visit, further strengthening the mentor-fellow relationships. The pre-meeting assignment required participants to gather information about the organizational culture of their home institutions.

Williams

For me, this was the most valuable content presented through the program. Timing was a key issue, as it came shortly after starting at my new institution. As I had not been at my institution long enough to develop an understanding of the culture, I met with my director to go through the preparatory exercises. At that point, my director had been at the institution for less than two years. Nevertheless, we had an in-depth discussion of what he had observed about the organizational culture of the library and the overall institution.

We had both come from West Coast public universities, so we shared similar frames of reference while discussing our new East Coast private institution. For example, both of our former institutions had fairly relaxed atmospheres, with less overt attention paid to the formalities around hierarchy. In contrast, we were both adapting to the more formal atmosphere and hierarchical undercurrent of our current institution. Another observation the director shared was realizing how important it was that the library was a department within the organization. He learned that this allowed the library to enjoy more visibility, resources, and a place at the table that would not be possible otherwise.

McKinnell

While working on this topic, I met with long-term and new employees who represented librarians and non-librarian staff. I was surprised to learn that the long-term employees were highly cynical of management's ability to successfully direct change. These attitudes were in contrast to those of newer employees, who indicated they were amazed at management's attempts to be open and honest throughout the change process. Moreover, the information provided by librarians suggested that although they were satisfied with their current work environment, they were eager to try shifting the organizational culture to one that was more dynamic and cohesive.

For me, the diversity of responses gathered from my workplace was confusing. The face-to-face discussion in Seattle helped me work through the information. Placing issues of organizational culture into a theoretical context gave me the ability to sort through the information and start thinking about how I could create positive change in my workplace. The information provided me with a framework I could use to do future planning. Using this approach, I was able to modify my personal goals as part of my annual performance review at work.

DIVERSITY AND INCLUSION

With promoting diversity in leadership across academic health sciences libraries an expressed goal of the program, this was an important learning topic for the cohort.

Williams

The pre-work was a useful way for me to become more familiar with my institution and my library's approach to promoting diversity and inclusion. I learned that my institution did not have a formal diversity and inclusion plan, but there were a number of other expressions of the institution's support for diversity and inclusion.

McKinnell

Like some of the other content, there were elements of this topic that initially seemed unrelated to my circumstances in Canada; legislative requirements and workplace expectations did not seem pertinent to my situation. As the group discussion unfolded, these perceptions shifted. The regional difference in workplace diversity issues at the home institutions of the participants was remarkable. This helped me understand my own work situation, in which the staff had vastly different cultural backgrounds from library users.

POWER AND INFLUENCE

Since the primary goal of the program was developing future directors of academic health sciences libraries, the learning topic on power and influence was highly relevant.

Williams

The topic was also closely related to my main personal learning goal around relationship building. Power and influence was the last topic discussed before the final capstone event and included a series of required readings and a short assignment. By attempting to relate what I learned through the readings to a case study that I was required to develop, I could better analyze the drivers in my case study and reflect on what I might have done differently. With hindsight, some distance, and the support of the readings and discussion on power and influence, I realized that many of the drivers at play in my case study were broader and deeper than I had originally perceived. Realizing that these issues at my former library were just one instance of bigger trends across the profession helped me better understand the situation described in my case study.

McKinnell

Compared to previous assignments, I found the discussion of power and influence more theoretical. Using the readings provided as a framework, the fellows were asked to describe a situation in their professional life wherein they had to use power and influence. The exercise in itself was thought provoking. Not all of the fellows felt they had real power over the situations they described, but all of the fellows could see areas where they had, or would have liked to have had, influence over the final outcome. Unfortunately, I was not sure that all of the participants learned as much as they could from this particular activity. It may have been the timing in the calendar year (mid-summer) or the placement of this topic in the program (the last online discussion), but the quality of the discussion was not as insightful as the previous sessions.

I found the power and influence readings valuable. Coincidentally, the timing of the exercise allowed me to apply the content to a situation at work. I was able to share the readings with colleagues who were struggling with the issues related to power and influence within the scope of their jobs. We continued to share articles as we discovered new information that might help us realign our thinking around workplace power issues. I cannot be sure if it was simply the timing, or the overall design of this unit, but either way, the issues raised and the ideas shared continue to play a role in problem solving in my workplace today.

SITE VISIT

Williams

My mentor and I decided that two one-week site visits gave more opportunity for supporting my learning goal than a single two-week visit to the mentor's university. We had multiple discussions about the focus of each of the visits. This was partly influenced by logistics, issues such as respective schedules and when certain meetings were taking place. A bigger influence was the mutual goal of aligning the site visits to support my learning goals. Based on this, we decided that the focus of the first site visit would be to understand the library and its role in supporting the health sciences at the mentor's university. This was accomplished by a number of one-on-one meetings between me and my mentor and attending team and committee meetings within the library and outside the library. The focus of attending these meetings was to understand the activities and initiatives involving the library from both the internal library perspective and the perspective of schools and departments with whom the library was working. During these meetings, I was able to observe the leadership approach of my mentor in his role as director of the library and how he interacted with administrators and other campus leaders. My main takeaway from these meetings was the active approach my mentor took to looking for opportunities where the library could help support the efforts of the schools and departments the library serves.

The goal of my second site visit was investigating the leadership styles of health sciences administrators while engaging them in discussions of the role of the library in supporting their schools and departments. Over the course of the week, my mentor and I met with five health sciences administrators. During these meetings, I continued to learn how much these administrators appreciated my mentor's active approach to supporting their departments and activities; they all said that this has led them to think of the library as a full partner with their departments. I also learned a lot about their approach to leadership, especially in relationship to how they were adapting to rapid changes in higher education.

McKinnell

I also chose two separate, one-week visits, one to the main campus and one to the medical center campus. My first visit addressed all three of my learning goals. I was able to explore the broader issues of library management and organizational change at the main campus undergraduate library. This library had recently undergone a senior library administration reorganization and a major renovation of student learning space. During the visit, I was able to meet one-on-one with librarians in senior leadership roles and participate in regularly scheduled faculty meetings.

I also visited one of the distributed medical campuses located near the main campus. My time there gave me the opportunity to meet with individual librarians and senior faculty administration in the School of Medicine and participate in regularly scheduled faculty and librarian meetings. The magnitude of change I witnessed in all of these environments was remarkable, and yet the people immersed in the change process barely recognized it. This observation was significant for me as I frequently, and perhaps mistakenly, considered my own work environment to be too static.

The second site visit was similar to the first, except that it also included a "road trip" to a neighboring city to visit two additional academic health sciences library directors. Visiting the other libraries allowed me to gain perspective on health sciences librarianship in general and insight into the variability that can exist across different, albeit successful, leadership styles. The meetings also highlighted the variability in administrator, staff, and user expectations.

The overall benefit to my personal learning resulting from these two site visits cannot be measured. Taking time to step away from immediate workplace pressures and learning from the successes and failures of others helped me define my own leadership style and professional aspirations.

Theoretical Framework

The multifaceted reflective elements of the NLM/AAHSL LFP can be viewed through the lens of a number of theoretical contexts. In addition to meeting stated objectives, the overall program design supported growth in the areas of self-directed, inquiry-based learning and emotional intelligence.

The work of Malcolm Knowles indicates that self-directed learning describes a process in which individuals take the initiative, with or without the help of others, in diagnosing their learning needs; formulating learning goals; identifying human and material resources for learning; choosing and implementing appropriate learning strategies; and evaluating learning outcomes.[10] In many ways, this definition provides an overview for the NLM/AAHSL LFP format, which encouraged participants, fellows, and mentors to use the resources provided and work through the learning opportunity in front of them. Although information was provided in the form of articles, discussion content, and supporting documentation, the onus was on each individual to weave this content into their own knowledge base. We have indicated that some of the program elements resonated with us, while others did not, suggesting that the delivery methods and materials provided accommodated a wide variety of self-identified learning styles.

Knowles also provided a strategy for implementing a self-directed learning initiative, which included completing self-assessment learning activities to diagnose learning needs; outlining learning objectives; identifying a variety of learning strategies and information resources (human and otherwise) to address individual learning needs; and evaluating learning outcomes.[11] While LFP did not explicitly cite this model, it appeared to be influenced by Knowles' proposed strategy as various program elements echoed several of his ideas.

The inquiry method used to deliver program content resembled Neil Postman and Charles Weingartner's definition of self-directed learning, which indicates that "student[s] generate their own stories by becoming involved in the methods of learning."[12] In particular, the site visits allowed participants to work with their mentors to develop experiences that met their preferred learning styles and stated objectives. All participants were encouraged to provide in-depth and ongoing evaluation, in effect influencing program design for future participants. This feedback loop also resembled the inquiry method wherein the teacher's lessons develop from the responses of the students and not a previously determined "logical" structure.[13]

The self-reflection element of the program appeared to support and reinforce learning outcomes. Jennifer Moon's work on reflection in a professional context supports reflection as an essential element to successful lifelong learning.[14] Many of the practical approaches to developing reflective practice in the professional context outlined in her work include journaling, studying case study evaluation exercises, and developing networks to support dialogue and discussion. These same activities were woven into the LFP design.[15]

Another influence on program design seems to be the work of Daniel Goleman, who brought the concept of emotional intelligence to the forefront of the business world with his *Harvard Business Review* article, "What Makes a Leader?" He presented five components of emotional intelligence at work:

- **Self-Awareness:** the ability to understand our own moods and emotions, what drives our performance, and how these factors impact our relationships with others. [16]
- **Self-Regulation:** controlling and redirecting negative impulses and thinking before acting to avoid hasty judgments.[17]
- **Motivation**: energy and persistence in pursuing goals and finding satisfaction in work beyond money and status.[18]
- **Empathy:** awareness and understanding of emotional drivers in colleagues and skill in navigating emotion-based reactions.[19]
- **Social Skill:** being effective at building and maintaining relationships and finding common ground.[20]

The NLM/AAHSL LFP supports growth in areas of emotional intelligence through a number of components. Participants' completion of the MBTI and FIRO-B instruments provided a foundation of self-awareness of one's personality characteristics and tendencies while working with others. Discussing and comparing the results of individual instruments with mentors built on understanding the emotional drivers in colleagues, the ability to better maintain relationships, and the importance finding common ground when dealing with conflicts.

Goleman suggests that although emotional intelligence varies in individuals, abilities in this area can be improved through motivation, practice, and feedback. He suggests enlisting a coach to help with improving performance in weak areas.[21] The design of the program was built around the concept of growth through the coaching of mentors and experienced faculty. Furthermore, many of the curricula topics provided were designed to promote meaningful conversations with the fellows' directors and offer opportunities for further mentoring at the fellows' libraries. All of this allowed the fellows to enhance their strengths in the area of emotional intelligence.

Conclusion

The NLM/AAHSL LFP reinforced the importance of participants stepping out of their day-to-day responsibilities and reflecting on how important issues in the profession impact their home institutions. The program design established a foundation that allowed participants to establish valuable relationships within and outside their institutions. Although the LFP was established to support the participants' career progression and respond to an anticipated shortage of future library leaders, we believe it also allowed us to be more effective in our current roles by promoting leadership skills development. We believe that our combined experiences have honed our abilities to shape the strategic visions of our libraries.

After reflecting on our experiences, we have identified four ways that we believe could improve the program's effectiveness:

1. **Reframe the themes**. Although the discussion of challenges related to intergenerational collaboration in the workforce was beneficial, we recommend broadening this discussion to include changing skills, training, and experience required of staff as academic health sciences libraries adopt new roles in their organizations.

The discussion of e-science could be incorporated into this discussion as one example of these new roles and its resulting impact on the library workforce.

2. **Expand the diversity and inclusion curriculum.** Awareness of the issues related to diversity and inclusion in the workplace was an underlying theme for the entire AAHSL/NLM LFP. Although meant to be a core element of the LFP, when compared to the other topics covered in the program, the sum of the activities supporting this issue was too basic. The topic of diversity and inclusion must be expanded to allow an in-depth examination of issues and a more expansive discussion of distinctive ways that this topic can manifest itself in varied environments. Alternatively, this particular topic may be better addressed as a horizontal theme running throughout the LFP.

3. **Experiment with content delivery methods.** As the year progressed, we found that the content delivery methods became repetitive. Experimenting with assignment design and discussion preparation strategies is recommended.

4. **Highlight power and influence in the workplace.** While referring to understanding how power and influence is weaved into a director's role, we believe the discussion of this topic should be expanded in scope within the LFP. There needed to be an approach that would allow fellows to address and reflect on this topic across the program year, providing for substantive growth in understanding and depth of knowledge rather than the limited impact of a single discussion.

For those looking to move into a director position within the academic health sciences library community, the NLM/AAHSL LFP provides an unmatched opportunity for preparation to succeed in this challenging role. Perhaps the most critical aspect is the fact that the participant funding is guaranteed, making this program merit based, rather than dependent on the ability of participants to secure funds through other venues, including their home institutions. The ongoing investment that the NLM and AAHSL have made in developing future leaders will undoubtedly help ensure the vitality of academic health sciences libraries in the future.

Notes

1. Martin, "The Leadership Reconsidered Symposium," 251–52.
2. AAHSL (http://www.aahsl.org) supports academic health sciences libraries and directors in advancing the patient care, research, education, and community service missions of academic health centers through visionary executive leadership and expertise in health information, scholarly communication, and knowledge management; Martin, "The Leadership Reconsidered Symposium," 254.
3. Bunnett et al., "The National Library of Medicine."
4. Lipscomb, Martin, and Peay, "Building the Next Generation," 848.
5. Lipscomb et al., "Building a Farm Team."
6. Howe and Strauss, "The Next 20 Years."
7. Gold, "Data Curation and Libraries"; Association of Research Libraries, "E-Science Institute"; University of Massachusetts, "UMass Medical Center."
8. "Power Sources," Harvard Business Essentials; Vecchio, "Power, Politics, and Influence."
9. Myers & Briggs Foundation, "The Myers & Briggs Foundation"; High Performing Systems, "The FIRO Community."
10. Knowles, *Self-Directed Learning*, 18.
11. Ibid., 18–24.
12. Postman and Weingartner, *Teaching*, 29.
13. Ibid., 35.
14. Moon, *Reflection*.
15. Ibid., 165–202.
16. Goleman, "What Makes a Leader?," 84–85.
17. Ibid., 85–87.
18. Ibid., 88–89.
19. Ibid., 89–90.
20. Ibid.
21. Ibid., 87.

Bibliography

Association of Research Libraries. "E-Science Institute." Accessed December 16, 2013. http://www.arl.org/rtl/eresearch/escien/escieninstitute/index.shtml.

Bunnett, Brian, Nancy Allee, Jo Dorsch, Gabriel Rios, and Cindy Stewart. "The National Library of Medicine/Association of Academic Health Sciences Libraries (NLM/AAHSL) Leadership Fellows Program: A Year in Review." *Journal of Library Administration* 49 (2009): 869–79.

Gold, Anna. "Data Curation and Libraries: Short-Term Developments, Long-Term Prospects." Self-published manuscript, last modified April 4, 2010. PDF file. http://works.bepress.com/agold01/9.

Goleman, Daniel. "What Makes a Leader?" *Harvard Business Review* 82 (2004): 82–91.

Harvard Business Essentials. "Power Sources: How You Can Tap Them." In *Power, Influence, and Persuasion.* Boston: Harvard Business School Publishing, 2005.

High Performing Systems. "The FIRO Community." Accessed December 20, 2013. http://www.hpsys.com/firo.htm.

Howe, Neil, and William Strauss. "The Next 20 Years." *Harvard Business Review* 85 (2007): 41–52.

Knowles, Malcolm S. *Self-Directed Learning: A Guide for Teachers and Learners.* New York: Association Press, 1975.

Lipscomb, Carolyn E., Elaine R. Martin, and Wayne J. Peay. "Building the Next Generation of Leaders: The NLM/AAHSL Leadership Fellows Program." *Journal of Library Administration* 49 (2009): 847–67.

Lipscomb, Carolyn E., Barbara A. Epstein, Lynn Kasner Morgan, and M.J. Tooey. "Building a Farm Team: Ten Years of Developing New Academic Health Sciences Library; The National Library of Medicine/Association of Academic Health Sciences Libraries Leadership Fellows Program." Poster presented at the annual meeting of the Medical Library Association, Seattle, Washington, May 18–23, 2012.

Martin, Elaine. "The Leadership Reconsidered Symposium: Report." *Journal of the Medical Library Association* 91 (2003): 251–57.

Moon, Jennifer A. *Reflection in Learning and Professional Development: Theory and Practice* New York, RoutledgeFalmer, 1999.

Myers & Briggs Foundation. "The Myers & Briggs Foundation." Accessed December 20, 2013. http://www.myersbriggs.org/.

Postman, Neil, and Charles Weingartner, *Teaching as a Subversive Activity.* New York: Dell Publishing, 1969.

University of Massachusetts Medical School in Worcester. "UMass Medical Center for Librarians E-Science Portal." Accessed December 16, 2013. http://esciencelibrary.umassmed.edu.

Vecchio, Robert P. "Power, Politics, and Influence." In *Leadership: Understanding the Dynamics of Power and Influence in Organizations*, 69–95. Notre Dame, IN.: University of Notre Dame Press, 2007.

PART 3

Programs for ARL and Large Research Libraries

CHAPTER 6

ARL's Leadership Career Development Program for Underrepresented Mid-Career Librarians

Jon E. Cawthorne and Teresa Y. Neely

THE ASSOCIATION OF Research Libraries (ARL) "is a nonprofit organization of 125 research libraries at comprehensive, research-extensive institutions in the US and Canada that share similar research missions, aspirations, and achievements."[1] Established in 1932 by directors from 42 major university and research libraries, the ARL is governed by a board of directors and has led or cosponsored national and international efforts on collections, preservation, copyright, open access, diversity, statistics, assessment, and leadership.[2] The majority of ARL member libraries (94 percent) are academic. Motivated by member libraries, ARL is committed to leadership and diversity recruitment efforts for the profession of librarianship, specifically academic research libraries.[3] A review of the leadership and diversity literature for library and information science professionals of color reveals the ARL is one of only a few library organizations offering leadership programs on a national scale for this population. In 2010, Charlene Maxey-Harris and Toni Anaya surveyed ARL libraries on various diversity topics and found that "very few libraries are designing mentoring programs specifically for librarians from underrepresented ethnic or cultural groups."[4] Responding libraries reported that they relied on external programs, such as the ARL Library Career Development Program (LCDP) or the University of Minnesota Training Institute for Early Career Librarians, for skill-building opportunities and training to "advance these librarians to leadership positions."[5]

The ARL LCDP is the longest-running leadership program at ARL. Established in 1997, the program was developed to prepare librarians from diverse racial and ethnic groups for leadership positions in ARL libraries. To date, 149 librarians have participated in the program, with curriculum elements that include residential institutes, career coaching and support from an ARL library administrator, and a research component.[6] The ARL LCDP is just one of the diversity leadership programs offered by the ARL, and the only one focused on mid-career library professionals. Table 6.1 shows the participating classes and the number of individuals participating in the program since its inception. With the exception of the Inaugural Class, it is unclear how the participants for the cohort years were selected. All data for table 6.1 was taken from the ARL LCDP webpages.

TABLE 6.1. **ARL LCDP Participant Groups by Year**		
Year	Class	Number of Participants
1997–1998	Inaugural Class	21
1999–2000	Millennial Class	18
2001–2002	New Century Class	20
2003–2004	Intentional Visionaries Class	21
2007–2008	Renaissance Class	20
2009–2010	Vanguard Class	10
2011–2012	Luminary Class	18
2013–2014	LCDP Fellows	21
Total		149
Source: Association of Research Libraries, "LCDP."		

Program Curriculum

In 1997, Corrine Nelson and Evan St. Lifer reported on the program's beginnings, noting it "hopes to encourage minority librarians to make particular use of the cultural experience and knowledge they gain outside the organization to inform and enhance their careers, leadership development, and upward professional mobility."[7] The LCDP would consist of two "intensive, hands-on institutes with an off-site individual-based project."[8] The main objectives "include[d] the opportunities to strengthen management and decision-making skills through training; develop a network of mentors to foster career development; and provide participants" with an opportunity to pursue special projects and contribute to the library profession.[9]

In 1999, nine participants from the Inaugural Class (1997–1998) collaborated to describe their experiences in the program.[10] The authors reported that the LCDP revolved around mentoring and research projects, writing assignments, and team-building experiences designed to challenge participants. Additionally, participants attended two five-day residential institutes purposely located in geographically isolated venues to promote and facilitate group interactions and insure "a committed audience for the guest speakers."[11] During the first institute, participants were engaged in work sessions up to 10 hours a day, covering topics including "effective leadership, strategic planning and priority setting, decision-making systems, project development, and cross-cultural communication."[12] It was during this first institute in Palm Coast, Florida, that ARL deans Camila A. Alire of Colorado State University; James Williams of the University of Colorado Boulder; and Robert Wedgeworth of the University of Illinois at Urbana-Champaign presented. Three more ARL deans, Nancy Baker of Washington State University; Gloria Werner of the University of California, Los Angeles; and Gerald Lowell of the University of California, San Diego, presented three months later at the second institute in California. The LCDP listserv was established between the two institutes, and participants were also provided with mentoring and coaching for their research projects. The authors concluded that the "mentoring component was one of the most nurturing facets of the Leadership and Career Development Program."[13] Additionally, the authors noted, "in the brief time spent together during the first one-week institute, participants created a culture of sharing, openness, learning, collaboration, and trust."[14] The authors believed the isolated, residential nature of the institute was a significant contributor to its success. "We were disengaged from our work routine and thus free to give undivided attention to investigating and challenging beliefs, attitudes, and assumptions about ourselves as individuals and about issues of librarianship."[15]

Program components for the Millennial Class (1999–2000) and the Intentional Visionaries (2003–2004) cohort remained unchanged from the Inaugural Class: a mentoring relationship, a research project, and two five-day institutes. In 2001, Camille Hazeur reported that the 2001–2002 LCDP would include two leadership institutes to be held at the University of Kansas and the University of Arizona, the mentoring relationship, and the research project. Three online lyceum courses with topics on motivation, fundraising, and influencing skills were added to the curriculum to maintain participant engagement throughout the year.[16]

In 2009, Teresa Neely, one of the authors of this chapter, reported that LCDP had been newly redesigned with two goals: to provide experience with strategic issues shaping the future of research libraries and to prepare participants for leadership roles in ARL libraries.[17] According to the ARL website, the focus of LCDP remains the preparation of "mid-career librarians from traditionally underrepresented racial and ethnic minority groups" for "increasingly demanding leadership roles in ARL libraries."[18] The curriculum is tied to the strategic directions of ARL, and the program design includes "three institutes; a career-coaching relationship with an ARL library director or senior staff member [the former mentoring relationship]; training on identifying, developing, and conducting a research project during the fellowship; online discussions and webinars related to the ARL strategic directions; and a closing event and poster session held during the American Library Association annual meeting."[19]

Program Reflections

Prior to participating in the LCDP, both of us participated in the Snowbird Leadership Institute. Additionally, Cawthorne has attended the Emerging Leaders Institute, the Frye Leadership Institute, and UCLA Senior Fellows. In reflecting on our individual LCDP experiences, the our views reflect our career aspirations and trajectories to date.

CAWTHORNE

The LCDP marked a turning point in my career. It was the first time I was surrounded by people who aspired to lead research libraries. While the design of the program has changed over time, I believe the length and focus on developing lifelong colleagues remains. The program and relationships I've maintained over my career are responsible for expanding my thinking on future career options and directions. At the time I participated in LCDP, I was just starting my career. I knew I wanted to serve in leadership positions, but I had little understanding of what skills and competencies I needed to serve successfully in leadership positions. As I look back, I recall thinking more about being in the position, maybe holding the title, without a deeper understanding of the actual work. When I think about one of the memorable workshops at LCDP, I am reminded of how much I did not know.

Camila Alire's presentation, "A Day in the Life of a Library Dean," has inspired me my entire career. It was really the first time anyone ever explained the work of a library dean. She began by describing her appointment as a library director at the age of 24. The lessons she learned and the mistakes she made helped her be an even better leader later in her career. Because I was not serving in a leadership position during LCDP, I know I did not absorb as much from the leadership lessons as I did from the specific details of a day in the life of a dean. Looking back, I can say the inspiration planted by Alire remains with me to this day. I also know that aspiring to any leadership position requires a certain amount of personal growth. This is the element in Alire's presentation that I didn't absorb but had to live through to fully understand. Given what I know now about being a dean of libraries, I can say that all experiences, including successes, failures, and considering and reconsidering a personal vision for libraries, are essential and lay the foundation for success in leadership positions.

Alire's presentation started with some context and background. She detailed the content of e-mails received from staff and an e-mail from a faculty member who believed that journals he needed for his research were being canceled under the guise of a serials substitution project. She talked about continuing projects, letters of reference, and follow-up for national committee work. Most importantly, she ended by sharing her criteria for prioritizing and organizing her work. The question to participants was, "What do you focus on first?" Alire said she focused on personnel because they are really important; e-mail responses to staff would be first. More than any other LCDP session, Alire's motivated me to pursue a dean of libraries position, but I have learned some valuable lessons along the way that have helped me understand myself and Alire's presentation even better.

Alire discussed her failures and what she learned from them. Now, as dean of libraries, I finally understand the complexity, nuance, and passion necessary to lead and sustain leadership. The specifics of her presentation are now vivid, tangible, and I now remind myself of the importance of failure to personal growth. I understand that a positive outlook and a deep sense of personal integrity are critical for making leadership decisions. In the 17 years since the LCDP, I have learned the ability to prioritize comes from trial and error (successes and failures), a deep knowledge of self (developing a personal vision), and understanding how to adapt to the changing environment. Almost like a three-legged stool, experiencing and perfecting this balance taught me the valuable lessons I initially missed from Alire's talk. Looking back, I would say I missed each leg of the stool because I was not working in a leadership position, but that would be too simplistic. Throughout my career, I have accepted increasingly more responsible positions; this has allowed me to gain experience and develop myself. I learned from my journey that it was important to ask, "What is my comfort level with change? What is my comfort level with failure? What is my comfort level with taking a risk when the prevailing thought is to remain in the status quo?" Although my journey is far from anyone's standard, I believe that having a high tolerance for change and failure forced me to reconsider my own beliefs, approaches, and what I thought about myself.

Alire knew the context and subtleties that factored into leadership decisions, but she had learned this through experience. In order to be an effective leader, she also understood that leaders inspire staff at all levels and connect their work within the larger campus culture. Her presentation made decisions look easy, but in fact, library dean jobs are not straightforward—there are many factors that play into successful leadership. I believe constant personal growth is an essential element in making good decisions and inspiring the respect of the organization. The career journey makes you who you are, and you have to be open to exploring and understanding yourself. If you cannot lean into and shed light on blind spots and personal fears in your own life, how can you expect to effectively lead people? Yet, the good news is that I believe leaders are certainly made and it is all a process. Alire ended with the good news that leadership can be learned; this has definitely been the case for me.

NEELY

Up until the writing of this chapter, I have viewed my experience in LCDP as a part of my leadership research agenda. I've focused more on assessing the major components of this and other leadership programs for librarians than I have reflected on my personal experiences in the programs.

Unlike my coauthor, I was not inspired to become a dean by Alire's presentation or my participation in any of the leadership programs I have been involved with. On the contrary, I actively worked to *not* be the person in the leadership position, without really fully acknowledging or recognizing that leadership does occur at many points throughout the organization. I was happy being a director of a program or unit, but I did not aspire to lead an entire organization. I would routinely find ways to position myself strategically among and in alliance with my colleagues within larger groups with decision-making responsibilities or in strategic-planning situations. For example, as a member of the group of directors and unit heads in my position as director of a unit, I would routinely volunteer to take meeting minutes (which would go out to the entire organization, from me); I would also volunteer to present small group findings to the larger group during planning retreats. I was indeed leading and effectively facilitating change at a high administrative level, but I still had one foot in the trenches with the worker bees, actually getting the work done.

Listening to Alire's presentation, I had a different reaction to her message than my coauthor did. I was not really affected by what she was faced with, but by how she started her day and how much of a commitment her position as dean required. As she began her "A Day in the Life" presentation, she set the scene by describing how she began her days, incredibly early, reading e-mail in her pajamas. My first thought was "Work does not start until I get there!" I had absolutely no desire to be a dean or director of anything if that is what it entailed. Little did I know that the level of engagement and dedication and commitment she was describing would be something I would embrace wholeheartedly as I have advanced in my career. I've also come to realize that the behavior she was describing was not necessarily reserved for the dean. I cannot point to the time where I stopped thinking about my work as a job and fully accepted it as a career, but I have.

At some point in this journey, I accepted that I cannot do well or be effective in my role if I am not engaged and responsive. Thankfully, innovations in technology have made that part easy. I check for e-mail, voice mails, and texts as soon as I roll out of bed. I have been employed at my current institution for nearly 10 years, and during that time, we have had two major floods in two of our four library facilities and a fire that ravaged our print newspaper and journal holdings.[20] So, when I say I need to check to make sure there are no fires to put out that developed over night, I am being literal. Disasters notwithstanding, I sincerely believe my responsibilities for the people I work with, the collections I oversee, and the services I implement do not end when I leave the building. I think that is a part of what Alire was trying to convey. Perhaps I internalized the lessons from her presentation after all. From what I can recall, her presentation was the only one that was practical. I believe both Cawthorne and I recall that one so vividly because it had real life, real time examples. Here are these things that come across my desk, here is how I deal with them, and here is why I deal with them that way. Those real life examples provided a lot of food for discussion, thought, and introspection.

The two perspectives presented here on Alire's presentation illustrate that participants do have a role in the effect of leadership institutes and programs on participants' career development and trajectories. The literature on senior library leadership programs clearly indicates evidence of this.[21] Reflecting on their experiences in ARL LCDP, Maria de Jesus Ayala-Schueneman and her colleagues wrote, "It became clear early on that the greatest challenge of leadership is the task of self-management. To lead others requires tremendous self-knowledge, including understanding one's strengths, weaknesses, goals, values, and beliefs."[22] Therefore, participating in a leadership development program does not absolve participants from directing their actions in a thoughtful way to develop their careers.

Minorities in Library Leadership Positions

In 2006, Kaylyn Hipps set out to track the progress gained or lost in diversifying the professional research library workforce for people of color holding leadership positions in ARL libraries. She characterized progress as "demonstrated by increased percentages of minority librarians and minority managers, including library directors."[23] Using data from the *ARL Annual Salary Survey* for 1986–1987, she concluded that in the 20-year time span, "ethnic and racial minorities remain underrepresented among ARL Librarians."[24]

Looking at the data Hipps used and comparing it with data from the *2011–2012 ARL Annual Salary Survey* (see table 6.2), not much has changed. In the FY 1986 *ARL Annual Salary Survey*, minorities held 9 percent of the positions in 105 US ARL libraries. By the time the FY 2005–2006 survey was released, minorities held 13 percent of the positions in 99 US ARL university libraries. That number only increased marginally to 14 percent, or 1,003 of the total 7,260 positions in 99 libraries by FY 2011–2012.[25]

TABLE 6.2. Distribution of Minorities and Whites in US ARL University Libraries within Each Position

	FY 1986		FY 2005–2006		FY 2011–2012	
	Minority (%)	White (%)	Minority (%)	White (%)	Minority (%)	White (%)
Director	2	98	5	95	8	92
Associate or Assistant Director	5	95	6	94	9	92
Branch Head	8	92	10	90	11	89
Department Head	6	94	10	90	10	90
Subject Specialist	12	88	20	80	21	79
Functional Specialist	7	93	13	87	13	87
Reference	10	90	14	86	14	86
Cataloging	14	86	17	83	17	83
Other	9	91	8	92	12	88
Total	9	91	13	87	14	86

Source: Calculations made from using data from Fretwell, Tables 16 and 19; Kyrillidou and Young, Tables 21 and 27; Kyrillidou and Morris, Tables 21 and 27.

There was an overall increase in all positions held by minority librarians between FY 1986 and FY 2011–2012; however, the increase of 5 percent is dismally slow growth over a 27-year time period. Hipps also looked at the distribution of positions within the minority and white populations and found that for FY 1986, whites held 37 percent of the managerial positions, compared to 23 percent of minority librarians in managerial positions. Managerial positions were defined as department head, branch head, associate or assistant director, and director. Both groups' percentages of managerial positions held within their respective communities decreased in FY 2005–2006, with minorities holding 21 percent of the managerial positions and whites holding 33 percent. The *2011–2012 Salary Survey* revealed that 21 percent of minorities remained in managerial positions within the minority population, while whites fell to 31 percent. See table 6.3 for the compilation of this data.

TABLE 6.3. Distribution of Positions within Minority and White Populations in US ARL University Libraries

	FY 1986		FY 2005–2006		FY 2011–2012	
	Minority (%)	White (%)	Minority (%)	White (%)	Minority (%)	White (%)
Director	0	2	1	1	0	1
Associate or Assistant Director	3	5	3	6	3	6
Branch Head	7	8	5	7	4	5
Department Head	13	22	14	19	12	17
Subject Specialist	14	10	19	11	22	13
Functional Specialist	5	7	22	22	26	27
Reference	19	17	19	17	13	13
Cataloging	26	16	12	9	11	8
Other	13	13	5	7	7	9
Total	100	100	100	99	98	99

Source: Calculations made from using data from Fretwell, Tables 16 and 19; Kyrillidou and Young, Tables 21 and 27; Kyrillidou and Morris, Tables 21 and 27.

Application of the Trends to LCDP

How does the upward movement within the ranks of LCDP compare with these statistics? Is there evidence that the number of minority librarians in leadership positions has increased?

A look at the participant positions and their institutions at the time of participation in the LCDP compared to their current positions and institutions reveals that participants of this program are moving into leadership positions in ARL and other libraries. Examining the eight cohorts between 1997 and 2014, 149 mid-career library and information professionals participated in the LCDP. Using participants list from the ARL website and information gathered from the websites of institutions where participants are employed currently, the current employment status for 134 (90 percent) of the participants was determined and is displayed in table 6.4.

TABLE 6.4. ARL Participant Positions Held during Program Participation and Currently (2014)				
Positions Held	During LCDP (N=147)	% During LCDP	Currently (Post LCDP) (N=134)	% Currently (Post LCDP)
Director or Dean	4	2.72	16	11.94
Associate (or Assistant) Director (or Dean)	4	2.72	9	6.71
Branch Head	5	3.40	9	6.71
Department Head	28	19.04	27	20.15
Subject Specialists, Functional Specialists, Reference, Cataloging	106	72	73	54.47
Total	147		134	
N/A—unable to confirm participant positions or participants are in current cohort	2		15	
Source: Positions held and during LCDP identified from the ARL website, websites of current places of employment, and ARL publications.				

The largest change in table 6.4 is actually a decrease in the general librarian category, which includes reference librarians, subject specialists, bibliographers, and catalogers. The nearly 18 percent decrease is indeed encouraging and appears to correlate well with the corresponding minor increases in positions at the associate and assistant director, branch head, and department head levels. The next notable change is the increase in the individuals in director or dean positions. Nearly 12 percent of participants are currently holding positions at the dean or director levels, compared to less than 3 percent at the time they participated in the program. Although the numbers are still small, the data gathered shows more than a 50 percent increase in program participants holding associate or assistant dean or director positions and nearly a 50 percent increase in those holding branch head positions.

Conclusion

LCDP is ARL's program to prepare ethnically and racially diverse librarians for senior positions. ARL was interested in bringing in minorities and training them for leadership positions when they were at early points in their careers. We have had different career experiences and goals since participating in LCDP. While one of us aspired to become a dean of libraries, the other recognized that leadership happens at all levels and feels she has had leadership success in positions other than as library dean. From our experiences, attending LCDP is not a guarantee of advancement, especially for individuals from underrepresented minorities. Aside from the LCDP, which focuses on "mid-career librarians from traditionally underrepresented racial and ethnic minority groups" and on preparing these librarians for "increasingly demanding leadership roles in ARL libraries," there are few programs that maintain this commitment. For example, Research Library Leaders Fellows, another ARL program with a strong track record preparing individuals to compete for ARL director openings, has only accepted three people who had previously participated in LCDP.[26]

There are other large scale library leadership programs developed to promote and support mid-career librarians including the now-defunct Urban Library Council's Executive Leadership Institute, which focused on public librarians, and the Snowbird Leadership Institute; the Australian Aurora Leadership Institute; and the Canadian Northern Exposure to Leadership Institute (NELI).[27] Other library leadership programs aimed at mid-career librarians include the Historically Black Colleges and Universities (HBCU) Library Alliance Leadership Program, the Online Computer Library Center (OCLC) Diversity Fellowship Program, and the University of Hong Kong Libraries Leadership Institute, all of which are aimed at ethnically diverse librarians.[28] To date, statistics on career progression and leadership attainment aren't readily available for any of these programs, particularly those aimed at providing support for advancing library and information professionals of color, except for the LCDP. It was noted previously that the LCDP focus is now integrated with ARL's strategic directions. Future research on the LCDP should incorporate findings from assessment of the impact of these program elements on participants as well as any demonstrated impact on the leadership within ARL libraries and ARL strategic priorities. Only then will we begin to see a more holistic picture of the value of the program to ARL in particular and the profession in general; the impact of participation on program participants; and, more uniquely, the role of LCDP participants in ARL strategic priority directions. In the meantime, conducting program assessments and surveying participants of the other programs listed above, several which may be found in other chapters of this book, and making the findings available would go a long way towards contributing to the published literature on this growing area of interest and the increasingly data-driven environments in which we operate.

Notes

1. Association of Research Libraries, "About ARL."
2. Association of Research Libraries, "History of ARL."
3. Dewey, "The Imperative for Diversity."
4. Maxey-Harris and Anaya, *Diversity Plans and Programs*, 15.
5. Ibid.
6. Neely, "Assessing Diversity Initiatives."
7. Nelson and St. Lifer, "ARL Makes Strides."
8. Ibid.
9. Ibid.
10. Ayala-Schueneman et al., "Creating a Legacy."
11. Ibid.
12. Ibid., 2.
13. Ibid., 4.
14. Ibid.
15. Ibid.
16. Hazeur, "ARL Welcomes."
17. Neely, "Assessing Diversity Initiatives," 813.
18. Association of Research Libraries, "Leadership & Career Development Program (LCDP)."
19. Ibid.
20. Wilkinson et al., *Comprehensive Guide*; Cole et al., *The Zimmerman Fire: (re) collections*.

21. See Rumble and MacEwan, "The UCLA Senior Fellows Program," 272; Garten, "The ACRL/Harvard Leadership Institute"; Urban Libraries Council, "Leadership Experts"; Kalin, "Reframing Leadership."
22. Ayala-Schueneman et al., "Creating a Legacy."
23. Hipps, "Diversity in the US ARL," 1.
24. Fretwell, "Table 16," "Table 19"; Hipps, "Diversity in the US ARL," 1.
25. Kyrillidou and Morris, "Table 21," "Table 27."
26. Association of Research Libraries, "Leadership & Career Development Program (LCDP)."
27. Urban Libraries Council, "About; Neely and Winston, "Snowbird Leadership Institute" (see Chapter 14 for an in-depth review of Snowbird); Barney, "Evaluation of the Impact"; Phelan, "Creating Leaders."
28. Historically Black Colleges and Universities Alliance, "HBCU Library Alliance Leadership Program" (see Chapter 4 for an in-depth review of this program); OCLC, "OCLC Diversity Fellowship Program"; Sidorko, "Fostering Innovation."

Bibliography

Association of Research Libraries. "About ARL." http://www.arl.org/about#. UzGv-qhdV8E.

———. "History of ARL." http://www.arl.org/about/history#.UzG0eKhdV8E.

———. "Leadership & Career Development Program (LCDP)." [http://www.arl. org/leadership-recruitment/leadership-development/leadership-career-development-program#.UzIR5ahdV8E.

Ayala-Schueneman, Maria de Jesus, Glendora Johnson-Cooper, Poping Lin, Nerea A. Llamas, Johnnieque Blackmon Love, Neville Durrant Prendergast, Gloria Rhodes, Denise Stephens, and Valerie Wheat. "Creating a Legacy, Sustaining a Vision." *Leading Ideas: Issues and Trends in Diversity, Leadership and Career Development* 7 (April 1999): 2–6.

Barney, Kay. "Evaluation of the Impact of the 2003 Aurora Leadership Institute—'The Gift that Keeps on Giving.'" *The Australian Library Journal* 53, no. 4 (2004): 337–48.

California State Library. "Eureka! Leadership Institute." http://eurekaleadership. org/.

Cole, Deborah A., and Fire/Watch Book Group (Claire-List Benaud, Pat B., Mary Ellen Hanson, and Heidi Perea). *The Zimmerman Fire: (re)collections.* Albuquerque, NM: University Libraries, University of New Mexico, 2008. https://repository.unm.edu/handle/1928/6707?show=full.

Dewey, Barbara. "The Imperative for Diversity: ARL's Progress and Role." *portal: Libraries in the Academy* 9, no. 3 (2009): 355–61.

Fretwell, Gordon. "Table 16: Number and Average Experience of ARL Minority University Librarians, Fiscal Year 1986." *ARL Annual Salary Survey 1985.* Washington, DC: Association of Research Libraries, February 1986.

———. "Table 19: Number and Average Salaries of ARL University Librarians by Type of Institution, Fiscal Year 1986." *ARL Annual Salary Survey 1985.* Washington, DC: Association of Research Libraries, February 1986.

Garten, Ed. "The ACRL/Harvard Leadership Institute: A Five-Year Old Spreads Its Wings." *College & Research Libraries News* 65, no. 2 (2004): 81–83.

Hazeur, Camille. "ARL Welcomes the 2001–02 Leadership and Career Development Program Participants." *ARL: A Bimonthly Report on Research Library Issues and Actions from ARL, CNI, and SPARC*, no. 217 (August 2001): 16.

Hipps, Kaylyn. "Diversity in the US ARL Library Workforce." *ARL: A Bimonthly Report on Research Library Issues and Actions from ARL, CNI, and SPARC*, no. 246 (June 2006): 1–2.

Historically Black Colleges and Universities Alliance. "HBCU Library Alliance Leadership Program." http://www.hbculibraries.org/html/leadership.html.

Jones, DeEtta. "Editor's Note." *Leading Ideas: Issues and Trends in Diversity, Leadership and Career Development* 1 (March 1998): 1.

Kalin, Sally. "Reframing Leadership: The ACRL/Harvard Leadership Institute for Academic Librarians." *Journal of Business and Finance Librarianship* 13, no. 3 (2008): 261–70.

Kyrillidou, Martha, and Shaneka Morris. "Table 21: Number and Average Salaries of ARL University Librarians by Position and Type of Institution, FY 2011–2012." *ARL Annual Salary Survey 2011–2012.* Washington, DC: Association of Research Libraries, 2012.

———. "Table 27: Number and Average Salaries of Minority US ARL University Librarians by Position and Sex, FY 2011–2012." *ARL Annual Salary Survey 2011–2012.* Washington, DC: Association of Research Libraries, 2012.

Kyrillidou, Martha, and Mark Young. *ARL Annual Salary Survey 2005–06.* Washington, DC: Association of Research Libraries, 2006.

Maxey-Harris, Charlene, and Toni Anaya. *Diversity Plans and Programs: ARL SPEC Kit 319.* Chicago: Association of Research Libraries, 2010.

Neely, Teresa Y. "Assessing Diversity Initiatives: The ARL Leadership and Career Development Program." *Journal of Library Administration* 49 (2009): 811–35.

Neely, Teresa Y., and Mark D. Winston. "Snowbird Leadership Institute: A Survey of the Implications for Leadership in the Profession." In *Racing Toward Tomorrow: Proceedings of the Ninth National Conference of the Association of College and Research Libraries, April 8–11, 1999*, edited by Hugh A.

Thompson, 313–24. Chicago: ACRL, 1999. http://www.ala.org/acrl/sites/ala.org.acrl/files/content/conferences/pdf/winston99.pdf.

Nelson, Corinne, and Evan St. Lifer. "ARL Makes Strides for Diversity." *Library Journal* 122, no. 15 (1997): 18.

OCLC. "OCLC Diversity Fellowship Program." https://oclc.org/about/professional-development/minority-fellows.en.html.

Phelan, Daniel. "Creating Leaders: A Study of the Northern Exposure to Leadership Participants—Before and After." February 3, 2005. PowerPoint, 65 slides. http://www.slideserve.com/claral/creating-leaders-a-study-of-the-northern-exposure-to-leadership-participants-before-and-after.

Rumble, Juliet, and Bonnie MacEwan. "The UCLA Senior Fellows Program." *Journal of Business & Finance Librarianship* 13, no. 3 (2008): 271–86.

Sidorko, Peter Edward. "Fostering Innovation in Library Management and Leadership: The University of Hong Kong Libraries Leadership Institute." *Library Management* 28, no. 1/2 (2007): 5–16.

Urban Libraries Council. "About." http://www.urbanlibraries.org/about-ulc-pages-13.php.

———. "Leadership Experts find ULC Executive Training 'Exceptional.'" Press release, 2008.

Wilkinson, Frances C., Linda K. Lewis, and Nancy K. Dennis. *Comprehensive Guide to Emergency and Disaster Preparedness and Recovery.* Chicago: American Library Association, 2009.

CHAPTER 7

A Year of Discovery:
Leadership Development at the Library of Congress

Catherine Dixon and Karen B. Walfall

A CONVERSATION BETWEEN General Colin Powell and the Librarian of Congress, Dr. James Billington, inspired Billington to begin the Leadership Development Program (LDP) at the Library of Congress. Powell spoke to Billington about the benefit of receiving leadership training before he assumed leadership duties and how that helped him perform effectively. The LDP was launched in 1993, with a generous endowment from the late John W. Kluge, in an effort to revitalize the profession and to prepare a diverse group of minority staff members at the Library of Congress for leadership roles in the 21st century.[1]

Kluge was born in eastern Germany on December 21, 1914, and came to the United States with his mother and stepfather in 1922. He never knew his father, who was killed in World War I. He graduated from Columbia University; worked to build a communications empire, Metromedia; and became a generous benefactor to the Library of Congress. Never forgetting his own roots, Kluge identified with minority status. He once said, "As an immigrant, you are a minority. If minorities get the proper tools, they'll do as well as anyone else."[2] Kluge covered the cost of training, conference registration, travel, printing, receptions, all costs associated with the graduation ceremony, and other costs related to the administration of the program.

At its inception in 1993, five participants were recruited from the Library of Congress staff, and five were selected from other cultural institutions in library science and other professions for a 15-month developmental experience.[3] The LDP fellows were given work assignments, received management training, attended seminars, and were assigned to a senior library manager for mentoring. Upon completion of the first year of the program, all components of the program were evaluated and changes were recommended. In subsequent years, the content and format of the class continued to be evaluated, and discussions were held with Library of Congress executive committee members, who considered how institutional needs might impact the training needs for future classes. Beginning with the second cohort of fellows, all 10 participants were chosen from the Library of Congress staff for a 12-month developmental assignment at the beginning of the fiscal year. Not all of the fellows selected were librarians; in the 2005–2006 cohort, for example, the group of fellows included a preservation specialist, an exhibits specialist, a human resources specialist, and a copyright and licensing technical specialist. Kluge's support continues to assist with the costs of all activities related to the library's LDP.

The Curriculum

The participant experience in the program consisted of library-wide orientations, individual work assignments, a group project, and developmental assignments that included a two-week external work assignment and many varied training opportunities.[4] The library-wide orientations consisted of information sessions on each service unit within the Library of Congress, during which a service unit representative presented an extensive overview of that unit and talked about how that unit contributes to the mission of the library. Some of these sessions included a tour of the public and staff work spaces within the unit. By the end of the orientations, the fellows had received an in-depth look at how the Library of Congress's seven service units were connected and needed to be able to work together.[5]

During 2005–2006, each staff member selected for the program was reassigned from their current position to being an LDP fellow and moved into an office space that was shared by the fellows participating in that year's LDP. In addition to a wide variety of developmental training classes, each fellow was assigned two four-month work assignments and a two-week detail at another institution or organization. The purposes of the work assignments were to ensure that each fellow worked on developmental assignments at a grade level above their current grade level and outside of the service unit or division under which they were employed. This practice was established so that each fellow would be required to work at a higher level of expectation within an operational unit that was unfamiliar to them. The placements for the two work assignments were determined after an interview with the fellow, the LDP program manager, and a team of consultants. At that interview, assignment choices for the two four-month details and a two-week detail off-site were presented to the fellow based on the initial program questionnaire completed by the fellow. The discussions centered on which of the available assignments were most suitable to the fellow considering the fellow's knowledge, skills, and abilities as well as future professional goals and aspirations. For example, one reference specialist was assigned a four-month detail as the acting assistant chief of a cataloging division, a four-month detail working with an instructional designer in the library's Center for Learning and Development, and a two-week detail at the Institute for Museum and Library Services. Another reference specialist was assigned four-month details in the Federal Library and Information Center Committee Division and the library's Strategic Planning Office and a two-week detail working with the library director at a local university.

Additionally, the fellows attended many developmental training sessions throughout the 12-month program. The final report of the second class explained,

> Developing a general program for a group of individuals with varied grade levels, backgrounds, and previous work experiences was very challenging. However, using the responses from the participants' questionnaires as a guide, core courses were identified and coordinated for all Fellows.[6]

During our year in the program, there were many hours of formal training related to the development of leadership skills, librarianship, technology skills, and administrative issues. Titles of the classes included

Federal Financial Management Overview, Leadership and Communication Strategies, Grant-Seeking Basics, Presentation Skills, Media Training, Strategic Planning, Business Protocol and Etiquette, Managing Projects, Accounting for Non-Accountants, Negotiation Skills, Project Management Certification Boot Camp, and Time Management. The length of the classes ranged from one-day to one-week, and most of the classes introduced knowledge or ideas participants might never have encountered during a normal workday.

For example, in the two-day Media Training class, fellows learned media characteristics, created an interview checklist, developed a clear message, and became familiar with common pitfalls when dealing with media outlets. The last portion of the class included a mock "live" interview with a member of the media, including the use of a spotlight shining on fellows who were "grilled" by the media representative. After the interview, participants watched the videotape of the interview with the instructors and were given constructive feedback on their responses.

A week-long Project Management Course was offered by the George Washington University School of Business that culminated in fellows taking the Project Management Prep (PMP) Test. A passing grade on that test enabled any interested fellows to go on to register for a PMP certification test. The course on Business Protocol and Etiquette covered a wide array of topics, including information on proper dining and seating etiquette for various functions, how to address and greet dignitaries from other cultures or countries, and even the proper location for one's nametag at a conference or event when nametags are required. Many of the courses had practical, role-playing elements to them, so that as fellows tried out new techniques, they were coached on behaviors. The Presentation Skills class provided another opportunity to experiment with some tips on how to make presentations more engaging and successful. Again, at the end of their presentations, fellows were provided with feedback.

Beginning with the first LDP class, all fellows participated in the five-day National Leadership Institute at the University of Maryland University College in College Park, Maryland. This program, appropriate for mid- to upper-level managers, is recognized for its unique design, which incorporates assessment instruments, experiential exercises, and feedback to help leaders gain insights about their leadership behavior and become more effective, successful leaders.[7] Some special features of the program included 360-degree assessments; videotaped exercises to develop coaching skills; confidential, one-on-one consultation with professional feedback coaches; and leadership and team experiential exercises. During this week, training and professional development opportunities consisted of team building, coaching skills, a survival exercise, in-the-moment feedback from peers, and emotional intelligence skills. Fellows benefited from the evaluation of industrial psychologists concerning the variety of personality tests administered to reveal strengths and areas to improve.

Another component of the program was mentoring. Each fellow was matched with a Library of Congress manager who volunteered to serve as a mentor. The mentors received training on coaching and the mentoring relationship. The objective of this session was to teach the mentors about their responsibilities and provide guidance on how to help the fellows understand their role in self-empowerment. In this mentoring capacity, each mentor committed to foster and develop a relationship with the fellow and to offer support and guidance in his or her professional growth and development. The matching of the mentors to fellows was similar to the selection of the work assignments. Personalities as well as professional, educational, and special interests were considered. Diversity was also considered as a potential benefit in these developmental relationships.

The LDP fellows in the 2005–2006 cohort formed a cohesive and effective operating team through which each person was able to participate in activities well beyond their perceived potential. For example, placements in the two four-month detail work assignments were made at least at one grade level above the fellow's current grade level. Also, each fellow was further challenged by being placed in a division or unit of the library that was outside his or her area of familiarity and level of comfort. In so doing, the cohort members were pushed to "figure things out" and to do whatever was needed to get up to speed with the work of that division or unit. It was these kinds of experiences that helped fellows to see firsthand what kind of work was necessary to become a leader.

In addition to the classes and training sessions, the four-month assignments, and the two-week detail, fellows were assigned a group project with the expectation that they would plan and manage every aspect of the project to final implementation. In 2005–2006, the assignment was to create a communication plan to inform the Library of Congress staff of developments regarding the new Visitors Experience (VE), now called the Library of Congress Experience. The fellows became familiar with all aspects of the VE, met with staff members involved with the creation of the VE, kept up with developments and timelines for various aspects of the VE, and then planned for and presented the promotional materials and events that were to inform the staff. As with all of the other aspects of the program, the group project taught the fellows in an applied way about multitasking, juggling, and prioritizing responsibilities.

The LDP program provided an environment where the level of responsibility, authority, and accountability was enhanced for the participants. Fellows were expected to work independently, which gave them the opportunity to use skills they had not yet been trained to use, but which were within their ability. They were also expected to work as a team and in doing so came to know each other and gained an appreciation of different personalities, boundaries, knowledge, expertise, and ways of working. As a result, participants learned to respect each other and gained a better understanding of how all the units of the library must work together. Each fellow developed an individual needs assessments and created individual development plans and were provided with many opportunities to build a network of resources through access to senior managers and staff throughout the library. The 2005–2006 class became aware of the greatest challenges facing the Library of Congress during the coming years and the need for the library to develop leaders who would be able to cope with and offer solutions to these issues that would bring great changes to the library. Through our work assignments and other activities, many of the fellows worked on these issues.

For Future Consideration

At the end of the program, fellows completed an evaluation of the program. The 2005–2006 cohort identified a few opportunities for improvement in the program. Although the service unit orientations provided an excellent management overview of the library and its culture, and were helpful for gaining a broad perspective of the work of the Library of Congress, all of the orientations were scheduled at the beginning of the program. The cohort reported feeling totally overwhelmed with many full days of extensive information being provided and not having enough time to absorb and compartmentalize this information. To alleviate this, it would be helpful to schedule the orientation sessions throughout the year rather than scheduling them one after the other at the beginning of the year. Another potential improvement for the program to consider would be a placement component at the program's conclusion for those fellows who wanted to move in a different direction after their experiences in the LDP. Additionally, the creation of a skill-set pool of LDP fellows, so that fellows could be sent on details to fill staffing voids throughout the library could be a useful outcome for the fellows and the Library of Congress.

The LDP provided fellows with the opportunity for critical self-reflection. Through the course sessions and work assignments, the program provided experiences that increased participant confidence in communication skills, that taught participants how to listen and delegate more effectively, and that gave participants the flexibility to change at both a personal and professional level. The program emphasized the importance of teamwork to accomplish significant goals and the importance of creating a cooperative climate rather than a competitive one for everyday leadership. In short, the program's major strength was the 10 culturally and ethnically diverse fellows who possessed strong, diverse, and independent personalities, and yet managed to become a united, effective, and productive management team.

Notes

1. Library of Congress, *Leadership Development Program*. John H. Kluge established the Leadership Development Program Gift Fund to assist with all activities related to the Leadership Development Program. In total the John W. Kluge Foundation provided $1 million towards the establishment of the program.
2. Urschel, "Greater Knowledge."
3. The head of Harvard's Littauer Library, the associate curator for public services for University of Virginia's Special Collections Department, and the manager of media services for Brown University were a few of the participants from the other cultural institutions.
4. We participated in the 2005–2006 cohort. This chapter constitutes our personal recollections and perceptions and should not be construed as representing the Library of Congress or as a formally conducted evaluation or assessment of the program.
5. The seven service units were Copyright, Congressional Research Services, Law Library, Library Services, Office of the Librarian, Office of Strategic Initiatives, and the Office of Support Operations. To see an organization chart

that details the Library of Congress Service Units, go to http://www.loc.gov/about/lcorgchart.pdf.

6. Library of Congress, *Leadership Development Program*.
7. University of Maryland University College Center for Creative Leadership, *National Leadership Institute*.

Bibliography

Library of Congress. *Leadership Development Program Final Report, 1999–2000*. Washington, DC: Library of Congress, 2000.

Library of Congress. "Organization Chart." Accessed September 4, 2013. http://www.loc.gov/about/lcorgchart.pdf.

University of Maryland University College. *National Leadership Institute: Leadership Development Program*. Loose-leaf notebook given to 2005-2006 Library of Congress Leadership Development Program participants. Baltimore, MD: University of Maryland University College, 2002.

Urschel, Donna. "Greater Knowledge and a Better Life: Kluge's Life Leaves Sweeping Legacy for Library." *Library of Congress Information Bulletin* 69, no. 10 (2010). http://www.loc.gov/loc/lcib/1010/kluge.html.

CHAPTER 8

Big Place, Big Challenges:
ARL's Leadership Fellows Program

Ann Campion Riley

ALL TYPES OF organizations need to do succession planning, and large complex research libraries are no exception. In the early years of the 21st century, a group of North American research librarians chose to address the need for succession planning together. That group, the library deans and directors of the Association of Research Libraries (ARL), an organization of the 120 largest libraries in North America with specific membership criteria, began conversations on how to address the issue.[1] ARL has a history of offering leadership programs since the 1970s through its Office of Leadership and Management Services, and in 2004, ARL's then executive director, Duane Webster, after study and in consultation with the ARL board of directors, decided to begin a leadership program that would focus on developing a pool of trained leaders from ARL member institutions who might be interested in eventually becoming deans and directors of large research libraries. These potential leaders had to be sponsored by their home institutions, go through a competitive selection process, and be willing to travel to other campuses for five days, at least three times over the course of the program. The participants would retain their positions at their home libraries, and the home libraries were required to cover the costs of travel in addition to the program fee.

The different types of universities within the ARL lent themselves to comparison, and typically the Research Libraries' Leadership Fellows

(RLLF) site visits reflected the various types of places that have research libraries. For example, Columbia University in New York City, a private Ivy League institution in one of the world's largest cities, offers a very different atmosphere than the University of Colorado Boulder, a public university that plays a defining role in its town, or the University of British Columbia in Vancouver, offering the Canadian perspective on higher education. No other leadership program within librarianship offers the opportunity to spend time at diverse locations over the course of several years, with access to top campus leadership. Elliott Shore, executive director of ARL, described the RLLF as "the Cadillac" of leadership programs because of its quality as well as its cost (pers. comm.). Webster commented that it was "one of the least expensive" to run because all the deans and directors as well as campus administrators donate their time and expertise (pers. comm.). The willingness of member directors to donate their time demonstrated their belief in the value of the program and their dedication to its success. Whether the ARL operated the program through contracting with outside consultants or through its own staff and members' time, the multiple campus visits were a clear strength and important aspect of the program.

History of the Program

This program was called the Research Libraries Leadership Fellows (RLLF) until 2013, when it was renamed the ARL Leadership Fellows.[2] The program included campus visits and interactions with campus leaders. These interactions were intended to give participants an introduction to the roles research library directors played in their institutions and the profession and allowed participants to experience the difference between the external campus focus of the dean or director in contrast to the internal library focus most participants experienced in their current positions. Only ARL member libraries could nominate participants until 2013. Nominees' credentials went forward to a selection committee of sponsoring ARL deans and directors who made the final selection, with a limit of 25 participants per cohort. The program ran, and still runs, over two academic years.

Webster and consultant De Etta Jones Young described the first three times the program was offered, 2004–06, 2007–08, and 2009–10, in their article on the program, "Our Collective Wisdom."[3] They described the theoretical intent of the program, to provide practical, research-library based experiences, along with the program's history and planning process. They included the instructional design of the program and its inclusion of group sessions, visits, and themed programming, with a focus on campus leadership in relation to libraries. The program was designed to approach the challenges of leading research libraries in four areas: strategic domains, issue arenas, learning outcomes, and key questions.[4] The designers chose to emphasize the importance of the involvement of the directors or deans of the sponsoring libraries. The focus was on the special issues that the size and complexity of research libraries added to common management and leadership challenges. In particular, the role of research library leaders in shaping the future of scholarly publishing and communication was an emerging issue.[5] The sponsoring deans or directors chose the themes used to structure the three week-long institutes held onsite at the sponsoring libraries. In addition to the institutes, leadership fellows were also offered site visits to four other ARL institutions, plus visits to OCLC's headquarters and the Mellon Foundation's office in New York.[6] Attendance at the ARL spring and fall meetings and at the Coalition for Network Information meetings was also suggested for the leadership fellows.[7] Participants also had webinars on various themes, a 360-degree assessment, and some opportunities for leadership coaching related to the strengths and weaknesses identified in the 360 assessment. Fellows were also expected to complete a group project on a topic of interest to research libraries and had an ARL member director assigned to each of them during the fall and spring ARL meetings, to be a mentor just for that meeting, as a way to meet more people and learn more at the meetings.

The library deans or directors from each of the campuses that hosted institutes for the fellows formed the selection committee for those who applied to participate in the program. This linking of the hosting library administrators with the selection of participants added a personal dimension to each program as the hosting directors had the opportunity to see career details and read professional statements from those chosen as fellows. Each iteration of the program from 2006–2012 involved a different set of campuses for both the institutes and the site visits, allowing interested ARL deans and directors the chance to showcase their operations. The hosting libraries' dean or director and staff developed the content of the meetings and arranged for speakers around the strategic issue themes. For example, two strategic issue themes during the 2011–12 institutes were "The

Politics of Technology" and "Community Engagement." In both cases, the chosen themes addressed areas deemed important by the hosting libraries and were areas in which the libraries considered themselves to have special strength or expertise.

Literature Review

Relatively few articles have been published on the ARL Leadership Fellows program, and topics include descriptions of the program, use of the program as a model for other programs, and a study of the program's effect on participants. Young and Webster described the ARL Leadership Fellows program from the point of view of its creators.[8] Their article provided a history of the program, information on its instructional design, and its original content, which has changed over time. Another even earlier article by Paula Kaufman, the former dean of libraries at the University of Illinois at Urbana-Champaign, detailed reasons for starting the program from the point of view of one of the founding library sponsors.[9]

James Neal, Victoria Owen, and William Garrison refer to the program as "creating a best practice" in leadership training for library leaders.[10] Martha Bedard, in her introduction to a special issue of the *Journal of Library Administration*, highlights positive statistics as a hallmark of the program's effectiveness.[11] Another article describes how the program was used as a model for a Canadian program for public library leadership development.[12]

A 2009 study based on a survey of the participants of two cohorts and written by members of those groups reviewed the outcomes of the program and the perceptions of the participants.[13] It contained information on the age of the participants and statistics on how many had changed positions since the program commenced, with over 60 percent reporting that the program encouraged them to pursue more ambitious career paths and to consider library leadership.[14] Comments from the participants indicated the experiences they had were highly valued both for the experiences of meeting with campus leadership and the increased perspective gained about the library's role on a campus.

Program Content

A key concept underlying the ARL Leadership Fellows program is the idea that research libraries are so large and complex that they pose special challenges in leadership that are addressed most effectively by people who have experience in the research library environment. The early restriction of participants to those employed at ARL institutions was an expression of that concept. No evidence exists that ARL experience is a primary predictor of new director success. Much research has been done on the need for management training and the types of management training library supervisors and directors should receive, but none on the backgrounds of research library directors and the correlation of their ARL experience, if any, with their long-term success as administrators and leaders. Indeed, administrative success is difficult to quantify. An element of success ARL program participants are able to observe is the interactions between the library administrators and the campus administrators during the institutes and site visits. There was a perception of success among the fellows where campus administrators demonstrated confidence and familiarity with library issues and personal warmth toward the library deans and directors, resulting in good working relationships.

A typical five-day institute began with an optional dinner Sunday night with the two fellows from the hosting institution. On Monday, fellows had an optional tour of the city, followed by lunch on their own. After that, an afternoon session addressed a topic, such as success strategies for new directors of research libraries, with a brief presentation followed by questions and discussion from 2:00–5:00 pm. Then after a brief break, the hosting institution held a reception in a museum or other campus venue. The next morning, the official program began, starting with a continental breakfast and a welcome and orientation session from the hosting dean or director. After that, the sessions related to the theme of the institute began, continuing with lunch and breaks throughout the day and culminating with a hosted dinner at a local restaurant. The next two days continued with discussions; presentations; and the most important session, the open discussion with the campus provost, vice chancellors, or other administrators. Lunches were sometimes at varying campus dining facilities, and one visit included dinner at the college president's house. Transportation was always provided back to the hotel or residence hall where the fellows were staying. The final session of each institute included time for the fellows to discuss their observations during the visit after the formal programming had ended, and some of the most frank discussions occurred at the end of the visits. Often the host library provided readings on the theme of the institute before the visit, but these were generally not directly discussed.

Another portion of the program was the formation of small groups to work on projects related to the themes of the institutes or other issues that arose during the discussions. Some of these arose during the visit to the Mellon Foundation offices in New York City. The group projects allowed participants to pursue an issue more fully, such as the use of ARL statistics. Some group reports were presented at an ARL meeting, while others became publications or grant applications.

Theoretical Leadership Model

Theories of leadership and the academic study of leadership had minor roles in the ARL program; rather, the emphasis was on interaction with campus leadership. The four frames philosophy developed by Lee G. Bolman and Terrence E. Deal, described in their 1994 book, *Reframing Organizations*, arose as a model during discussions and was recommended reading for participants unfamiliar with it, but it was not a major focus of the program.[15] The four frames are the structural frame, the human resources frame, the political frame, and the symbolic frame. Leaders were able to see different aspects of situations by viewing them within the various frames, and the authors provided examples from complex organizations as diverse as Kodak, large hospitals, and the US Marines. The four frames model has been used in educational administrators' training institutes, such as the one cosponsored by the Association of College and Research Libraries and the Harvard Graduate School of Education, and is cited by many recent articles on leadership in education.[16]

Most of the library administrators articulated some variation of transformational leadership style.[17] A constant theme was the need for libraries to be transformed from their traditional roles as holders of books and materials to key players in campus instruction and research. Observation during the individual visits with leaders introduced a variety of leadership styles, rather than any specific theories.

Personal Experience

I was a participant in the fifth iteration of the program, from January 2011 to October 2012. Although I saw the value of the themed content, I found the content overshadowed by the information gleaned from observing the interactions of library staff with their administrators and the relationship of the libraries to campus priorities. While in theory each library organization played a similar role in the support of research and student learning on its respective campus, each successive visit served to highlight the variations of campus engagement and library priorities. The personal styles of the library administrators and their relationships with campus leaders who came to speak to the RLLF participants demonstrated these differences. While the need for a library dean or director to have an effective professional relationship to his or her supervisor, typically a provost or vice president for academic affairs in research institutions, may seem obvious, the depth of the alignment of library priorities with those of the rest of the campus emerged as an indicator of my perception of the library leadership's success. The unique structure of the RLLF program, which allowed participants to see the library administrators interacting with other campus upper-level administrators, offered a very valuable and hard-to-acquire experience. I found my own leadership skills developed specifically in my improved ability to assess situations and see the role of each library in the context of the mission and political climate of each institution, based on what participants heard from the local leaders we met. I also developed a much greater appreciation of the differences among research libraries. The demands faced by the university librarian at a public flagship university differed more than I realized from those faced by the same position at private institutions. However, the situations faced by Canadian librarians were more similar to those of US librarians than I had previously understood. Issues with the role of the libraries on campus, tenure for librarians, and the politics of dealing with information technology staff, for example, seemed very similar between US and Canadian research libraries.

Conclusion

The ARL Leadership Fellows program benefits mid-level librarians with some years of supervisory experience and experience in research libraries. The focus on research libraries and large universities may also be an important experience for potential participants who had most of their experience at smaller libraries. More emphasis on the development of vision and the differences between high-functioning managers and successful leaders would also strengthen the program. A tremendous advantage the program provides is the opportunity for participants to become well acquainted with others in the program who share the aspiration to become an ARL director. The friendships that formed helped create camaraderie within the group of

ARL directors, which should eventually lead to improved effectiveness and smoother functioning of the ARL. The pairing of participants with current ARL directors for membership meeting mentoring also helped build rapport. The projects offered an opportunity to work on an issue in depth, often enough to produce a publication or grant to benefit the participants.

Direct comparisons between short-term leadership training experiences of a few days versus programs such as the ARL Leadership Fellows are difficult to effectively make. The only truly valid comparison would be between a short program versus a long one with the same content and same leaders. Assessing the effectiveness of the program would still be difficult if the measure were a survey of participants who brought different levels of leadership experience and knowledge to the program; however, a survey could then be done to compare the two delivery methods. The number of leaders that ARL Leadership Fellows can observe and interact with face to face over the length of the program would be impossible to duplicate in a week-long program, and those interactions are the heart of the program. The reality of life as a campus leader when seen by observers on that campus, however briefly, is also impossible to duplicate and adds depth to the program experience.

The program was spread out over two years, so that both the cost of the travel and the time away from the workplace would be less difficult for the institutions and the participants to manage.[18] The time between visits was also helpful, allowing participants time to think about the content of each of the visits and time to test some of the ideas and techniques observed at their home institutions. For example, after the institute at the University of British Columbia (UBC), which had as its theme "Community Outreach," I became more observant of the community outreach activities of my library. UBC seemed to echo work done at US land grant universities with which I was familiar. In weeklong leadership programs, there is no time for the testing and reevaluation of ideas with the benefit of live group discussion. Some programs do offer follow-up meetings such as reunions at American Library Association annual or midwinter conferences or online discussions, but I have not found those as fruitful as live, focused group discussions.

The 2009 article by Lisa German and others offers some quantitative assessment of the program and indicates that many participants consider the program to have influenced their decisions to pursue administration.

Almost two-thirds of those completing the program have changed positions within several years. All the assessments in that study indicate that participants moved to leadership positions, which may indicate positive results, although perhaps not a direct correlation since there was no control for other factors.[19]

If the succession of its graduates to ARL dean and director positions is used as an assessment measure for meeting the programs objectives, the program would appear to be meeting that need. Each year at the ARL meeting at which new deans and directors are welcomed, part of the official announcements include information on former ARL leadership program participation. Shore indicated that a review of the program was done internally at ARL, with the board of directors and the committee on the program from 2012. The results of that review informed the ARL's decision to continue offering the program (Elliot Shore, pers. comm.).

Notes

1. See http://arl.org for more information about the Association of Research Libraries.
2. For further information, see ARL Leadership Programs, http://arl.org
3. 3 Young and Webster, "Our Collective Wisdom."
4. Ibid., 781.
5. Ibid., 782.
6. OCLC is the international not-for-profit corporation that provides cataloging, research, and interlibrary loan services for its member libraries and offers the bibliographic resource WorldCat (see more on OCLC's history at http://oclc.org); information about the Mellon Foundation may be found at http://www.mellon.org/.
7. For information about CNI, see http://www.cni.org/.
8. Young and Webster, "Our Collective Wisdom."
9. Kaufman, "Where Do the Next 'We' Come From?"
10. Neal, Owen, and Garrison, "Research Library Leadership Development."
11. Bedard, "Introduction to Our Commitment," 777.
12. Barrie and Raven, "Building Our Future."
13. German et al., "RLLF in the Rear-View Mirror."
14. Ibid.
15. Bolman and Deal, *Reframing Organizations.*
16. Details at http://gse.harvard.edu; over 50 dissertations in higher education reference Bolman and Deal in an online search of Dissertations Abstracts International *done in October 2013.*

17. Transformational leadership is described by Bass in "From Transactional to Transformational Leadership" as the leader elevating the interests of employees beyond their self-interests to support of the broader mission and goals of the institution and the group.
18. Young and Webster, 781.
19. German et al., 801.

Bibliography

Albino, Judith. "Personal Leadership Identity and Leadership Frames: Understanding What Happened at Penn State." *The Psychologist-Manager Journal* 16, no. 3 (2013): 131–46.

Barrie, Lita, and Rebecca Raven. "Building Our Future: The Public Library Leadership Fellows Program." *Partnership: The Canadian Journal of Library and Information Science Practice and Research* 7, no.1 (2012): 1–3.

Bass, Bernard M. "From Transactional to Transformational Leadership: Learning to Share the Vision." *Organizational Dynamics* 18, no. 3 (1990): 19–31.

Bedard, Martha. "Introduction to Our Commitment to Building Leaders: Programs for Leadership in Academic and Special Libraries." *Journal of Library Administration* 49, no. 8 (2009): 777–79.

Bolman, Lee G., and Terrence E. Deal. *Reframing Organizations: Artistry, Choice, and Leadership*. San Francisco: Jossey-Bass, 1994.

German, Lisa, Victoria Owen, Jill Parchuck, and Beth Sandore. "RLLF in the Rear-View Mirror: A Report on the Impact and Value of the ARL Academic Library Leadership Fellows Program." *Journal of Library Administration* 49, no. 8 (2008): 795–809.

Kaufman, Paula. "Where Do the Next 'We' Come From?" *ARL Bimonthly Report* 221 (2002): 1–8.

Neal, James, Victoria Owen, and William Garrison. "Research Library Leadership Development: Creating a Best Practice." In *Continuing Professional Development: Pathways to Leadership in the Library and Information Science World*, edited by Ann Ritchie and Clare Walker, 153–165. Munich: Saur, 2007.

Young, DeEtta Jones, and Duane Webster. "Our Collective Wisdom," *Journal of Library Administration* 49, no. 8 (2009): 781–93.

CHAPTER 9

Leadership and Fellowship:
The UCLA Senior Fellows Program

Marianne Ryan, Kathleen DeLong, and Julie Garrison

THE UCLA SENIOR Fellows program is a management institute for senior-level academic librarians. The program's unique aspects include its
intensive, residential framework and its in-depth exploration of issues concerning higher education and problems facing academic library administrators. A cohort of 15 fellows spends three weeks together on the UCLA
campus. Within this context, the group participates in a range of learning
and professional development activities. The Senior Fellows experience includes a variety of components such as traditional classroom lectures, vibrant discussions, library visits, field trips, small group conversations, and
personal reflection. Because the fellows live together for the better part of a
month, close bonds form. A stipulation of the program is that fellows leave
their jobs behind and remain in residence, except in extraordinary circumstances, to afford the greatest immersive learning and deepest community
building experience.

Established in 1982 as a five-week program, the initiative evolved from
the vision of the Council on Library Resources (CLR) President Warren J.
Haas and the work of its advisory committee on university libraries.[1] The
program is now based at UCLA's Graduate School of Education and Information Science (GSEIS).[2] When the initiative began, it was fully funded by
CLR, with the idea that it would eventually become self-supporting. This

has been the case since 1991. After the initial offering in 1982, the intent was to offer the program every year. A cohort was selected in 1983, but 1984 was skipped to avoid the challenging logistics of Los Angeles being the site of the Olympics that year. When the program resumed in 1985, it became annual and remained so until 2007. Today the program is conducted every other year, and the last two groups of fellows studied in 2012 and 2014. With the exception of 1995 and 1997, the program has always been hosted at UCLA.

The first director of the Senior Fellows program was Robert Hayes, dean of UCLA's School of Library and Information Science (LIS) and a member of the aforementioned CLR advisory committee. Hayes led the program through 1985 when he was succeeded by Dorothy J. Anderson, assistant dean of LIS. In 1991, leadership of the Senior Fellows program was taken over by Beverly P. Lynch, then dean and professor of LIS. A member of the first Senior Fellows class, Lynch has guided the program continuously since then, codirecting with Anne Woodsworth in 1995 and 1997, the years it was based at Long Island University.

The original concept of the program to specifically attract librarians at ARL institutions gave way to selection centered instead on the individual. Fellows are now chosen from a variety of academic environments, including liberal arts colleges, master's-granting institutions, and research libraries. Since its inception, a total of 220 librarians have participated in the program, 77 males and 143 females. At their time of selection as fellows, 78 were library directors and 120 were assistant university librarians. A small number of department heads, library science faculty, and members of library consortia have also participated.

The Curriculum

The curriculum is organized around a set of planned speakers and topics focusing on current issues and the future direction of academic libraries and higher education. Speakers contribute readings in addition to the collection of books and articles selected by Lynch. Fellows also contribute to their own agenda, sharing their own priorities and hopes for the program and agreeing to discuss other shared issues during their time together. Speakers, readings, and agendas shift with each cohort group and are tailored to the group's needs and important issues at the time of the program. The program also offers a mix of social activities, including receptions and dinners with speakers, field trips, and other group activities.

Although the Senior Fellows experience offers a stable curriculum, each program addresses current topics and is customized to the needs and interests of participants. With the luxury of extended, uninterrupted time, reading is an important component of the fellows' experience. Initially, a research project was expected, but in more recent years this has become optional. Relaxing this requirement has not deterred fellows from designing research and publishing, either individually or collaboratively. Lynch describes a sample of these activities in her 1994 article.[3]

Literature Review

Although more than 200 academic librarians have participated as fellows since the program was founded in 1982, there has been relatively little written or research conducted about the experiences of participants or effect on their careers. Early in the program's history, Dorothy Anderson, coordinator of the 1989 class, compared the first two cohorts with a control group of ACRL members and tested hypotheses around visibility in the profession, geographic mobility, and responsibility.[4] Anderson found that fellows were more than twice as visible and nearly twice as mobile as the control group. They were also three times more likely to assume management positions than members of the control group. She also provided a basic profile of male and female fellows that demonstrated striking similarities, with the noteworthy exception that male fellows moved twice as quickly as their female counterparts into initial management positions, though after their first two management positions this difference was no longer evident. Also unique to the Senior Fellows classes was the leadership profile and image they created. While no causal relationships between participation in the Senior Fellows program and career progression could be drawn, fellows were regarded as leaders within their communities when they were nominated for the program. Anderson also found that this leadership capability was demonstrated in their professional lives and activities as evidenced in their individual profiles.

Lynch provided a descriptive overview of the program to the *Journal of Library Administration*.[5] Lynch's article included basic information concerning the development of the program and some follow-up on the careers of participants in the seven cohorts since the first class in 1982 (of which Lynch was a member). It also provided a detailed description of the issues challenging research libraries from the 1960s to the 1990s and a framework for the papers produced by the 1993 Senior Fellows class based upon their assessments of the environment of research libraries and the new ideas and solutions to issues they discussed. Lynch began with Keyes Metcalf's seminar on administrative problems in 1958 at Rutgers University and concluded with brief summaries of the papers produced by the 1993 Senior Fellows class, including unpublished papers by Joan Giesecke on organizational structures and Margo Crist's description of organizational change and redesign. Some of this work was later compiled and published as a resource on organizational change in academic libraries.[6]

Several individual fellows have written of the experience with their particular cohort and the value they found in the program content and interactions; examples include Gordon Aamot, James K. Bracken, and Jeffrey Horrell.[7] These were most often brief descriptions and intended to inform and encourage a particular audience to explore the program's benefits.

Juliet Rumble and Rose MacEwan provided the most recent and only evaluative study of the UCLA Senior Fellows program.[8] In 2007, they interviewed 11 academic library directors who participated in the program between 1987 and 2001. The majority of the study participants identified professional networking opportunities as the most beneficial aspect of the program for them. Also important were program content and the opportunity to step away from day-to-day responsibilities and focus on big picture issues and discussions. Study participants provided many insights regarding their personal development as leaders, particularly an understanding of their leadership style and individual strengths. Study participants mentioned Lynch's invaluable role as a mentor and facilitator of the program's objectives. Overall, the participants deemed the experience as most valuable for broadening awareness of leadership issues as well as highlighting the need for collaborative approaches through internal and external partnerships if research libraries were to continue to thrive in volatile campus environments.

Study and Results

Building on the work of Rumble and MacEwan, this study surveyed three Senior Fellows' cohorts, 2007, 2010, and 2012, to identify what participants continued to appreciate about the program. Participants were asked about what they most valued, insights they gained, support they feel they received from fellow participants and program faculty, and suggestions for improving the program. Invitations to participate in the survey were sent to 42 fellows, of which 30 responded (see Appendix 9.1 for the questions).

The 30 fellows respondents overwhelmingly indicated the tremendous value of the program to their careers and professional development. They considered networking one of the most important aspects of the program. A majority stated that the conversations and interactions with their colleagues, both inside and outside the classroom, were enormously meaningful as was networking time with the invited speakers (see table 9.1). Several fellows noted that the strong ties and relationships they formed with their cohort offered opportunities for exploring their own leadership struggles and sharing different solutions to problems. One respondent commented that "Each of us brought a different perspective to the program, and we learned from each other. I still reach out to my colleagues for advice, and I still use the advice I received during the program."[9]

TABLE 9.1. **Most Important Aspects of the Senior Fellows Program**	
Program Aspect	Responses
Networking with other Senior Fellows colleagues outside the classroom	26
Conversations with Senior Fellows colleagues in the classroom	25
Planned programming	18
Networking with invited speakers	17
Dedicated time away from the office	13
Content and readings	11
The social activities	8
Field trips	5
Other aspects of the program (please explain in the comment box)	1

Over two-thirds of respondents stated that gaining a better understanding of their own personal leadership style and developing a greater awareness of the challenges and opportunities facing academic libraries were the most critical lessons they learned during the program. The Senior Fellows experience validated their thinking, built confidence in their own abilities, and helped them learn from the perspectives of their colleagues. Respondents indicated that they discovered the self-assurance that they too have the skills and leadership qualities to be a dean or university librarian as well as insight into the fact that others also experienced leadership challenges. Another important realization was the power of the collective group wisdom and, again, the importance of having a community of colleagues. One respondent observed, "There is not a single correct approach. It was also refreshing to be able to disagree, but with respect and collegiality."

Fellows were asked whether the program had any impact on their professional development. Sixteen, just over half of survey respondents, indicated that they altered their approach to their current positions as a result of their experience. Nine acknowledged a shift or clarification in their career path as a result of participating in the program. Another six had a change in employment within a year of completing the program. Other stated effects included a deeper understanding of what it takes to be a university librarian or dean and the ability to discern whether to move to such a position.

Fellows were asked to explain the types of support they received from the faculty and their cohort during and after the program. In general, responses indicated that Lynch and the invited speakers were interested in the fellows, engaged in conversations, willingly answered questions, and were accessible throughout the program. Fellows also reported that when they contacted Lynch or speakers since the program ended, they received helpful replies. All survey respondents commented positively about the importance of the relationships that developed among members of their respective cohorts. These close connections and networks appear to have the most lasting effect. As one fellow described, "We continue to have one-to-one and group discussions online about things. And we meet twice a year for discussion and fun. I always know that I have a group of people who I can count on to ask questions or from whom I can seek advice." Many report consulting about professional concerns, getting together socially, and receiving personal support from their peers.

Respondents were asked how they provide support to up-and-coming leaders and whether their experience as a fellow influenced their involvement in mentoring. Based on survey responses, it appears that the Senior Fellows program has not necessarily had a major impact on whether individuals mentored overall; comments suggested that fellows mentor others in many ways. Some noted that the program reinforced the need for mentoring and that they expanded their approach based on their Fellows experience. Others remarked that the program reinforced or strengthened their commitment to mentoring others. One fellow stated that their approach to mentoring has changed, and

> I now am really looking to see who among my staff and others seems to have the interest and ability to move into a higher-level administrative position. When I first thought of applying to be an administrator I thought I might be wasting my effort/talent… I see many active younger professionals who think the same way and I really work to show them that if they do not look to this level as a goal, others who may be less able will (and that will be the field's loss).

Leadership Theories, Best Practices, and Lessons Learned

> Leadership is an illusive variable in terms of rationally deciding what it is and who has it. That it is essential to move academic librarianship forward is accepted. That leaders need to be identified and nurtured is agreed.[10]

The Senior Fellows program is not based upon a particular leadership theory or style. It can best be described as allowing individuals, who have already been identified as library leaders by their institutions, the time and space to commune with others who have significant knowledge and understanding of key issues in the field of librarianship and to learn from their experiences of leadership. The speakers and invited guests who are chosen for the Senior Fellows program are actively involved in libraries and in higher education and bring a nuanced and thoughtful approach to emerging issues and ongoing challenges facing academic libraries. Additionally, fellows are encouraged to read widely before the program begins and reflect broadly, bringing their own ideas and opinions to bear upon the topics under consideration. The opportunity to discuss and debate with cohort members from a multitude of institutions is reported as being invaluable. Discussions emphasize the ever-changing and increasingly complex nature of academic libraries, and the focus is on reflecting and thinking about the conditions and the culture of the organizations in which fellows are playing a key role as well as about their own values and behaviors. While some discussions may incorporate descriptions of best practices, the program is structured so that participants learn from others and enrich their individual understandings. These "lessons learned" will be taken back to the fellows' home institutions and provide the potential for significant impact on their continuing growth and development.

Future of the Program

With the advent of new library leadership programs and the inherent challenges facing potential participants to get away from demanding workplaces for an extended period of time, some have asked if the Senior Fellows program should continue. The answer is a resounding yes. According to participants, the value of the experience is unparalleled. Survey respondents offered suggestions for ways to enhance the program in the future. Some individuals commented that better facilities and possibly varying the location so that the program isn't always on UCLA's campus might be considered. Other recommendations for improving the program included moving materials online (currently participants get most communications and other information in print), recruiting new speakers, making sure there is enough time for fellows to reflect on conversations and experiences, and incorporating more content about the future of higher education and broader issues facing universities. A few respondents also commented that the program should remain three weeks and not be shortened as the extended time is so essential to a meaningful Fellows experience.

Survey participants identified the need for leadership succession planning. Fellows recognize that while Lynch has been a fantastic leader and program facilitator for many years, should she choose to retire or not to direct any longer, the program could end. It may be time to consider appointing an advisory board, as the program initially had, to begin exploring possibilities and perhaps pave the way for another alumnus to eventually become coordinator, following the path to leadership that

Lynch followed. Involving former fellows in planning and developing the curriculum for future groups was another suggestion.

To ensure the ongoing relevance of the program, reinstating what is now an optional scholarly project may have merit. Additionally, it could be worthwhile to invite former fellows back to discuss their scholarship and engage with members of future cohorts.

Conclusion

The UCLA Senior Fellows program remains an exceptional and unique learning and professional development experience for participants. The fact that the perceptions and perspectives of former fellows have remained stable over time lends substantial credibility to the program. Members of the three cohorts surveyed for this study, echoing the findings of Rumble and MacEwan, noted that the most important aspects of the program were professional networking opportunities, big picture discussions, and dedicated time away from the workplace. Key takeaways included a better understanding of leadership issues and greater personal insight and self-awareness. The emphasis on relationship building, both among members of the cohort and with the program coordinator, are among the elements that set the Senior Fellows experience apart from other library management institutes. It is a program that facilitates leadership development through intensive and sustained fellowship.

Appendix 9.1. Survey Questions

Q1. Please rate the overall value of the Senior Fellows program to your career and professional development.

Q2. What aspect(s) of the program were most important?

Q3. What were the most valuable lessons you learned during the program?

Q4. What was the most important insight you gained during this program?

Q5. What impact has the program had on your professional development?

Q6. What type of support did you receive from the Senior Fellows faculty (Beverly Lynch and/or invited speakers) during the program?

Q7. What type of support did you receive from the Senior Fellows faculty (Beverly Lynch and/or invited speakers) after the program?

Q8. What type of support did you receive from your Senior Fellows cohort during the program?

Q9. What type of support did you receive from your Senior Fellows cohort after the program?

Q10. What kind of support do you provide to up and coming leaders? How has your involvement with mentoring changed since you participated in the Senior Fellows program?

Q11. Do you have any suggestions for improving the Senior Fellows program?

Notes

1.   For more information about CLR, see http://www.clir.org/.
2.   For more information about UCLA's GSEIS, see http://gseis.ucla.edu/.
3.   Lynch, "Taking on the Issues."
4.   Anderson, "Comparative Career Profiles."
5.   Lynch, "Taking on the Issues."
6.   Giesecke, *The Dynamic Library*.
7.   Aamot, "UCLA Senior Fellows Program"; Bracken, "A Continuing Library Leader"; Horrell, "Leadership Development in Libraries."
8.   Rumble and MacEwan, "The UCLA Senior Fellows Program."
9.   Due to the specifications of the survey submitted for IRB approval, all quotations from respondents are anonymously submitted to this chapter with no identifying differentiation.
10. Lynch, "Taking on the Issues," 14.

Bibliography

Aamot, Gordon. "UCLA Senior Fellows Program." *Library Directions: A Newsletter of the University of Washington Libraries* 16, no. 1 (2006): n.p. http://www.lib.washington.edu/about/news/libdirections/ldspr06-web/view.

Anderson, Dorothy J. "Comparative Career Profiles of Academic Librarians: Are Leaders Different?" *Journal of Academic Librarianship* 10, no. 6 (1985): 326–32.

Bracken, James K. "A Continuing Library Leader Education: The 2003 UCLA Senior Fellows Program." Trans. Kazuko Takagi. *Journal of Information Processing and Management* 46 (2003): 603–07. https://www.jstage.jst.go.jp/result?cdjournal=johokanri&item1=4&word1=bracken.

Giesecke, Joan, ed. *The Dynamic Library Organization in a Changing Environment.* New York: Haworth Press, 1994.

Horrell, Jeffrey. "Leadership development in Libraries: Theory and Practice." *ILA Reporter* 19, no. 5 (2001): 6–8.

Lynch, Beverly P. "Taking on the Issues in a Changing Environment: The Senior Fellows Program." *Journal of Library Administration* 20, no. 2 (1994): 5–15.

Rumble, Juliet, and Bonnie MacEwan. "The UCLA Senior Fellows Program." *Journal of Business & Finance Librarianship* 13, no. 3 (2008): 271–86.

PART 4

Programs for
Multiple Types
of Libraries

CHAPTER 10

Developing Practical Library Leadership Skills:
The Sunshine State Library Leadership Institute

Rachel Besara

THE SUNSHINE STATE Library Leadership Institute (SSLLI) is not focused purely, or even primarily, on the needs of academic librarians. The institute's curriculum is designed for flexibility and works across a variety of library types. Many college and research library participants have graduated from the program. This diversity in institutional affiliation brings an unexpected richness and diversity to the perspectives, resources, leadership approaches, and discussions in the institute.

Program Description

The goal of the SSLLI is "to assist in preparing library leaders to provide the highest quality library services to the citizens of Florida in the most effective and innovative manner that will meet today's needs and tomorrow's challenges."[1] One of the driving motivations behind this goal is the current crisis in library leadership that the State Library of Florida identified in a 2002 needs assessment.[2] This leadership crisis is two-pronged: (1) the aging of the profession and (2) the disruption that technological change is bringing to traditional library models.[3] These two factors contributed heavily to the overall objectives of the institute.

The results of the needs assessment is stated within the objectives of the institute:

- retain staff currently working in the library and information management profession by reenergizing and developing new leadership skills,
- develop leaders who will have the skills to replace those who will retire from the library and information management profession,
- build collaborative networks within the library community across the state that are sustained over time, and
- establish professional support systems using recognized leaders as mentors.[4]

The program is selective and enrolls approximately 40 participants a year. SSLLI recruits librarians from all types of libraries as well as management-level paraprofessionals who wish to become leaders in the profession. The group of paraprofessionals is specifically targeted by the program as part of a long-term strategy for library leadership recruitment.[5] Applicants to the program are required to have at least two years of professional library experience and have a track record of success.[6]

The call for applications goes out in the spring with the institute beginning in October of every year. The length of the institute is 10 months. Each month there is one face-to-face meeting or two online meetings. Participants are scattered throughout the state, so the meetings are held at two different locations. A few of the sessions are held with the entire cohort. Often these whole-cohort sessions are held the day before the Florida Library Association Conference in the spring and at the SSLLI graduation session, which usually takes place in July at the State Library and Archives of Florida in Tallahassee.[7]

SSLLI's pilot cohort began in October 2003.[8] Originally, the institute was partially based on *The Leadership Challenge* and modeled on two successful regional leadership programs within the state, the Southeastern Florida Library Information Network's Sun Seeker Leadership Program and the Southwestern Florida Library Information Network's leadership program.[9] However, while the pilot year was underway, an extensive needs assessment was completed.[10] This needs assessment guided the final structure of the curriculum, which remains relatively static. The details of the SSLLI curriculum within that structure are adjusted to meet the changing needs of Florida libraries as seen through the feedback of key stakeholders and participants.[11]

Because of the breadth of its objectives as well as the diversity of its participants, the program is focused on a down-to-earth, practical approach, flexible enough to fit the needs of all library types and sizes. The curriculum is adjusted yearly by the faculty members who facilitate the sessions. During my year of participation, the faculty members were DeEtta Jones, a leadership consultant and trainer from DeEtta Jones and Associates and former director of the Association of Research Libraries' Organizational Learning; Pat Wagner, a library trainer and consultant from Siera; and Jill Canono, a leadership consultant from the State Library and Archives of Florida.[12] The curriculum is focused on four professional development foundations: core leadership competencies, shared learning experiences, practical application assignments, and mentoring.

CORE LEADERSHIP COMPETENCIES

The SSLLI core leadership competencies encompass eight constructs that all of the institute's activities, instruction, and projects are centered on. Rather than being tied to one leadership approach, these core competencies relate to the theories contained in several different popular leadership texts.[13] The competencies are develops self and others, sets direction, focuses on results, thinks and acts strategically, demonstrates resilience, builds and sustains relationships, empowers others to act, and understands the value of patrons as partners.

Develops Self and Others

This core competency involves greater self-awareness, awareness of others, and how that knowledge can be used to foster productive interactions. It is related to the James M. Kouzes and Barry Z. Posner's admonition to "challenge the process" and Warren G. Bennis's idea of creating an inspired vision.[14] It involves having a defined sense of mission, values, and goals as well as an overarching vision that helps guide all of the leaders' activities.[15] To demonstrate this competency, leaders should have a sense of urgency and be continually learning.[16]

Sets Direction

When leading by setting direction, it is key to create a shared vision for the organization and to manage by example.[17] In order to sustain this direction, it is important to maintain physical health and serve as a model of balance to prevent burnout.[18] Leaders must be confident, maintain a service focus, and create a group of employees or stakeholders to guide the rest of the organization.[19]

Focuses on Results

Leaders must focus on results. Other issues cannot sidetrack them. To do this, they need to enable those they influence to act and carry out goals on their own.[20] They must be visible in encouraging and working toward the desired results.[21] Leaders cannot indulge in showing frustration or other emotions that might take the focus off of the end goal; they must practice self-mastery.[22] Those in leadership positions must also be willing to share the "spoils" of achievement with their followers in order to keep organizational focus sharp.[23] Continual positivity and an adaptive vision and strategy are key to keeping an organization on course to the desired results.[24]

Thinks and Acts Strategically

SSLLI emphasizes the importance of not being solely reactive or short-sighted. It is very important for leaders to think and act strategically and take the long-term view. This involves communicating a vision of change and the future.[25] Leaders should display caring, support, and affection for their followers.[26] It is important to model the behaviors and attitudes valued by the organization and to listen attentively to employees so that any course adjustments can be made to avoid potential roadblocks.[27]

Demonstrates Resilience

Leading change can be difficult and requires leaders to demonstrate resilience in the face of the unexpected. In order to do this, one cannot shoulder the load alone. Leaders must empower broad-based action and delegate to those on the front lines while still staying results oriented and decisive.[28] To help the organization stay resilient, leaders should also encourage all of their followers and show appreciation to their team and the broader community.[29]

Builds and Sustains Relationships

It is vital that leaders build and sustain relationships both inside and outside of the organization. Bennis's recommendation is to treat employees with respect, doing less micromanagement and giving more leadership opportunities, which will result in closer internal relationships.[30] Leaders must demonstrate that they truly care about and are committed to their employees' projects.[31] If they do not, they risk losing support and buy-in. These relationships, both internal and external, are key to managing change, making it possible for an organization to negotiate it successfully.[32] Finally, when first entering an organization, leaders must try to cement relationships by producing short-term wins for those involved.[33] This sets up a pattern for future success and builds the trust necessary for leaders to be effective long-term.

Empowers Others to Act

Leaders must know their limitations; they will be able to accomplish very little and will quickly burn out if they try to do everything themselves. Teams armed with essential training should be developed to reach results.[34] To grow these teams, leaders must surround themselves with innovators and consolidate their gains to produce even more change in an organization.[35]

Understands the Value of Patrons as Partners

The last core competency of the SSLLI is understanding the value of patrons as partners. New approaches need to be anchored in a shared culture.[36] In today's climate of change for libraries, it is also crucial that leaders understand and encourage the advocacy role of patrons in true partnerships. This competency is closely related to the other competency of building and sustaining relationships.

These eight core leadership competencies are needed for participants to successfully complete the various assignments given to them during the SSLLI. Every session is mapped to one or more of these competencies, and they serve as the institute's shared leadership framework.

SHARED LEARNING EXPERIENCES

Most of the institute's activities are completed by groups. Like many leadership or management endeavors in a real setting, successful activities may require the input of large and small group discussion, partner sharing, and consultations with one's mentors and colleagues. This group approach allows for leadership issues to be viewed from multiple perspectives, leading to participants developing broader perspectives and varied approaches. Furthermore, shared learning builds a strong sense of participant community. This leads to valuable discussions and insights on issues faced across library types, and it contributes to a community of practice within the state. The cohorts stay connected long after the 10-month program is completed via listserv, through the wiki devoted to their year's cohort, and by informal meetings at state conferences.[37] The institute also brings together the different years' cohorts through events, targeted mentor recruitment, and the recognition of graduates' accomplishments. This provides a continuity of support for the program's graduates. Interestingly, as in many programs, when graduates look back, it is the shared experience and networking they remember more than the specific content.[38]

PRACTICAL APPLICATION ASSIGNMENTS

It has been shown that directly applying newly learned knowledge results in better understanding and retention of concepts, especially when it is tied to prior experience.[39] With this in mind, almost every exercise and take-home assignment given to the institute's participants are designed to have application or impact on their individual workplaces, communities, or peers. There are two types of applied assignments in the institute. The first is monthly curriculum assignments and the second is a leadership project designed and carried out by each participant, which is their "thesis" project. This is a practical and flexible approach that allows the cohort to learn together though their widely varied libraries and core populations.

One example of a take-home practical application assignment from the "Develops Self and Others" session involved a participant taking the DiSC assessment and applying the results in their work.[40] The assignment required each participant to identify a leadership project partner who had a different behavioral style and be especially self-aware during a conversation with him or her. The budding leader was then to reflect on the communication challenges that arose in the interaction and write a short paper considering how his or her behavioral preferences shaped the interaction and outcome. The participant was then urged to consider what techniques he or she would employ to ensure that a constructive relationship is maintained.[41] This type of activity was typical of the institute's approach to assignments.

The ultimate expression of the program's practical approach is the required leadership project. In order to receive a certificate, every participant of the institute must complete a leadership project where they will lead change in their library or community that solves a problem, involves partners, and has broader benefits for the wider library community.[42] One example of a completed project from the 2012 class is the development of a partnership with the Jacksonville Children's Commission to help prevent summer learning loss among summer camp attendees. Another example is the creation of a wiki to help One Person Libraries retain, recover, or discover institutional knowledge that might otherwise be lost.[43] More examples of leadership projects may be seen at the institute's webpage, which lists graduates and their projects and mentors.[44]

MENTORING

Mentoring is a key component of the institute. Each participant is responsible for identifying and establishing a mentor-mentee relationship with a leader who has expertise in his or her area of the library profession. SSLLI holds that a good mentor-mentee relationship can be key to the long-term success of a future leader, so the only mandatory book in the entire curriculum is on establishing and maintaining a productive relationship with a mentor, *The Mentee's Guide: How to Have a Successful Relationship with a Mentor*.[45] The institute also has guidelines that must be followed when choosing a mentor. Participants cannot have their direct supervisor as a mentor as this could curb frank and open discussion about sensitive issues. They are encouraged to choose someone who is local, so they can meet in person to strengthen the relationship. The mentor-mentee relationship is expected to last at least the 10 months of the institute, but the activities are designed to promote a connection that will last much longer in most cases. A mentor serves as a resource for the mentee and gives advice, suggests resources, praises, sponsors his or her protégé, and is a confidante. Participants are also encouraged to choose mentors who have experience in the area of the mentee's leadership project.[46]

To help ensure a healthy and active mentoring relationship, SSLLI has suggested discussions and activities, primarily those outlined in *The Mentee's Guide* to be completed by the participants and their mentors.[47] There are also scheduled calls that the institute's faculty makes to the mentors to

ensure that the participants are progressing with their projects and to discuss growth in their leadership skills and mindset.[48]

The four professional development foundations (core leadership competencies, shared learning experiences, practical application assignments
and leadership projects, and mentoring) shape all of the activities of the
SSLLI. However, the foundations only address the framework of activities
within the program. They do not describe the desired participant outcomes.

Participant Outcomes

The institute has concrete outcomes that it wants its graduates to achieve.
It is designed to have participants

- understand their own talents and how to most effectively use
  them as a leader;
- move from managing to leading people;
- formulate, articulate, and communicate a vision that inspires
  others to act;
- prepare for and address a current crisis focusing on the future;
- develop public and private partnerships with other agencies and
  community-based organizations;
- identify and solve existing but unaddressed problems within their
  library;
- target library services to individuals of diverse geographic, cultural, and socioeconomic backgrounds, with disabilities, and with
  limited functional literacy or information skills;
- target library and information services to persons having difficulty using a library and to underserved urban and rural communities, including children from families with incomes below the
  poverty line; and
- increase the level of visibility and value of the library within their
  broader community.[49]

These outcomes are assessed at the graduation meeting of each year's
cohort, where final projects are presented to all participants and mentors
as well as stakeholders from the Florida Department of State. Feedback and
discussion of successes and failures are designed to inform future progress
and further growth of the participants, who often stay in contact through
the SSLLI alumni wiki, listserv, or conferences.[50]

Literature Review

There has been relatively little published about SSLLI in journals. An editorial in *Community and Junior College Libraries* in 2005 and another 2005 article in *Florida Libraries* describe and discuss how SSLLI is aimed at recruiting and developing emerging leadership within Florida libraries.[51] Another descriptive piece was published discussing the structure and creation of the program from the State Library and Archives of Florida's perspective.[52] The institute has been mentioned in more recent literature among the examples of state library-led leadership programs with a nontraditional yearlong format, but SSLLI is not discussed individually at any length.[53]

A survey was done of the graduates of the first four classes, and the results were presented in a poster session at ALA in 2009. Approximately 15 percent of the respondents of the survey were from academic libraries.[54] The survey found that approximately 70 percent of participants found SSLLI better than other leadership training they had completed and that the primary reason participants enrolled in the institute were networking and professional development.[55]

While relatively little has been written about SSLLI in academic sources, there are many reports on the program, reflecting its roots in the Florida Division of Library Services and the institute's continued funding by the Florida Library Services and Technology Acts (LSTA) Grants. There was a founding report describing the structure of the program and how it fits within the other leadership programs in Florida.[56] The institute was also described in a report to the Institute of Museum and Library Services as part of the 2007 Florida LSTA report.[57] This was followed by an update in the current Florida LSTA Plan reflecting SSLLI's ongoing status and place within the Florida Department of State Division of Library and Information Services suite of services.[58]

These founding and descriptive reports are complemented by the *Evaluation of 2008–2012 LSTA Five-Year Plan*.[59] This is the first report that contains a significant evaluative component of the program. The institute is evaluated immediately following each meeting of participants, and these responses show that 80 percent of respondents reported that the content covered relates to their work, that the institute encouraged them to participate in statewide activities, and that their leadership skills had been enhanced. A majority of respondents indicate they had exercised an increased leadership role at their library because of the institute. The report also contains a qualitative summary based on a focus group held with SSL-LI graduates, finding that the program improved their management and communication skills. Networking opportunities were also mentioned as an important result of the institute. However, the report acknowledges that there is a lack of follow-up and long-term measurement of the impact of the institute on its graduates.[60]

A Participant's Perspective

I enrolled in the 2010–2011 SSLLI, the seventh cohort graduating from the program. I attended all of the sessions but one. My leadership project was the development and implementation of an ethnographic study of the science, technology, engineering, and mathematics (STEM) population at Florida State University (FSU). The results were used to shape changes at the science library. My mentor was the associate dean of public services and collection development at the University of Rochester. She was selected because of her leadership roles, science background, and participation in the ethnographic library studies at the University of Rochester.[61] I found the long-term, distributed nature of the program spread over 10 months to be very helpful in allowing time for reflection and application of concepts. Three main benefits came out of my participation in the program: an increased awareness and application of leadership skills coming from the institute's curriculum, an expanded network, and greater involvement in professional organizations.

One of our sessions discussed John French and Bertram Raven's five bases of social power.[62] My position as assessment librarian in my organization requires me to manage projects, such as my leadership project; partner with groups; and motivate colleagues. However, I do not have any traditional hierarchical management power over almost any of these groups, aside from the few students who work for me. An awareness of other bases of power allowed me to develop and apply them in order to be more effective. This allowed me to get further than I had anticipated in my STEM ethnography, working with the various academic departments on campus to recruit subjects, collaborating with the science librarians to gather data, and working with library administration to disseminate results internally. The project was so successful that it was not only used internally, but the American Library Association Library Research Roundtable also selected it as one of the top research library research projects in 2012.[63]

I also found the content dealing with the leadership and management of collaborative work extremely helpful when I have been in charge of managing group projects. In particular, the different stages of developing ideas in groups, specifically dealing with the management of the divergent and convergent aspects of the process and ensuring all voices are heard and respected.[64] I had never used this model for meeting management before, and it has been invaluable in the meetings I have led since. I have applied it successfully in potentially contentious meetings, such as when leading discussions about revising my institution's merit process in my role of chair of the Libraries' Faculty Assembly in 2012–2013. The merit process was successfully revised and is partially due to the use of application of these concepts.

Two social elements of my experience in the institute that particularly stand out to me are networking and mentoring. Because of the long-term, multiple meeting format of the institute, I formed relationships and connections in Florida that are lasting. Many of these are connections across library types that I would not have otherwise formed. These relationships have broadened my understanding and have allowed me enrich the dialog about assessment in the library community. This can be seen in some of the state and national discussions I have helped to arrange since completing SSLLI.[65]

The relationship with my mentor not only helped with completing my leadership project but has also continued beyond my graduation from the program. Her assistance helped me take the general leadership principles discussed in the curriculum and apply them effectively in my academic library context. Her assistance and support has been invaluable as I develop my leadership skills within the academic and research library milieu, particularly in my professional growth and increased leadership roles in professional organizations.

Finally, a major result of my experience in the program is an increased openness to leadership experience. Since my enrollment in the program, I have been elected chair of my libraries' Faculty Assembly, and I have been elected as chair of the American Library Association's Library Leadership and Management Measurement, Assessment, and Evaluation Section. I would have been far more hesitant in pursing these leadership roles had I not received the training provided in SSLLI.

Conclusion

Participants report finding SSLLI to be a rewarding experience. However, the program does have room for improvement. The groundwork for these improvements needs to arise from a foundation of program evaluation and assessment. Currently, SSLLI only gathers self-reported, short-term data.[66] The institute needs to now focus on other measures as well as longitudinal and outcomes-based assessment. A comparison to other leadership programs with similar approaches reveals some possibilities.

Synergy, the Illinois State Library Leadership program, is similar to SSLLI in crossing library types, mentoring, and a longer-term format. A participant of their program has surveyed the supervisors of their program's academic library graduates to gain a different view of participants' growth.[67] SSLLI might consider adopting a similar survey to supplement the self-reported data gathered from end-of-session evaluations.

The American Libraries' Association's Emerging Leaders program is also similar to SSLLI, particularly in their project-centric approach, time-distributed delivery, library-type inclusive design, and cohort community building.[68] However, it differs in its focus in the sense that it accepts only librarians new to the profession whereas SSLLI also enrolls mid-level library employees. It also varies from SSLLI in assigning participants projects rather than having them create the projects themselves. The Emerging Leaders program's culminating poster session is something that SSLLI might want to emulate. As SSLLI currently is configured, a select group of SSLLI graduates present their projects at the graduation ceremony. Perhaps if an inclusive and standard method of final project presentation was required, it could offer the institute a way to record, evaluate, and follow-up on the demonstrated community outcomes of the institute.

The Association of College and Research Libraries' College Library Directors' Mentor Program (CLDMP) also has some parallels with SSLLI. While CLDMP is limited to academic librarians who have reached a high level of responsibility, it is also longer-term in its scope and has a significant social component, involving mentors and a cohort of participants.[69] Like SSLLI, CLDMP's mentor and cohort component are highly praised by the participants as being very effective in helping participants overcome leadership challenges.[70] The CDLMP results were also evaluated, like Synergy, by the supervisors of the participants, although by requesting letters rather than through Synergy's survey approach. This also seems to indicate that it might be a wise practice for SSLLI to consider adopting.

With its 10-year anniversary, SSLLI is launching a survey of all graduates to try to discover some long-range outcomes reported by the graduates (Brad Ward, pers. comm.). While this begins to address the lack of data on long-term institute results, other more sustainable approaches should be considered. For example, participants' leadership projects could be required to have an outcomes assessment component that ties to SSLLI's desired program outcomes. These outcomes measures could be gathered and documented at the end of the institute's year. This could be done with a poster session approach similar to Emerging Leaders.

Regular, structured evaluation of the institute's contribution to participants' growth by their supervisors, as seen in the CDLMP and in Synergy, would also be an excellent addition to the SSLLI. Something somewhat similar to this is done by the SSLLI program coordinators when they check-in with participants' mentors. However, this should be further formalized and broadened to other stakeholders. This would help the program move beyond self-reported or informal data to document effectiveness.

Research enabled by better evaluations and assessments of the program could then be used to improve the program in other ways. While curricular revision already happens on a regular basis by the institute's faculty, a broader view of the long-term sweep and value of the curriculum would allow more effective curricular redesign. The effectiveness of methods used to deliver specific leadership content, online or in-person, could be researched as well.

Based on participants' feedback, SSLLI is already a valued and useful program. Further research and assessment will only strengthen the program and allow the program coordinators to increase its effectiveness and demonstrate its value in broader terms.

Notes

1. Florida Department of State, "Sunshine State Library Leadership Institute Overview."
2. Elizabeth Curry's Consulting Services, *Florida Library Leadership Program*, 4.
3. Golden, "Leadership Development," 17.
4. Florida Department of State, "Sunshine State Library Leadership Institute Overview."

5. Elizabeth Curry's Consulting Services, *Florida Library Leadership Program*, 12.
6. What constitutes success in this context is undefined by the institute.
7. Florida Department of State, "Sunshine State Library Leadership Institute Overview."
8. Golden and Roberts, "Florida's Library Leadership Program."
9. Kouzes and Posner, *The Leadership Challenge*; Curry and Smithee, "Developing Leadership." 31; Elizabeth Curry's Consulting Services, *Florida Library Leadership Program*, 8.
10. Ibid., 4–6.
11. Florida Department of State, "Sunshine State Library Leadership Institute Overview."
12. DeEtta Jones and Associates, "About DeEtta Jones"; Pattern Research, "About Pat Wagner"; Florida Department of State, "Sunshine State Library Leadership Institute Overview."
13. Canono, "Sunshine State Library Leadership Institute."
14. Kouzes and Posner, *The Leadership Challenge,* 37; Bennis, *Why Leaders Can't Lead,* 109–10.
15. Anderson, Ford, and Hamilton, *Transforming Leadership*, 62; Peters, *Thriving on Chaos*, 490–92.
16. Kotter, *Leading Change*, 35; Covey, Principle-Centered Leadership, 33–34.
17. Kouzes and Posner, *The Leadership Challenge*, 124; Bennis, *Why Leaders Can't Lead*, 36.
18. Anderson, Ford, and Hamilton, *Transforming Leadership*, 62.
19. Peters, Thriving on Chaos, 576; Covey, Principle-Centered Leadership, 34; Kotter, Leading Change, 51.
20. Kouzes and Posner, *The Leadership Challenge*, 184.
21. Bennis, Why Leaders Can't Lead, 29–30.
22. Anderson, Ford, and Hamilton, *Transforming Leadership*, 76.
23. Peters, Thriving on Chaos, 400.
24. Covey, Principle-Centered Leadership, 34–35; Kotter, Leading Change, 67.
25. Ibid., 85.
26. Peters, *Thriving on Chaos*, 510; Covey, Principle-Centered Leadership, 108.
27. Kouzes and Posner, *The Leadership Challenge*, 243–44; Bennis, Why Leaders Can't Lead, 141; Anderson, Ford, and Hamilton, *Transforming Leadership*, 63.
28. Kotter, Leading Change, 85; Bennis, *Why Leaders Can't Lead*, 109; Anderson, Ford, and Hamilton, *Transforming Leadership*, 63; Peters, Thriving on Chaos, 576.
29. Kouzes and Posner, *The Leadership Challenge*, 270; Covey, Principle-Centered Leadership, 35.

30. Bennis, Why Leaders Can't Lead, 80.
31. Peters, Thriving on Chaos, 303.
32. Anderson, Ford, and Hamilton, *Transforming Leadership*, 64.
33. Kotter, Leading Change, 117.
34. Bennis, Why Leaders Can't Lead, 23; Anderson, Ford, and Hamilton, *Transforming Leadership*, 63.
35. Peters, *Thriving on Chaos*, 306; Kotter, Leading Change, 131.
36. Ibid., 14.
37. Ward, "Sunshine State Library Leadership Institute Wiki."
38. Paul, "Just Do It!," 45.
39. Green and Farazmand, "Experiential Learning," 21.
40. Jones, "Sunshine State Library Leadership Institute"; DiscProfile.com, "What is DiSC®?."
41. Jones, "Sunshine State Library Leadership Institute."
42. Florida Department of State, "Sunshine State Library Leadership Institute Year 10."
43. Florida Department of State, "Florida Library Leadership Institute Participants and Mentors."
44. Ibid.
45. Phillips-Jones, The Mentee's Guide.
46. Florida Department of State, "Sunshine State Library Leadership Institute Overview."
47. Phillips-Jones, The Mentee's Guide.
48. Florida Department of State, "Leadership Mentors."
49. Florida Department of State, "Sunshine State Library Leadership Institute Overview."
50. Ward, "Sunshine State Library Leadership Institute Wiki."
51. Golden, "Talent Management," 5–6; Golden, "Leadership Development."
52. Golden and Roberts, "Florida's Library Leadership Program."
53. Arnold, Nickel, and Williams, "Creating the Next Generation," 445.
54. Martin and Woolard, "The Efficacy of a Statewide Leadership Program."
55. The other leadership training was not listed or described; Martin and Woolard, "The Efficacy of a Statewide Leadership Program."
56. Elizabeth Curry's Consulting Services, *Florida Library Leadership Program*, 7–9, 19–21.
57. Florida Department of State, *Gateway to Information through Florida Libraries*, 33.
58. Florida Department of State, *Strengthening Libraries and Services*, 17.
59. Florida Department of State, *Evaluation of the 2008–2012 LSTA Five-Year Plan*, 23–6.

60. Ibid., 25.
61. Clark, "Mapping Diaries."
62. French and Raven, "The Bases of Social Power," 262–68.
63. Besara and Kinsley, "Science, Technology, Engineering and Math (STEM)."
64. Harvard Business School Publishing, "Harvard Manage Mentor: Team Management."
65. Hodel, Svec, and Kinsley, "Assessment Across Library Types"; Nitecki, "What's the Return on ROI."
66.. Florida Department of State, *Evaluation of the 2008–2012 LSTA Five-Year Plan*, 25.
67. Sheehy, "Synergy," 65–66.
68. American Library Association, "ALA Emerging Leaders Program."
69. Association of College and Research Libraries, "The College Library Directors Mentor Program."
70. Hardesty, "College Library Directors Mentor Program," 286.

Bibliography

American Library Association. "ALA Emerging Leaders Program." Accessed April 24, 2013. http://www.ala.org/educationcareers/leadership/emerging-leaders.

Anderson, Terry D., Ron Ford, and Marilyn Hamilton. *Transforming Leadership: Equipping Yourself and Coaching Others to Build the Leadership Organization*. Boca Raton, FL: St. Lucie Press, 1998.

Arnold, Jennifer, Lisa T. Nickel, and Lisa Williams. "Creating the Next Generation of Library Leaders." *New Library World* 109, no. 9/10 (2008): 444–56.

Association of College and Research Libraries. "The College Library Directors Mentor Program." Accessed April 24, 2013. http://www.ala.org/acrl/about/sections/cls/collprogdisc/collegelibrary.

Bennis, Warren G. *Why Leaders Can't Lead: The Unconscious Conspiracy Continues*. San Francisco: Jossey-Bass Publishers, 1989.

Besara, Rachel, and Kirsten Kinsley. "Science, Technology, Engineering and Math (STEM) Students' and Faculty Academic Work Behaviors and Needs User Study." Presentation at the American Library Association Annual Conference, Anaheim, California, June 24, 2012.

Canono, Jill. "Sunshine State Library Leadership Institute." Presentation at the Sunshine State Library Leadership Institute, Ocala, FL, October 28, 2010.

Clark, Katie. "Mapping Diaries, or Where Do They Go All Day?" In *Studying Students: The Undergraduate Research Project at the University of Rochester*, edited by Nancy Fried Foster and Susan Gibbons, 48–54. Chicago: Association of College and Research Libraries, 2007.

Covey, Stephen R. *Principle-Centered Leadership: Strategies for Personal and Professional Effectiveness*. New York: RosettaBooks, 2009.

Curry, Elizabeth A., and Jeannette Smithee. "Developing Leadership in a Multitype Library Consortium: Ten Years of SEFLIN Sun Seekers." *Resource Sharing & Information Networks* 20, no 1/2 (2009): 18–34.

DeEtta Jones and Associates. "About DeEtta Jones." Accessed March 31, 2013. http://www.deettajones.com/about/deetta-jones.

DiscProfile.com. "What is DiSC®? Dominance, Influence, Steadiness, Conscientiousness." Accessed April 1, 2013. http://www.discprofile.com/whatisdisc.htm.

Elizabeth Curry's Consulting Services. *Florida Library Leadership Program: Developing a Statewide Approach 2004–2009*. Tallahassee, FL: State Library and Archives of Florida, 2004.

Florida Department of State, Division of Library & Information Services. "Florida Library Leadership Institute Participants and Mentors." Accessed April 1, 2013. http://dlis.dos.state.fl.us/bld/leadership/2011-2012/participants.cfm.

———. "Leadership Mentors." Accessed March 31, 2013. http://dlis.dos.state.fl.us/bld/leadership/mentors.cfm.

———. "Sunshine State Library Leadership Institute Overview." Accessed April 24, 2013. http://dlis.dos.state.fl.us/bld/leadership/institute.cfm.

———. "Sunshine State Library Leadership Institute Year 10 Application Form." Accessed April 24, 2013. http://www.pdffiller.com/21519760-SSLLIApplication-2013-2014pdf-Sunshine-State-Library-Leadership-Institute-Year-10-Application-Form-Various-Fillable-Forms.

———. Division of Library and Information Services. *Evaluation of the 2008–2012 LSTA Five-Year Plan*. Tallahassee, FL: State Library and Archives of Florida, 2012.

———.Division of Library and Information Services. *Strengthening Libraries and Services: Florida's Library Services and Technology Act Plan 2013–2017*. Tallahassee, FL: Florida Department of State, Division of Library and Information Services, 2012.

———.Division of Library & Information Services, State Library & Archives of Florida. *Gateway to Information through Florida Libraries: A Strategic Plan for Library Development: Years 2003–2007*. Tallahassee, FL: Florida Department of State, Division of Library and Information Services, 2007.

French, John, and Bertram Raven. "The Bases of Social Power." In *Studies in Social Power*, edited by Dorwin Cartwright, 259–69. Ann Arbor, MI: Research Center for Group Dynamics, Institute for Social Research, University of Michigan, 1959.

Golden, Janine. "Leadership Development & Staff Recruitment… Florida Style." *Florida Libraries* 48, no. 2 (2005): 17–20.

———. "Talent Management, Succession Planning, Leadership Development… What's Needed?" *Community College and Junior College Libraries* 13, no. 4 (2005): 3–6.

Golden, Janine, and Faye Roberts. "Florida's Library Leadership Program." *Association of Specialized & Cooperative Library Agencies* 28, no. 3 (2007).

Green, Robert, and Farideh A. Farazmand. "Experiential Learning: The Internship and Live-Case Study Relationship." *Business Education & Administration* 4, no. 1 (2012): 13–23.

Hardesty, Larry. "College Library Directors Mentor Program: 'Passing It On;' A Personal Reflection." *Journal of Academic Librarianship* 23, no. 4 (1997): 281–90.

Harvard Business School Publishing. "Harvard Manage Mentor: Team Management." Accessed April 24, 2013. http://www.cimaglobal.com/h-m-m-p/team_management/manage_divergent_and_convergent_thinking.html.

Hodel, Mary Ann, Deborah Svec, and Kirsten Kinsley. "Assessment Across Library Types." Panel presentation at the Florida Library Association Annual Conference, Orlando, Florida, April 20, 2012.

Jones, DeEtta. "Sunshine State Library Leadership Institute." Presentation at the Sunshine State Library Leadership Institute, Ocala, FL, February 3, 2011.

Kotter, John P. *Leading Change*. Boston: Harvard Business Review Press, 1996.

Kouzes, James M., and Barry Z. Posner. *The Leadership Challenge: How to Keep Getting Extraordinary Things Done in Organizations*. San Francisco: Jossey-Bass, 1995.

Martin, Jason, and David Woolard. "The Efficacy of a Statewide Leadership Program: A Study of SSLLI." Poster presentation at American Library Association Annual Conference, Chicago, Illinois, July 9–15, 2009.

Nitecki, Danuta. "What's the Return on ROI." Discussion group at the American Library Association Midwinter Meeting, Seattle, Washington, January 27, 2013.

Pattern Research. "About Pat Wagner." Accessed March 31, 2013. http://www.sieralearn.com/author/patwagner/.

Paul, Connie. "Just Do It! Leadership Training Builds Strong Networks." *American Libraries* 35, no. 9 (Oct. 2004): 44–45.

Peters, Thomas J. *Thriving on Chaos: Handbook for a Management Revolution*. New York: Knopf, 1998.

Phillips-Jones, Linda. *The Mentee's Guide: How to Have a Successful Relationship with a Mentor*. Grass Valley, CA: Coalition of Counseling Centers, 2003.

Sheehy, Carolyn A. "Synergy: The Illinois Library Leadership Initiative and the Development of Future Academic Library Leaders." *College and Undergraduate Libraries* 11, no. 1 (2008): 61–75.

Ward, Brad. "Sunshine State Library Leadership Institute Wiki." Florida Department of State. Accessed March 31, 2013. https://sslli-alumni.pbworks.com/w/page/13288220/FrontPage.

CHAPTER 11

The Stanford Institute:
A Brief California Experiment

Vicki D. Bloom

IN THE LATE 1990s Stanford University Librarian Michael Keller and State Librarian Dr. Kevin Starr developed a concept of a leadership institute that would elevate the quality of services libraries provided to information users in the 21st century through first, the development of library leaders, and second, greater awareness and adoption of best practices in information technology. They posited that only by understanding emerging concepts of information technology would current and future library leaders develop the kind of dynamic, risk-taking leadership needed to move libraries forward.

As a result of their discussions, Keller, on behalf of Stanford University, wrote and received LTSA funding from the California State Library to offer an intensive residential program for library staff "who believe in the future."[1] A key component of the institute was the formation of an advisory group composed of leaders from a variety of sizes and types of libraries in California. They assisted with planning, marketing, and the application process. Public library administrator Anne Marie Gold joined the institute as executive director in the summer of 1999.

Stanford's award was large enough to allow over 125 librarians to participate, 100 of which were to be from California. California participants were charged $275 for the week and out-of-state participants were charged $2,000.

The Stanford Institute was "aimed at library and information profession-al[s] from California, the nation, and around the world… from a wide vari-ety of libraries and information organizations. Participants would be part of [their] current leadership team, working at mid or upper management level, or in a supervisory capacity."[2] Print brochures describing the program were distributed widely in California, across the country, and at selected nation-al libraries abroad. The program was also promoted in library publications and on various listservs. A website provided detailed information about the speakers and the sessions, as well as logistical information for participants.

Applications consisted of resumes, two letters of recommendations, and "two essays on any six topics relating to leadership, libraries and tech-nology."[3] In the first year, 132 library professionals participated. While the majority came from California, there was representation from 17 states in the United States, plus three countries. In the second year, attendance grew to 143 participants with representation from 23 states and two other coun-tries. All types of libraries were represented as illustrated in table 11.1.[4]

TABLE 11.1. Percentage of Types of Libraries Represented by Attendees by Year		
Type	2000 (%)	2001 (%)
Public	48	61
Academic	23	19
School	14	11
Corporate	5	*
Law or medical	2	6
Source: Hinman and Williams, *Study of 21st Century Librarianship Initiatives*, 21–22.		

Approximately 15 percent of participants were from culturally diverse backgrounds.[5] Table 11.2 indicates that a substantial number of attendees had more than 10 years of experience.[6]

TABLE 11.2. Professional Library Experience of Attendees		
Experience	2000 (%)	2002 (%)
5 years or less	10	5
5–10 years	31	31
10–20 years	27	36
20 or more years	31	31
Source: Hinman and Williams, *Study of 21st Century Librarianship Initiatives*, 22.		

Once participants were selected, a listserv kept them informed with weekly communications about the institute. The participants also began posting short biographical statements to the listserv, which then were placed on a password protected section of the website.

Content of the Program

The institute, held on the Stanford campus, ran for seven days in August of 2000 and 2001. The event began with Starr, the California State librarian, urging participants to fully sample the many planned opportunities to learn and develop. The institute was organized into five main thematic tracks: leadership, information technology, library collections and services, organizational effectiveness, and preservation and facility planning. The following year, the institute's themes were slightly revised and included leadership, technology impacts, libraries in the digital age, organizational effectiveness, and into the future.

Distinguished speakers, most of whom came from outside the library world, gave each day's opening plenary session. Addressing one of the thematic topics, these speakers set the tone, spurring the audience to consider such issues as how to optimize technology in our libraries, what makes someone a great leader, and how to create services geared to generation Y students. We heard from such prominent figures as Pulitzer Prize-winning historian and Stanford professor David Kennedy about Dwight Eisenhower's adaptive leadership style; president and CEO of Alibris, Martin Manley, about developing effective organizations in the digital age; and former Superior Court of California judge and current Stanford University administrator and community activist, LaDoris Cordell, on the importance of building relationships.

Following the plenary sessions were discussion groups related to that session's theme. After lunch, participants chose from a number of concurrent afternoon programs related to the five themes with speakers from the library and non-library world. Sample topics included social entrepreneurship, cultural facets of leadership, building community partnerships, online artifacts, and human-computer interaction. The afternoon concluded with small groups working on case studies of real-world challenges of libraries, such as fair use and resource reallocation.

Based upon feedback and successes from the first institute, the 2001 program was changed slightly. The post-plenary discussion groups were replaced with a series of seminars on leadership styles, conflict management, stress management, and work-life balance led by management consultant, Dr. Marilyn Manning. The afternoon session was shortened, fewer concurrent sessions were offered, and the case study groups were composed by library type instead of mixing groups together. The evening format was revised as well. In 2000, the institute included two evening sessions with one focused on using a web tool, Dreamweaver, and the second, a leadership assessment exercise led by Manning. The next year more workshops were held in the evening, including a visioning workshop and evening discussion groups on topics such as school and public library cooperation, knowledge management, and e-books and e-reference. Also new in 2001 were six interns, participants of the 2000 program who assisted the executive director with logistics, participant requests, preparation of a short newsletter called the *Daily Pixel,* and mentoring.

The content was only one part of the institute. According to Gold, the executive director, "the experience had to be equal or better than the content. We rarely do that in libraries" (pers. comm.). Participants received an executive-level experience, lavish spreads of gourmet food and drink, well-coordinated social outings for several of the evenings, and individualized attention. These activities fostered an atmosphere of collegiality, promoted cohort formation, and kept participants engaged. With the beautiful Stanford campus as a backdrop, it was common to see people taking walks, small informal gatherings, and impromptu outings to one of the nearby museums.

Leadership Theories

No one approach, model, or theory of leadership was advocated during the institute due to the multiplicity of speakers and thematic areas. Each speaker who spoke on leadership and organizational effectiveness provided his or her own insight. While the curriculum was not consistent from year to year, or even day by day, some common assumptions emerged. Most notably that leadership involves vision, risk-taking, and the ability to influence others in order to move organizations forward. Stanford University's library director, Keller, declared, "good stewards invest assets and therefore take risks."[7] Also emphasized was the idea that self-knowledge and training can accelerate the progress and development of new leaders. Speaker Johnson told the audience that "to change the library environment, change yourself first."[8]

Are leaders born or made? A couple of the speakers touched upon the Great Man theory, which assumes that traits of leaders are intrinsic.[9] This idea received little credence. Instead participants heard a mélange of perspectives and theories, some of which combined more than one approach. A few talks were grounded in the theory that leadership is a transformative process. Described by James MacGregor Burns in his 1978 classic work, *Leadership*, transformational leaders work to inspire and mobilize change by helping people in the organization reach their fullest potential.[10] Likened to this theory is charismatic leadership proposed by R.J. House in 1976.[11] Charismatic leaders are dominant individuals with a strong set of values and being. They display charisma, confidence, and competency. Prime, one of the speakers, exemplified this type of leadership. Taking a different perspective, speaker Kennedy spoke of the significance of situational context on leadership.[12] Using Eisenhower as his study, Kennedy demonstrated how Eisenhower adapted his style for the circumstance of the situation. As a general in wartime, Eisenhower emphasized task, motivating by clarifying tasks and removing obstacles. Conversely in his presidency Eisenhower focused on process; he created structures, built teams, and formed relationships in order to lead the country.

In her leadership workshops, Manning emphasized a behavioral model to describe leadership, the style approach. According to, Peter Northouse, focusing on styles "provides a framework for assessing leadership in a broad way, as behavior with a task and relationship dimension."[13] Participants in Manning's workshops took a self-assessment tool using the Carlson Learning's DiSC Personal Profile System, which provided a ranking for the prominence of four components of behavior: dominance or driving, influence, conscientiousness, and steadiness. Strategies for growth and working with others were also supplied based upon these behavioral tendencies.

Literature Review

Little has been written about the Stanford program. This is not surprising given that the program lasted only two years. The exception was a 2004 article in *Library Trends* by Florence Mason and Louella Wetherbee titled "Learning to Lead: An Analysis of Current Training Programs for Library Leadership."[14] Their article provided a thorough overview and analysis of leadership theories, detailed the different library leadership programs and types of learning approaches used, and described program assessments and findings. Since few of the leadership programs had published evaluation reports, the Stanford Institute was highlighted in the article's section about leadership program evaluation. The authors noted that the Stanford program "endeavored to improve data collection and evaluation by using multiple methods of collecting data, control groups, and even longitudinal data."[15] They found problems, however, with some of the data interpretation. Because the participant and control group "seemed to be drawn from the same pool," the authors believed that "meaningful differences could not be detected between the two groups as a result of leadership development training."[16] The authors urged for more systematic research on the efficacy of leadership programs to determine if participants learned anything new, whether learning was retained, how it was applied in the workplace, and whether that knowledge or those skills improved the individual or improved the workplace.

In contrast to the research literature, there is a significant amount of descriptive information about the Stanford Institute at the institute's website (http://institute21.stanford.edu/) and the Infopeople website, the California-based library training organization (http://www.infopeople.org/resources/surveys/i2isurvey). Both sites were last updated in 2002 and included information about both years of the Stanford program. The institute's site includes daily schedules, information about the speakers, short summaries of sessions, descriptions of study groups and evening meetings, the *Daily Pixel* newsletter, a roster of the advisory council, photographs, and selected participant reports. Director Gold's presentation at the LITA National Forum 2000 can be found there as well. Holly Hinman and Joan Frye Williams' consultant report, Gold's paper presented at the International Federation of Library Associations (IFLA) meeting in 2001, and minutes from advisory council meetings are available on the Infopeople site. Only some of the links to the Stanford Institute participant survey are viable.

My Experience

The Stanford-California State Library Institute was one of the most positive, inspiring, and life-changing professional development opportunities of my career. I was able to spend a hectic week focusing on my own growth and development in a setting that was conducive to self-improvement. The institute provided access to prestigious speakers that I would not typically see at other venues; exposure to a wide range of topics, many of them new to me; along with a high level of attention from the program directors and other colleagues.

The overall experience benefit cannot be overstated. Unlike typical conferences, workshops, and institutes, Stanford participants were made to feel special, handpicked, and headed toward great success. I had been a department head in an academic library for five years when I participated in the institute and was seriously considering my next career move. Due to my participation in the institute, I had a renewed sense of confidence in my abilities and potential.

While it would be several years before I assumed a greater leadership role as a dean of libraries at a medium-sized academic institution, the institute reinforced what it takes to lead the library of the future, namely a greater understanding of the overarching confluence of technology coupled with vision, inclusiveness, honesty, accountability, risk-taking, and effective relationship building.

On a practical level, a visit to Stanford Libraries opened my eyes to more innovative ways of serving library users. Double-sided monitors were installed at the general reference desk, which allowed users to easily see the librarian's screen. I adapted this technology at my home institution. This proved to be so popular that additional library service desks at my library installed them as well. Later we added wireless keyboards and mouses to encourage in-person co-browsing. I also advocated for large monitors to be placed near the entryway displaying both televised news and library information, similar to Stanford's news wall. Back in 2000 these screens were very cutting edge. My institution's library took several years to install this technology. I also began incorporating what I had learned about gen Y in our library's instruction program, my work on a campus-wide first-year experience committee and pilot program, and as library liaison to the university's Center on Teaching Excellence.

The Stanford program also reinforced the importance of thinking broadly and taking advantages of new opportunities. As an example, I successfully advocated that a newly renovated periodicals and microforms information area be placed under my managerial control. I wrote job descriptions, hired and filled library assistant positions, set service hours, and requested appropriate equipment and furniture. In less than one year's time, over 10,000 users received personal assistance in this area. The once intimidating microfilm equipment became more palatable as users discovered they could receive one-on-one assistance. Later I campaigned for new equipment that would allow microform images to be printed to networked printers, e-mailed, or saved to flash drives. A complete shelf read of the collections in these areas was undertaken, which resulted in correcting numerous problems with the catalog records, boxes of discarded titles, label changes, and shifts of collections. Working with the head of preservation, I was able to secure funding to replace microfilm boxes that were in disrepair. To increase discoverability of the microform collections, I created an extensive web guide to major microform sets and their indexes.

My professional outlook and style as a manager and leader changed too. Two institute speakers made a difference on how I conduct my professional life: Eugenie Prime and Amal Johnson. In her presentation entitled "Assertive Leadership," Prime, then manager of Corporate Libraries at Hewlett Packard Labs declared, "Nice librarians finish last." Prime went on to note, "Power is not a four letter word; we need power to make things happen. True power is when you can influence others." She coached that "leaders inspire and create other leaders, not more followers."[17] While she purported that charisma is helpful to selling a vision, communication and storytelling are critical to getting the message across. Prime also cautioned us to "not just communicate with people in your organization when you need something from them! Get to know them, let them get to know you, show respect for their goals and decisions, and understand where they are coming from."[18] This dynamic woman further instructed us to encourage differences, reward risks, live and value ambiguity, and celebrate success.

Prime's presentation helped me to put my own strengths and weaknesses in perspective. While I embraced risk-taking, being assertive, goal achievement, and rewarding risks, I was less comfortable with ambiguity. Perhaps this is because I was in a management role where the boundaries were limited and outcomes fairly certain. To stretch, I had to create more opportunities to collaborate, widen participation in decision making, and negotiate to affect further changes. After months of troubleshooting queries from users trying to access library resources via the proxy server, I urged the deputy librarian to call a meeting with several library departments and Campus Computing and Communications to improve communication and services. This resulted in updated webpages explaining the proxy service, shared information about known issues and problems, and a stronger partnership between the library and campus computing services.

The other speaker whose message shaped my leadership philosophy was Johnson, general partner in a technology-focused venture capital firm. She spoke about the importance of hiring smarter, leading well, and building strong teams. Like Prime, she emphasized that one of the most critical roles of today's leader is to develop others: "I hate the word empowered because it implies you have to give something to them. They have it already! Create moments of leadership where people are able to solve problems on the spot."[19] Leadership was not limited to administrators; it could emerge and be fostered at any level of an organization.

I came away from the institute knowing that effective leadership is a sophisticated and complicated process that cannot easily be prescribed or described. The leaders we met and heard crafted their own approach to leadership based upon their personality and behaviors as well as the needs, personnel, and challenges facing their organizations.

Evaluation

The services of an independent organization, the Evaluation and Training Institute (ETI), was contracted to conduct an extensive evaluation and assessment of both institutes. ETI used a combination of onsite observation, pre- and post-tests, follow-up surveys, and comparisons with a control group to look at several factors:

- satisfaction, perceptions, and expectations;
- cadre formation;
- individual and organizational impact;
- changes initiated as a result of attendance; and
- impact on career mobility and advancement.

Their findings were published in a 78-page report in 2002. Overall ETI found participants of the 2000 institute were exceptionally pleased with the institute experience and gave it a "very satisfied" rating on the survey. According to the participants, the institute had a way of making them "feel special."[20] Findings for the 2001 institute were similar with 96 percent of the participants reporting that the institute met their expectations.

ETI noted that the high rating was "not only due to the formal aspects of the institute… but also due to the collegial and high-spirited atmosphere of the institute."[21] According to the report, it was not clear if a cohort developed over time. It was concluded, however, that the institute did "offer the kind of intense experience that promotes bonding and makes people comfortable enough to call on others who went through the same experience."[22] In both years, the plenary sessions were the most popular segment of the program and the case studies the least favorite. Interestingly, when asked what they wanted to learn, second year participants placed technology at the bottom of their interests.

After comparing institute participants with a control group of nonparticipants, the researchers concluded that there was not necessarily a cause-and-effect relationship between institute attendance and subsequent career developments and professional growth. But self-perceptions were markedly affected: Over 77 percent of attendees reported taking more risks, and 80 percent reported more confidence in taking a leadership role. Sixty-five percent reported mentoring someone since attending the institute while 79 percent reported voluntarily taking on a new professional project. Analysis of essay responses indicated that participants showed more creativity, demonstrated a grasp of the big picture, pursued more ambitious changes and projects, and implemented more "cutting-edge" technologies than the control group.[23] The final consultant report also included participant open-ended comments and reports of specific changes initiated as a result of the institute. A selective listing is provided in Appendix 11.1.

What the ETI report did not include was a definition of the term *leadership*. At an advisory council meeting in September 2002, one of the report's coauthors Hinman noted that shortcoming.[24] She also pointed out that those who attended the institute in 2001 were surveyed only one year after the institute, which might not have been sufficient time to see concrete behavioral change.

Due to financial reasons the institute did not continue after the second year. The two founders, Keller and Starr, had hoped to secure funding from library vendors and high-tech companies located in nearby Silicon Valley. They also initiated discussions with the Bill and Melissa Foundation Gates Foundation but were unsuccessful in securing additional funding.

Looking Back and Looking Ahead

The goals of the Stanford Institute were ambitious—to raise the quality of services libraries provided to information users in the 21st century by preparing current and future leaders to seize new positional and organizational opportunities in the face of rapidly evolving technology. Leadership and organizational effectiveness training went hand in hand with a technology agenda. Given the integration and high acceptance of technology in libraries today, perhaps less emphasis on technology would be needed if the institute were offered now. At the time, however, the cofounders of the institute felt that libraries were at a critical juncture due to new demands in information technology, such as digitization, electronic publishing, human computer interface design, and web tools.

This emphasis on technology left less time for specific skill-building exercises related to other areas such as transforming organizational culture, developing strategic plans, and formulating and articulating a vision. While additional self-assessments were added in the second year, all participants of the institute would have benefited from developing personal plans for growth.

Other leadership programs that I have attended before and after the Stanford Institute were smaller in scope, intimate in feel, and feedback intensive. The manager workshops offered by the Association of Research Libraries Office of Management emphasized skill development using feedback tools, role-playing, and learning experiences to address common components of supervision: team building, communication, conflict management, motivation, coaching, and decision making. To demonstrate how values affect decision making, groups examined a case study in which the supervisor/manager/leader had to lay off one of four staff members. Developing an agreed upon criteria and consensus proved quite difficult for many of the groups. In another exercise, teams were formed to observe and provide feedback to individuals trying to communicate problems to one another. My experience a few years ago with the College Library Directors' Mentor Program emphasized leadership development through mentoring and coaching. This program is particularly effective at providing targeted instruction to individuals, taking into account his or her organizational context and needs.

While these two programs were effective in their own right, several factors made the Stanford program unique. If the Stanford Institute were ever revived again, it would need to continue to offer similar opportunities to gain exposure to entrepreneurs, scholars, activists, and cutting-edge innovators from both outside and inside the field of librarianship. Their insights about the importance of creativity, contribution, influence, risk taking, and vision gave participants permission to look at the profession and themselves in a new light. The low cost allowed library professionals from all types and sizes of libraries to attend. Above all, the ambiance and tone of the program should be replicated. From the positive messages to the CEO treatment, attendees were not only made to feel special but destined to make a difference at their institutions and in their communities. Participants left revitalized with a new sense of mission.

Appendix 11.1. Reported Changes Suggested by Participants as Direct or Indirect Result of the Institute

Below are selected responses to the question: "Please describe up to three changes you suggested in your library/organization as a direct or indirect result of your institute attendance."

Full responses can be read at http://www.infopeople.org/sites/all/files/surveys/i2isurvey/PLSParagraphResponses.pdf.

- Started Self-Directed Work Teams. My staffs are given the authority and responsibility to direct their own day-to-day work progress and manage themselves.
- Outsource more functions (e.g., OCLC PromptCat) so we can concentrate on our core competencies.
- Reorganization of reference services systemwide.
- Expanded our library's teen council and institutionalized it system-wide.
- Suggested a formal mentoring program for new full-time employees.
- Use web to create electronic branch library that mirrors all services available at local libraries.
- Staff Intranet to better facilitate internal communication.
- Promoted web-based reference.
- Upgrade the technology used in the library to better position us for digital projects. We plan to digitize the senior projects and few other special collections and provide access over the web via our online catalog.

- Providing some user-friendly services such as pagers to notify students when reserve materials are available.
- Place a greater emphasis on purchase and preservation of local history materials.
- Incorporate e-books into the collection.

Notes

1. Keller and Gold, *The First Annual Stanford-California State Library Institute*, 2.
2. Ibid.
3. Gold, "Developing Leaders for Libraries," 2.
4. Hinman and Williams, *Study of 21st Century Librarianship Initiatives*, 21–22.
5. Gold, "Developing Leaders for Libraries," 5.
6. Hinman and Williams, *Study of 21st Century Librarianship Initiatives*, 22.
7. Stanford-California Institute on 21st Century Librarianship, "Quotes, Words and Phrases."
8. Ibid.
9. Northouse, *Leadership: Theory and Practice*, 15.
10. Burns, *Leadership*.
11. Ibid.,176.
12. Situational leadership is a model developed by Hersey and Blanchard as described in their book, Management of Organizational Behavior: Utilizing Human Resources. The model states that the leader adapts their style to the situation rather than applying their leadership style to the situation.
13. Ibid., 178–179.
14. Mason and Wetherbee, "Learning to Lead."
15. Ibid., 213.
16. Ibid.
17. Prime, "Assertive Librarianship."
18. Ibid.
19. Stanford-California Institute on 21st Century Librarianship, "Quotes, Words and Phrases."
20. Hinman, *Study of 21st Century Librarianship Initiatives*, 35.
21. Gold, "Developing Leaders for Libraries," 5.
22. Hinman, *Study of 21st Century Librarianship Initiatives*, 35.
23. Ibid., 37.
24. Advisory Council of the Study of 21st Century Librarianship Initiatives, "Advisory Council Meeting Notes September 26, 2002."

Bibliography

Advisory Council of the Study of 21st Century Librarianship. "Advisory Council Meeting Notes September 26, 2002." https://infopeople.org/sites/default/files/ACminutes092602.pdf.

Burns, James MacGregor. *Leadership*. New York: Harper & Row, 1978.

Dyer, Karen. "One Hundred Forty-Four Librarians and the Lone Trustee." Stanford-California Institute on 21st Century Librarianship: Summer 2001 Post Institute. Last modified September 2, 2001. http://institute21.stanford.edu/summer/logistics.html.

Gold, Anne Marie. "Yellow Lines and Dead Skunks: Choosing Our Lane on the Infobahn." Presentation at the LITA National Forum 2000, Portland, OR, November 5, 2000. http://institute21.stanford.edu/about/lita_presentation.pdf.

———. "Developing Leaders for Libraries: The Stanford-California State Library Institute on 21st Century Librarianship Experience." *IFLA Conference Proceedings* (2001): 1–15. http://files.eric.ed.gov/fulltext/ED459787.pdf.

———. "Stanford-California State Library Institute for 21st Century Library Leadership." *Final Narrative Report for the State Library, Library Services and Technology Act.* October 31, 2001.

Hersey, Paul, and Kenneth H. Blanchard. *Management of Organizational Behavior: Utilizing Human Resources.* Englewood Cliffs, NJ: Prentice-Hall, 1969.

Hinman, Holly, and Joan Frye Williams. *Study of 21st Century Librarianship Initiatives: Consultant Report.* Last modified December 2002. http://www.infopeople.org/sites/all/files/surveys/i2isurvey/FinalReport.pdf.

Johnson, Amal. "Challenging the Management Status Quo." Stanford-California Institute on 21st Century Librarianship: Summer Institute 2000 Proceedings from Last Summer's Conference. August 10, 2000. http://institute21.stanford.edu/Current_Programs/2000_Institute/Presenters/papers/summary/summ-johnson.htm.

Keller, Mike, and Anne Marie Gold. *The First Annual Stanford-California State Library Institute on 21st Century Librarianship* (brochure). Stanford, CA: Stanford University: 2000.

Mason, Florence M., and Louella V. Wetherbee. "Learning to Lead: An Analysis of Current Training Programs for Library Leadership." *Library Trends* 53, no. 1 (2004): 187–217.

Morris, Hal. "Instituting the Future: Report from the Stanford-California Institute on Twenty-First Century Librarianship." *CSLA Journal* 25, no. 2 (2002): 25–26.

Northhouse, Peter. *Leadership: Theory and Practice.* 4th ed. Thousand Oaks: Sage Publications, c2007.

"Paragraph Responses—Overall Institute on 21st Century Librarianship Participant Survey." Stanford-California Institute on 21st Century Librarianship. Last modified June 18, 2002. http://www.infopeople.org/sites/all/files/surveys/i2isurvey/PLSParagraphResponses.pdf.

Prime, Eugenie. "Assertive Librarianship." Plenary session presentation at the Stanford-California State Library Institute of 21st Century Librarianship, Stanford University, CA, August 11, 2000.

Reynolds, Diane C. "Intern's Perspective of Summer 2001 Stanford Institute." Stanford-California Institute on 21st Century Librarianship: Summer 2001 Post Institute. Last modified August 8, 2002. http://institute21.stanford.edu/summer/logistics.html.

Stanford-California Institute on 21st Century Librarianship. "Quotes, Words and Phrases from the Institute." *Daily Pixel* 1, no. 7 (2000). http://institute21.stanford.edu/Current_Programs/2000_Institute/whatsnew/saturdaypixel.html.

———. Homepage. Last modified August 8, 2002. http://institute21.stanford.edu/.

Weiner, Sharon Gray. "Leadership of Academic Libraries." *Education Libraries* 26, no. 2 (2003): 5–18.

Wolfgram, Derek. Untitled. Stanford-California Institute on 21st Century Librarianship: Summer 2001 Post Institute. Last modified August 8, 2002. http://institute21.stanford.edu/summer/logistics.html.

CHAPTER 12

Minnesota Institute for Early Career Librarians from Traditionally Underrepresented Groups

Trevor A. Dawes

THE MINNESOTA INSTITUTE for Early Career Librarians from Tradition-ally Underrepresented Groups (MNTIEL, or the Minnesota Institute) is offered every two years for librarians with less than five years' profession-al library experience and is intended to provide an "opportunity to learn about leadership and organizational behavior in institutions of higher ed-ucation."[1]

The program, housed at and sponsored by the University of Minnesota Libraries, is the brainchild of librarians Linda DeBeau-Melting and Peggy Johnson. Both Johnson and DeBeau-Melting worked with various library residents at the University of Minnesota and recognized that the residents, all from underrepresented backgrounds, were generally less connected to the profession than were their peers.[2] This disconnection was due in part to the demographics of librarians in the United States and the lack of racial and ethnic diversity represented in the profession. In 2006, the American Library Association's *Diversity Counts* study reported that 89 percent of credentialed librarians were white—not representative of the changing de-mographics in the country, or even the demographics of higher education.[3]

Although many residency programs existed—and still do—to provide greater employment and development opportunities for librarians from underrepresented groups, the University of Minnesota librarians wanted to provide a targeted opportunity for librarians to develop both leadership and practical library skills.

The week-long program on the University of Minnesota campus has brought together over 180 librarians since its inception in 1998. Participants' institutions are expected to provide financial support for the program, and some costs are covered by other support, such as vendors. Between 20–24 participants are accepted for each cohort. The initial participants were predominantly African American, but the institute program planners have actively sought partnerships with the ethic caucuses of the American Library Association to promote the program, and with some success in that now the participants are from a greater variety of ethnicities.[4] The earlier cohorts included a mixture of academic and public librarians, but because of some divergent needs of these types of librarians, and the belief that it was more difficult to recruit and retain minority librarians in academic libraries, the focus now is only academic librarians.

MNTIEL Content

The Minnesota Institute is more than a leadership development program; it aims to provide a broad understanding of some critical skills required of librarians. The institute's self-described goals are to

- provide intensive training in leadership, management, and decision-making skills;
- increase self-knowledge and understanding of behavior in complex organizations;
- develop skills in grant development, management, and outcomes and in professional writing and publishing; and
- facilitate the development of a community of peers with whom participants share common experiences and on whom they can rely over time and distance for support and encouragement.[5]

The program accomplishes these goals by inviting leaders in the field to facilitate sessions on particular topics. The principal instructors, however, are seasoned workshop facilitators, knowledgeable in leadership and organizational development.

The program content has been modified slightly over time, but some enduring topics include teamwork and problem solving, decision making, career development, writing for publication, successful grant writing, and assessment. In covering a broad array of topics the program aims to develop the participants' various needed skills for their current or future positions.

Although the facilitators discuss various types of leadership theories during the institute, they employ the skills leadership theory model in the program. This theory assumes a leader can be trained to develop certain skills and abilities. Skills-based theories are an outgrowth of Robert Katz's *Skills of an Effective Administrator*.[6] In his work, Katz described three types of necessary leadership skills: technical, human, and conceptual.[7] Katz further states that skills are what leaders can accomplish. Leaders have the ability to use a set of competencies to accomplish a set of goals or objectives.[8] The Minnesota Institute prepares the participants in each of the three broad areas defined above—technical, human, and conceptual. In doing so, the participants become more self-aware, understanding the leadership roles they play in organizations, whether in a titled leadership position or not.

The program coordinators invite experts in the fields of each of the subject areas (teamwork, problem solving, etc.) to facilitate the discussions. Some of these instructors may be from the University of Minnesota, either from the libraries or from the faculty, and others may be from other universities or libraries. Previous program participants also return to describe their experience in the program and discuss the effect participating in the program has had on their careers.

Over the course of a week participants interact with the instructors, program facilitators, and each other in a fairly structured learning environment. In general, each of the topics is covered in half-day sessions comprising both lecture and interactive discussion. Participants are required to prepare for the sessions by completing readings on each of the topics and to actively engage in the discussion. Appendix 12.1 contains a selection of the readings used in the 2002 Institute. The program also builds in sufficient time for social functions and networking.

Literature Review

To date no one has written specifically about the Minnesota Institute, but as early as 1990, leaders within the Association of Research Libraries (ARL) formed a task force "charged with developing proposals for ARL initiatives in the areas of recruitment, retention, and workplace integration of minorities in professional positions in research libraries."[9] Although not specifically addressing leadership development, these conversations recognized the need to increase the representation and overall diversity of the professional staff in large research libraries.

In "Learning to Lead: An Analysis of Current Training Programs for Library Leadership," Florence M. Mason and Louella Wetherbee described various library leadership development programs. At the time of their writing, ARL's Leadership and Career Development Program (LCDP), the American Library Association's Spectrum Scholars Program, and the Minnesota Institute were the only programs geared towards librarians from traditionally underrepresented groups.[10] According to Mason and Wetherbee, library leaders determined a need for leadership development programs as they anticipated a wave of retirements among the existing leadership.

Surveying the Program

With the permission of the program coordinators, an informal survey was conducted of the MNTIEL alumni. Thirty-one alumni from the 1998–2010 cohorts responded to an e-mail message sent to the alumni listserv with a link to a Survey Monkey instrument. (The 2012 participants are not added to the alumni listserv until the next cohort group has been selected, and therefore were not solicited for survey responses.) From a total of 155 possible respondents, 20 percent responded to the survey. The survey (Appendix 12.2) was open for a two-week period from late March to early April 2013.

There was representation from each of the cohort groups, although a quarter of the respondents were from the 2010 class. Only three respondents had been librarians for more than three years at the time they participated in the program. Eighty percent of those surveyed (25 respondents) had moved on to a different position after completing the program, and of those, 70 percent moved into a position of greater responsibility. All but one of those who had moved into a position of greater responsibility attributed at least some of their success to their participation in the program.

When asked about the aspect of the program from which they benefited most, respondents provided the following statements:

> "The portions of the program that helped me to develop
> career goal-setting and review of goals. Also, I learned

a lot about where my strengths are and how to develop them in relation to challenges I have had."—Respondent 2

"Exposure to other early career librarians of color and all the mentors and instructors in the program provided the chance to build an invaluable professional network early in my career." —Respondent 5

"I learned a lot about organizational culture, how to use it to your advantage, and about leveraging formal and informal leadership." —Respondent 11

"Being given the language to understand and discuss the complex culture of a large academic library. Also, the creation of a network of peers who could relate to similar struggles and successes. It was both therapeutic, but encouraged me to hold my course, especially on the tenure track." —Respondent 16.

"I benefited from a better understanding of organizational culture, which up until that time I did not understand why I would come in to an organization who chose me over numerous candidates and then once I got to the institution, I felt like there were many barriers to change that I could not identify. This program gave me a better understanding of what an important role I could play in an organization and it gave me a renewed sense of purpose. It also exposed me to other colleagues that I respect and admire for the work they do." —Respondent 25

The comments provided a clear picture of the program, which in addition to developing the "hard" skills of writing for publication or undertaking assessment projects also helped the participants to understand the various cultures of academic libraries. Further, it built a network of colleagues who tended to rely on each other for advice and support well beyond the end of the program's formal schedule. Based on the feedback from this sample of respondents, the program appeared to be perceived by participants as meeting its stated goals.

Personal Experience

I participated in the Minnesota Institute leadership program in 2002 and agree with the other participants surveyed with respect to their positive experience. Although I had only recently completed my master's in library science at the time I participated, I had been working in libraries, supervising staff, and managing projects for over 10 years. The program helped to affirm some of the behaviors I learned at my place of employment through mentoring or in-house training and development. One area I found to be particularly helpful was on assessment of library services. More than 10 years later, the profession places emphasis on assessment of library services and demonstrating our value. I find myself reflecting on the information learned during MNTIEL, especially on managing focus groups, as I work on assessment in my current position. Of course, as is the case with any program of this sort, I, like several of the survey respondents, have developed many close professional contacts and friendships as a result of participating in the Minnesota Institute. These relationships have been invaluable, providing a cohort of friends and colleagues on whom I have called with questions, for advice, or just to maintain contact. Having participated in the Minnesota program over 10 years ago, and having participated in other leadership development programs, such as the Frye Institute, it is difficult to say exactly how much this particular program contributed to my current leadership abilities. The program does cover the foundations of leadership, and I do believe that my participation in the program either helped to solidify, or to lay the groundwork for, leadership skills and abilities I learned in other programs.

Future Work

The informal survey of the MNTIEL alumni suggests that the program is a perceived as a success in meeting its goals. Several of the respondents have moved into positions of greater responsibility, and all respondents have very positive comments about their experience in the program. This survey, however, fails to draw any direct correlation between participating in the program and career movement. Nor does it demonstrate any tangible ways in which the skills learned have helped the participants be more effective in their positions. Slightly less than half (47 percent) of the respondents indicate they had gone on to participate in other leadership development programs after participating in MNTIEL.

Future studies may want to more critically examine the effect participating in this program had on the careers of the librarians; this preliminary data suggests a positive relationship. The MNTIEL is a program for new librarians and provides a good overview of leadership competencies in the library context. Because the participants are new to the profession, and perhaps not yet in positional leadership roles, this program provides knowledge and leadership development that is believed to be appropriate for librarians new to the profession. It appears that the program provides participants with the knowledge, skills, and abilities to integrate themselves into the library culture at the institutions they work at or choose to work at later. There have been no formal reunions of program's participants, but some participants gather informally at library or related conferences to maintain the personal bonds they formed during the program. These informal reunions are not limited to any particular cohort as the invitation to join is shared on the listserv for all program alumni. This informal gathering fosters the types of networking and supportive relationships that the program intended, but did not explicitly create or support. Perhaps the program organizers could seize on the opportunity to extend the learning at events where the participants are already attending. Beyond this suggestion, it is difficult to say how the program could be improved, especially since the participants have all had such positive experiences.

Appendix 12.1 . Selected Bibliography from 2002 Minnesota Institute

Conger, Jay. "The Necessary Art of Persuasion." *Harvard Business Review* (May–June 1998): 84–95.

Deiss, Kathryn, and Maureen Sullivan. "The Shared leadership Principle: Creating Leaders throughout the Organization." *Leading Ideas: Issues and Trends in Diversity, Leadership and Career Development*, no. 2 (1998): 3–10.

Drucker, Peter. "Managing Oneself." *Harvard Business Review* (March–April 1999): 65–74.

Elias, Dean, and Paul David. "A Guide to Problem Solving." *The 1993 Annual for Facilitators, Trainers and Consultants* (1993): 149–56.

Jones, DeEtta. "The Significance of Race." *Leading Ideas: Issues and Trends in Diversity, Leadership and Career Development*, no. 8 (1999): 6–7.

Jurow, Susan. "Preparing For Library Leadership." In *Training Issues and Strategies in Libraries*, edited by Paul M. Gherman and Frances O. Painter, 57–73. Binghamton, NY: Haworth Press, 1990.

Krueger, Richard A., and Mary Anne. *Focus Groups: A Practical Guide for Applied Research*. 3rd ed. Thousand Oaks, CA: Sage Publications, 2000.

Rees, Fran. "From Controlling to Facilitating: How to L.E.A.D." *The 1992 Annual: Developing Human Resources* (1992): 213–22.

Walker, Carol A. "Saving Your Rookie Managers from Themselves." *Harvard Business Review* (April 2002): 97–102.

Appendix 12.2. Survey Questions

1. In what year did you participate in the MNTIEL program?
   a. 2012
   b. 2010
   c. 2008
   d. 2006
   e. 2004
   f. 2002
   g. 2000
   h. 1998
2. At the time of your participation in the program, how many years had it been since you graduated from library school?
   a. 1
   b. 2
   c. 3
   d. 4
   e. 5
   f. 6+
3. Have you changed positions since participating in the program?
   a. Yes
   b. No
4. If you answered yes to the above question, is your current position one with greater responsibilities than the position you held at the time you participated?
   a. Yes
   b. No
   c. Lateral move to different institution
   d. N/A
5. If in your current position you have greater responsibilities than you did at the time, do you attribute any of this success to your participation in the program?
   a. Yes
   b. No
   c. N/A
6. From what **specific** aspects of the program do you believe you benefited the most? [Open ended question]

7. Have you subsequently participated in any other professional development programs?
   a. Yes
   b. No
8. Are you of Hispanic, Latino, or Spanish origin?
   a. Yes
   b. No
9. What is your race? Please choose one or more.
   a. American Indian or Alaska Native
   b. Asian
   c. Black or African American
   d. Native Hawaiian or other Pacific Islander
   e. White
   f. Some Other Race

Notes

1. University of Minnesota, Minnesota Institute for Early Career Librarians.
2. Library residents are recent graduates of library and information science graduate programs who spend one or two years gaining practical experience in the library.
3. American Library Association, *Diversity Counts.*
4. Vilankulu, "Bright Stars."
5. University of Minnesota, Minnesota Institute for Early Career Librarians.
6. Katz, *Skills of an Effective Administrator.*
7. Ibid., 48–54.
8. Northouse, *Leadership.*
9. Dewey, "The Imperative for Diversity."
10. Mason and Wetherbee, "Learning to Lead."

Bibliography

American Library Association. "Diversity Counts." Presentation at ALA Annual Conference, Washington, DC, June 24, 2007. http://www.ala.org/offices/sites/ala.org.offices/files/content/diversity/diversitycounts/Diversity_Counts_CORS_Diversity_Aug07.pdf.

Dewey, Barbara I. "The Imperative for Diversity: ARL's Progress and Role." *portal: Libraries and the Academy* 9, no. 3 (2009): 355–61.

Katz, Robert L. *Skills of an Effective Administrator.* Boston: Harvard Business School Press, 2009.

Mason, Florence M., and Louella V. Wetherbee. "Learning to Lead: An Analysis of Current Training Programs for Library Leadership." *Library Trends* 53, no. 1 (2004): 187–217.

Northouse, Peter G. *Leadership: Theory and Practice.* 6th ed. Thousand Oaks, CA: Sage Publications, 2012.

University of Minnesota Libraries. Minnesota Institute for Early Career Librarians from Traditionally Underrepresented Groups. Accessed March 23, 2013. https://www.lib.umn.edu/sed/institute.

Vilankulu, Lucy. "Bright Stars: The Institute for Early Career Librarians Changes the face of Librarianship." *Continuum*, no. 3 (2004): 14–15. https://www.lib.umn.edu/sed/institute/brightstars.

Young, Ann-Christe. "University of Minnesota has received a…" *College & Research Libraries News* vol. 61, no. 2, February (2000): 139.

CHAPTER 13

Growing Our Own:
A Regional Leadership Challenge

Melissa Jadlos

IN 2001, LIBRARIANS in the Rochester, New York area realized a large number of library administrators and managers were expected to retire over the next five years. In order to create strong leaders to fill these vacancies, a training program was developed to create and sustain a library leadership development program. The goal of the program was to create a leadership curriculum aimed at middle managers, developed and taught by a nationally recognized leadership-training consultant. At the same time, the consultant would train five local library staff members to facilitate future leadership training programs.

In 2002 and 2004, the Rochester Regional Library Council (RRLC) and the Monroe County Library System hosted "Accepting the Leadership Challenge: A Library Leadership Institute." Funded by Library Services and Technology Act grants from the New York State Department of Education, the purpose of the program was to "train select staff from member libraries in the skills most needed in order to successfully lead libraries in the technologically complex environment of today and the near future. This training is intended to enhance leadership at all levels of library service."[1] A secondary goal of the 2004 institute was to create a faculty of library staff trained to present this curriculum to future cohorts. The session included a separate train-the-trainer component to educate five library staff, growing our own regional cadre of library leaders.

About the Institute

RRLC is a network of all types of libraries from the Greater Rochester, New York region. The Monroe County Library System is comprised of 30 public library branches in the city of Rochester and throughout Monroe County. As a joint program, the institute was open to 20 participants from each organization (i.e., 20 public library staff from Monroe County and 20 staff from libraries of all types in the Greater Rochester area).

The Leadership Institute was facilitated by Louella V. Wetherbee in 2002 and 2004, and Florence M. Mason in 2002. The institute was based on the book *The Leadership Challenge* by James M. Kouzes and Barry Z. Posner.[2] The two institutes varied slightly in format. The 2002 institute consisted of six sessions spread over four months; the 2004 institute was compressed into three and one-half days to reduce travel costs. Five alumni of 2002 participated again in 2004 with the intent to become future institute facilitators.

Leadership Institute participants were selected based on a competitive application process. Applicants provided an essay, a letter of support from the applicant's supervisor, and a description of a project the participant would lead while attending the institute. The essay was to describe how the institute would benefit both the applicant's career and institution. The first year there were not enough successful applicants to fill the program, so members of the steering committee reached out to likely candidates, encouraging them to apply.

Before the beginning of each institute, applicants were asked to fill out the Kouzes and Posner Leadership Practices Inventory 360 (LPI) and solicit colleagues to fill out the survey form intended for their supervisors and direct reports. Developed in the mid-1980s, the LPI is a formative evaluation tool that assesses "the frequency with which people engage in The Five Practices of Exemplary Leadership."[3] This is based on research by Kouzes and Posner that "the more frequently you demonstrate the behaviors included in the LPI, the more likely you will be seen as an effective leader."[4]

The curriculum was framed around the Five Practices of Exemplary Leadership as created by Kouzes and Posner.[5] Both institutes included an introduction to the research behind the theory, followed by a section focusing on each practice. The sections included a definition of the practice, examples from the world of libraries, and practical exercises to build the participant's skill in each practice. Since we had the results of our self and peer LPI evaluations, we could target areas for improvement and were given suggestions on how to practice and improve our skills in those areas. In 2002, each session was a full day with a month between. In 2004, approximately half of each day was devoted to each practice, and the sessions were held consecutively. The course materials included the most recent edition of the book *The Leadership Challenge*, supplemental readings and exercises created by the facilitators, and the *Leadership Practices Inventory Participant's Workbook*.[6]

The Five Practices of Exemplary Leadership program is based upon leadership trait research conducted by Kouzes and Posner over two decades beginning in the early 1980s. The researchers identified 20 qualities looked for or admired in leaders. They surveyed over 20,000 people on four continents and asked them to list the top seven qualities they "most look for and admire in a leader, someone whose direction they would willingly follow."[7] The results have been consistent over time and across cultures and industries. These 20 qualities could be considered the core competencies of leadership as described by Kouzes and Posner. The top five leadership qualities, reflected in the Five Practices of Exemplary Leadership are model the way, inspire a shared vision, challenge the process, enable others to act, and encourage the heart.[8] Kouzes and Posner contend that leadership can be observed and learned. By developing skills in the area of the Five Practices and using them consistently, ordinary people can become extraordinary leaders.

Literature Review

The theories of Kouzes and Posner have been discussed in relation to libraries since 1990.[9] The facilitators, Wetherbee and Mason, used this concept in Florida, Texas, and Indiana. The Rochester Leadership Institute was discussed in Mason and Wetherbee's article, "Learning to Lead: An Analysis of Current Training Programs for Library Leadership," wherein it is referred to as the Library Leadership Institute (Monroe County Library System) and described as a six-day program for librarians and support staff, with selective admission and a primary emphasis on personal assessment and leadership skills development.[10] Based on the use of the Kouzes and

Posner Leadership Practices Inventory, Mason and Wetherbee described the institute as "feedback intensive."[11] As stated in "Learning to Lead," Mason and Wetherbee cited the research of Leanne Atwater, Paul Roush, and Allison Fichthal, when they write, "Research on 360 feedback approaches has shown that use of these tools does lead to increased job performance."[12]

Theoretical Framework for Viewing Leadership

In their 2004 article, Mason and Wetherbee indicated there was no agreed upon statement of leadership skills for librarians or a list of core competencies.[13] Therefore it was difficult to develop a leadership education program without knowing what the learning objectives of the program should be. Also, without measurable objectives, it could not be determined whether the training was effective. In her 2013 article, Mary Wilkins Jordan describes her research study to identify a set of competencies for public library leaders.[14] By first identifying terms mentioned in the literature as being important for library leaders and then refining the list by surveying successful public library directors (results are listed in table 13.1), Jordan developed a list of nineteen competencies "most important to the profession for the next decade."[15]

TABLE 13.1. Core Competencies Defined by Successful Public Library Directors

Competency	Definition
Enthusiasm	Optimism, positive emotional connection
Demonstrating leadership	Being perceived as a leader; taking charge of situations effectively
Delegation	Handing off both responsibilities and sufficient authority to accomplish tasks
Accountability	Taking responsibility for results—positive and negative
Planning	Setting goals and developing strategies to achieve those goals
Integrity	Following professional code, being honest, being a role model for how to behave; honesty
Risk taking	Not taking the easy way; taking a chance of failure; bold or courageous action
Credibility	Building trust in others; doing what you say you will do; being consistent in speech and actions

Resource management	Finding money, facilities to accomplish goals
Creativity	Seeing different ways to accomplish goals; bringing forward new ideas
Customer service	Both internal and external; remembering that patrons are the focus of the library
Interpersonal skills	Effectively working together with others of different levels or different positions (staff and public); good social skills; building rapport
Communication skills	Speaking, writing, listening; understanding your message and conveying it to others
Flexibility	Changing course when necessary, changing plans to be successful
Vision	Looking at the future and seeing where the library can go; articulating directions
Political understanding	Government relations, board relations, working with city/county departments, understanding organizational structure
Maturity	Calm and in control, emotional intelligence, thinking of others first
Problem solving	Assess a situation and see what needs to be done
Advocacy skills	Being visible in the community and library, active in community organizations, building relationships with decision makers
Source: Jordan, "Developing Leadership," 42.	

In 2008, the Library Leadership Administration and Management Association (LLAMA) of the American Library Association (ALA) began the task of creating a list of competencies for library leaders.[16] The authors of the list were members of the 2008 class of the ALA's Emerging Leaders Program.[17] The project design included research, a literature review, and interviews of current leaders in the profession. The model proposed by the LLAMA Emerging Leaders group included 17 broad competencies divided into four central leadership competencies. They were cognitive ability, vision, interpersonal effectiveness, and managerial effectiveness. When the leadership competency model was presented at a poster session at the 2008 ALA Annual Conference, an additional category was included: personal attributes. Listed below in table 13.2 are the broad competencies grouped by the central leadership competencies.

TABLE 13.2. ALA LLAMA Core Competencies		
Cognitive ability	Culturally competent	Strategic planning
Problem-solving	Accountability	Collaboration
Decision making	Team building	Flexibility or adaptability
Reflective thinking	Development	Personal attributes
Vision	Inspirational or motivational	Principled or ethical
Global thinking	Communication skills	Honest
Creative or innovative	Managerial effectiveness	Humble
Forward thinking	Manage change	Gracious
Interpersonal effectiveness	Resource management	Teachable
Source: Ammons-Stephens et al., "Developing Core Leadership Competencies," 68–71.		

Table 13.3 compares the LLAMA and Jordan competencies with the leadership qualities identified by Kouzes and Posner. There are many common terms and phrases among the lists. Separately, two library organizations have developed competencies that align with Kouzes and Posner's characteristics. This suggests using training based on the concepts of Kouzes and Posner may develop leadership skills recognized as such by the library community.

TABLE 13.3. Competencies Compared with Characteristics		
Core Competencies Defined by Public Library Directors	Core Competencies According to ALA LLAMA	Kouzes and Posner's Characteristics of Admired Leaders
Enthusiasm	Cognitive ability	Honest
Demonstrating leadership	Problem-solving	Forward-looking
Delegation	Decision making	Inspiring
Accountability	Reflective thinking	Competent
Planning	Vision	Fair-minded
Integrity	Global thinking	Supportive
Risk taking	Creative/innovative	Broad-minded
Credibility	Forward thinking	Intelligent
Resource management	Interpersonal effectiveness	Straightforward

TABLE 13.3. **Competencies Compared with Characteristics**		
Core Competencies Defined by Public Library Directors	Core Competencies According to ALA LLAMA	Kouzes and Posner's Characteristics of Admired Leaders
Creativity	Culturally competent	Dependable
Customer service	Accountability	Courageous
Interpersonal skills	Team building	Cooperative
Communication skills	Development	Imaginative
Flexibility	Inspirational/ motivational	Caring
Vision	Communication skills	Determined
Political understanding	Managerial effectiveness	Mature
Maturity	Manage change	Ambitious
Problem solving	Resource management	Loyal
Advocacy skills	Strategic planning	Self-controlled
	Collaboration	Independent
	Flexibility/adaptability	
	Personal attributes	
	Principled/ethical	
	Honest	
	Humble	
	Gracious	
	Teachable	
Source: Jordan, "Developing Leadership"; Ammons-Stephens et.al, "Developing Core Leadership Competencies"; and Kouzes and Posner, *The Leadership Challenge*, 25th ed.		

Mason and Wetherbee summarized the evaluations of three leadership programs.[18] They were primarily based on post-training evaluations, and the article pointed out the weaknesses inherent in self-reported evaluations. In their conclusion, Mason and Wetherbee stated the need for longitudinal research and further study to determine if the programs achieved their stated objectives.[19] In the follow-up survey discussed below, I used questions similar to those summarized by Mason and Wetherbee.[20] By surveying participants nine and 11 years after their participation, I hoped to provide more information on the long-term effects of a trait-based, feed-back-intensive program such as the Library Leadership Institute.

What I Learned

At the start, I did not apply for the first Leadership Institute because I did not consider myself a leader. I subscribed to the theory that leaders are born, not made, and you either had it or you didn't. However, there were not enough applicants for the cohort in 2002 and I was invited to attend. Participation in the 2002 Leadership Institute played a pivotal role in my personal development and had a direct result on my decision to interview for a position as a library director. From the first day of the institute, when the facilitators explained the research behind the theory of Kouzes and Posner, I was hooked. Not only did the Kouzes and Posner research results trend across time, gender, culture, and industry; my institute colleagues' responses to the survey fell right in line. Table 13.4 compares the survey results in Kouzes and Posner's 1995 edition of *The Leadership Challenge* with our group exercise in 2002 and survey results from the 2012, 25th anniversary edition of *The Leadership Challenge*.[21] The numbers refer to the percentage of respondents who selected the characteristic as a quality they would look for in a leader. The "X" notes the top seven characteristics selected by the participants in the 2002 cohort in no particular order.

TABLE 13.4. Comparison of 2002 Institute Results with Kouzes and Posner

Characteristics	1995 (%)	2012 (%)	2002 Librarians
Honest	88	89	X
Forward-looking	75	71	X
Inspiring	68	69	X
Competent	63	69	X
Fair-minded	49	37	X
Supportive	41	35	X
Broad-minded	40	38	
Intelligent	40	45	X

Source: Kouzes and Posner, *The Leadership Challenge*, 2nd ed., 21; Kouzes and Posner, *The Leadership Challenge*, 25th ed., 34; Jadlos, "Leadership Institute Survey."

By demonstrating at the beginning of the first session that the theories of Kouzes and Posner held up over time and were directly aligned with my personal values, the facilitators validated the premise of the workshop for me, and I was prepared to continue with an open mind. As the days went on, I discovered that some of the actions I took instinctively and deemed common sense were leadership. For example, on the first day of the workshop, when we broke for lunch, there was a buffet set up against the wall. We had a short time to eat and there were over 40 people in line. I asked a colleague to help me move the table away from the wall so people could serve themselves from either side of the buffet. Even though it was a small gesture, it was a light bulb moment when I realized this action fell under the practices of challenge the process and enable others to act.[22] I began to assess past actions as activities described as leadership actions, and I began to think of myself as someone with leadership ability. After this, my confidence in my leadership abilities soared. With the results of my LPI in hand, I knew what areas I needed to strengthen in order to become a better-rounded leader. I also learned the value of hiring and relying on staff with strengths in areas that complement mine.

As a result of participating in the Leadership Institute and learning about the traits that people look for in leaders, I have consciously incorporated the practice of those traits in my daily life. I also learned that while acting like a leader is vital, it is also important to communicate what I am doing and why it is important. One of the five practices is model the way, which means set the example for how you expect others to behave, or "walk the walk." Instead of quietly setting an example and expecting others to follow, I will explain why I act the way I do. For example, copying a supervisor on an e-mail thanking a student for doing a good job or explaining why I am communicating with administration in a certain way. Sharing the why helps others to become more effective leaders, giving examples to learn from. In addition to using what I learned on a daily basis, I have also trained others: facilitating workshops for local library organizations, the State University of New York Librarians' Association, and the New York Library Assistants' Association.

In preparation for writing this chapter, I retook the LPI to compare with my 2002 results. Although I no longer have the LPI 360 survey results from my 2002 colleagues' point of view, I distinctly remember being surprised by the vast differences between the ways I viewed myself and how others viewed me. My colleagues observed more frequent demonstrations of leadership behaviors than I observed in myself.

Now that I recognize leadership behaviors and consciously incorporate them into my life, my self-study scores are very different. Each leadership practice score is based on a 60-point scale. My scores increased an average of 22 points, a 36 percent improvement. I believe now that I have an understanding of which behaviors are recognized as leadership behaviors, my scores would be more in line with how my colleagues would perceive me if I repeated the 360 evaluation.

Survey Results

In 2013, I surveyed participants in both the 2002 and 2004 Leadership Institutes.[23] The purpose of this survey was to understand the long-term effects of a feedback-intensive program such as the Leadership Institute.

In February 2013, the survey was distributed to participants in the 2002 and 2004 Leadership Institute Cohorts. The survey was designed to collect information on whether the participants believed the institute had achieved its stated outcomes and if the institute had any long-term effect on the participants. With the assistance of the Rochester Regional Library Council, I found contact information for 36 of the 2002 and 34 of the 2004 cohorts. (Each cohort contained 40 participants.) Since five members of the 2004 cohort were also 2002 participants selected to attend as facilitators in training, they did not receive the 2004 survey. For the 2002 cohort, 21 surveys were completed for a 57 percent response rate. The rate of return for the 2004 cohort was 24 percent, or 7 completed surveys. The institutes contained similar content, differing only in timing. The 2002 institute was spread out over four months, and 2004 was a continuous session held over three and one-half days. Leadership development expert Jay A. Conger writes, "A single, one-time course is insufficient to create and support lasting behavioral change. Instead, courses should be designed as a week-long session followed by a break... and then a follow-up course."[24] The increased response rate for the 2002 cohort may indicate that spreading the curriculum over four months had a more lasting effect on the participants. Table 13.5 summarizes the responses and compares the results from the 2002 and 2004 cohorts.

TABLE 13.5. **Leadership Institute Survey Results**				
	2002 (n21)		2004 (n7)	
Survey Question	Agree (%)	Disagree (%)	Agree (%)	Disagree (%)
The Leadership Institute gave me the opportunity to explore the many dimensions of leadership as described by Kouzes and Posner in *The Leadership Challenge*.	95	5	100	0
The institute gave me the opportunity to build practical and concrete skills to enhance my leadership abilities.	100	0	100	0
The institute changed my view of my potential as a leader.	90	10	100	0
The institute enhanced my view of the leadership potential of others.	90	10	100	0
My confidence in my leadership ability increased as a result of the Leadership Institute.	86	14	100	0
Eleven years later, are the Kouzes and Posner Five Practices of Exemplary Leadership relevant to your daily activities?	90	10	100	0
	Yes	No	Yes	No
Have you used any part of the curriculum to mentor others?	38	62	71	29
Note: N = number of completed surveys.				

Responses to the survey were overwhelmingly positive about the institute and the participants' experiences. The first two questions in table 13.5 refer to the learning objectives of the institute. Among the respondents, 95–100 percent, depending upon the cohort year, agreed or strongly agreed that the institute met the stated learning objectives. A respondent commented, "The skills given were practical and easy to remember and practice."[25] Participants agreed or strongly agreed the institute changed their view of their potential as a leader and changed their view of the leadership potential of others. One participant stated, "A better understanding of leadership attributes helped me discover my own and other peoples' abilities."[26] In the results of the survey, 2002 cohort members responded with 86 percent agreeing the institute increased their confidence in their leadership ability and from the 2004 cohort, 100 percent of respondents agreed their confidence levels increased. A 2002 respondent stated, "I had never thought of myself as a leader, but began to understand how we can all be leaders."[27] From the 2002 cohort respondents 90 percent and from 2004 100 percent agreed or strongly agreed the Kouzes and Posner Five Practices are still relevant to their daily activities. Participants commented that they keep course materials such as the poster and bookmark where they can see them every day. Since the institutes, 57 percent of participants have changed jobs or received a promotion. Although, most reported that the change was not related to the institute, several respondents commented they "felt more comfortable applying for jobs with a greater responsibility"[28] or it gave them the confidence to apply for leadership positions. Fourteen of the 29 participants who responded to the survey have continued to use the curriculum both formally and informally to train and mentor others. The 2004 cohort reported a much higher percentage of respondents who said they used some part of the curriculum to mentor others than the 2002 cohort. Since one of the purposes of the second cohort was to train future institute facilitators, there may have been more emphasis on mentoring during that session.

Discussion

According to the survey results, the Library Leadership Institutes were perceived as successful. Nine and 11 years after the institutes, more than 95 percent of survey respondents agreed that the institutes achieved the stated objectives. The institutes gave library staff an understanding of what leadership qualities are, how to recognize them in themselves and others, and how to strengthen their skills in these areas. Even after so many years, the Leadership Institutes are relevant and memorable. Participants continued to use the skills they gained and reported increased confidence in their ability to lead in the workplace and in their personal lives. The Leadership Institute facilitators had positive results training library staff, and the program has achieved its purpose to "train select staff from member libraries in the skills most needed in order to successfully lead libraries in the technologically complex environment of today and the near future."[29]

Conclusion

Since the year of the last institute (2004), library leadership core competencies have been identified by public librarians and the ALA LLAMA section.[30] The Kouzes and Posner qualities of leadership closely align with these competencies. Therefore, it seems the Library Leadership Institute used competencies very similar to those that have been identified by library organizations since 2009 in their leadership development program.

It would be a significant addition to library leadership training if the Leadership Institute could be continued. Kathy Miller, director of the Rochester Regional Library Council, stated "formal institutes have not been offered by RRLC since 2004 due to cost and a smaller pool of eligible candidates remaining after two cohorts of 40 participants" (pers. comm.). Offering the institute every three to five years using the trained local facilitators may address the need to generate a pool of participants and contain facilitator costs.

Going forward, the survey results and other research, such as reported by Conger, indicate that the most effective format for this kind of learning was the multiple-session syllabus spread out over several months.[31] The curriculum should remain based on *The Leadership Challenge* with additional discussion of how these qualities align with emerging library leadership core competencies such as the competencies being developed by ALA LLAMA. Creating a local team of facilitators may reduce overall costs and encourage replication of the institute curriculum throughout many types of libraries across the country.

Notes

1. Joyce. "Leadership Institute."
2. Kouzes and Posner, *The Leadership Challenge*, 2nd ed.
3. Kouzes and Posner, *The Leadership Challenge*, 25th ed., 85.
4. Kouzes and Posner, *The Leadership Practices Inventory*, 6.
5. Kouzes and Posner, *The Leadership Challenge*, 2nd ed.
6. Kouzes and Posner, *The Leadership Challenge*, 25th ed; Kouzes and Posner, *Leadership Practices Inventory*.
7. Kouzes and Posner, *The Leadership Challenge*, 2nd ed., 20.
8. Ibid., 1.
9. Jurow, "Preparing for Library Leadership."
10. Mason and Wetherbee, "Learning to Lead," 198.
11. Ibid., 205.

12. Atwater, Roush, and Fichthal, "The Influence of Upward Feedback"; Mason and Wetherbee, 205.
13. Ibid., 192.
14. Jordan, "Developing Leadership."
15. Ibid., 39.
16. Ammons-Stephens et al., "Developing Core Leadership Competencies." LLAMA is a division of the ALA (http://www.ala.org). More information about LLAMA may be found at http://www.ala.org/llama/.
17. More information about the ALA's Emerging Leaders Program may be found at http://www.ala.org/educationcareers/leadership/emergingleaders
18. Mason and Wetherbee, 208–213.
19. Ibid., 213.
20. Ibid., 210.
21. Kouzes and Posner, *The Leadership Challenge*, 2nd ed; Kouzes and Posner, *The Leadership Challenge*, 25th ed.
22. Kouzes and Posner, *The Leadership Challenge*, 2nd ed.
23. St. John Fisher College Institutional Review Board approval, File No: 3178-022113-06, was received on February 11, 2013.
24. Conger, 56.
25. Jadlos, "Leadership Institute Survey," Respondent 4.
26. Ibid., Respondent 2.
27. Ibid., Respondent 6.
28. Ibid., Respondent 1.
29. Joyce, "Leadership Institute."
30. Jordan, "Developing Leadership"; Ammons-Stephens et al., "Developing Core Leadership Competencies."
31. Conger, 56.

Bibliography

Ammons-Stephens, Shorlette, Holly J. Cole, Keisha Jenkins-Gibbs, Catherine Fraser Riehle, and William H. Weare. "Developing Core Leadership Competencies for the Library Profession." *Library Leadership & Management* 23, no. 2 (2009): 63–74.

Atwater, Leanne, Paul Roush, and Allison Fichthal. "The Influence of Upward Feedback on Self- and Follower Ratings of Leadership." *Personnel Psychology* 48, no. 1 (1995): 35–59.

Conger, Jay A. "The Brave New World of Leadership Training." *Organizational Dynamics* 21, no. 3 (1993): 46–58.

Jadlos, Melissa E. "Leadership Institute Survey Results 2002, 2004." Unpublished manuscript, 2013. Microsoft Word file.

Jordan, May Wilkins. "Developing Leadership Competencies in Librarians." *IFLA Journal* 38, no. 1 (2012): 37–46.

Joyce, Carole. "Leadership Institute: Developing Libraries in a Technological Era." New York State Library Services and Technology Act. Unpublished grant application, 2001. Microsoft Word file.

Jurow, Susan. "Preparing for Library Leadership." *Journal of Library Administration* 12, no. 2 (1990): 57–74.

Kouzes, James M., and Barry Z. Posner. *The Leadership Challenge.* 2nd ed. San Francisco: Jossey-Bass, 1995.

———. *The Leadership Challenge.* 25th ed. San Francisco: Jossey-Bass, 2012.

———. *Leadership Practices Inventory: Participant's Workbook.* Rev. 2nd ed. San Francisco: Jossey-Bass, 2001.

Mason, Florence M., and Louella V. Wetherbee. "Learning to Lead: An Analysis of Current Training Programs for Library Leadership." *Library Trends* 53, no. 1 (2004): 187–217.

McCauley, Cynthia D., and Stéphane Brutus. "Leader Training and Development." In *The Nature of Organizational Leadership: Understanding the Performance Imperatives Confronting Today's Leaders*, edited by Stephen J. Zaccaro and Richard J. Klimoski, 347–83. San Francisco: Jossey-Bass, 2001.

CHAPTER 14

Taking Flight at Snowbird:
Reflections on a Library Leadership
Institute

Shellie Jeffries

WHEN I WAS working as a reference librarian at Wayne State University
and the director of Wayne's library and information science program mentioned he wanted to nominate me to attend the Snowbird Library Leadership Institute, I experienced a "What, me?" moment. I thought of myself as a fairly average librarian and would never have identified myself as
someone with leadership potential. That experience, the opportunity to see
oneself differently, is one of the gifts of being part of a leadership program.

The Development of the Snowbird Institute
However, despite the confidence others had in me, I was not sure I had what
it took to be a leader, and I had absolutely no idea what the Snowbird Library
Leadership Institute was, beyond that it was held at the Snowbird Ski Resort
in Utah. After doing some research, I discovered that the Snowbird Institute
was founded in 1990 by J. Dennis Day, then director of the Salt Lake City
Public Library. According to F. William Summers and Lorraine Summers,

> Day was a strong supporter of 1987–88 American Library
> Association President Margaret Chisholm's call for special

training for young leaders, and when ALA's proposal for a much broader project to carry this out was not funded, he decided to do something on his own.... Dynix President Paul Sybrowsky perceived the value of making a major investment in the training of leaders for the profession his company serves. Thus, Dynix... has been the sponsor of... Snowbird Institutes.[1]

Margaret Chisholm, in a letter to Warren Horton, director-general of the National Library of Australia and an early advocate of the Snowbird Institute in Australia, described the program thus,

The Snowbird Leadership Institute offers a unique set of opportunities to librarians in the early years of their professional career. Through a variety of informal and structured activities, institute participants can identify their personal leadership style, explore alternative styles for effective leadership, experiment with leadership skills and techniques, and interact with a select group of outstanding leaders in the library world. The Institute offers those attending unparalleled opportunities to develop networking contacts with today's library leaders and to meet and interact with the leaders of tomorrow.[2]

To limit the number of applications to the program for "strategic effectiveness... rather than creating an indiscriminately large pool [of nominations]," deans of American Library Association (ALA) accredited library schools, state librarians, and presidents of ALA chapters were invited to nominate librarians who exhibited leadership potential and had been working in professional positions for between one and three years.[3] While the institute did not employ permanent staff, Nancy Tessman, then the deputy director of the Salt Lake City Public Library, played a significant role in selecting participants, organizing the events, and handling logistical concerns. Although Tessman was responsible for coordinating the institute's daily activities, it was library consultants Becky Schreiber and John

Shannon who provided the content. Experts in "organizational development for organizations in transition," they developed the curriculum of Snowbird, building on previous library workshops they had facilitated by adding leadership to the Snowbird program.[4]

Perched in the Wasatch Mountains

Held annually over five days at the Snowbird Ski Resort located in Utah's beautiful Wasatch Mountains, the Library Leadership Institute at Snowbird welcomed 32 librarians from across the United States, representing a variety of different types of libraries: high school, state, academic, public, corporate, and special. During the first evening's welcome reception, participants were divided into four groups of eight and introduced to their mentors, two for each group. Throughout the years the institute was held, it was able to attract leaders in the profession to be mentors and "share their wisdom and experience with participants."[5] During the 1999 institute year, the mentors included Martin Gomez, then executive director of the Brooklyn Public Library; George Needham, then OCLC vice president of member services; and Lana Porter, then president and CEO of Ameritech Library Services.

The remaining four days of the program consisted of a combination of individual reflection; small group meetings; larger group shared feedback; presentations by Shannon and Schreiber; communal meals; outdoor activities, which were both related to the program and recreational; and mentor insights.

The substance of the program revolved around what Schreiber and Shannon called "key leadership competences": know yourself, assess the environment, stand in the future, act with courage, embrace change, and promote individual and relationship power.[6] Prior to arriving in Utah, participants were encouraged to take the Keirsey Character and Temperament Sorter online questionnaire and the Enneagram personality type online survey and bring the results with them.[7] These results were discussed during the first full day of the program as Schreiber and Shannon described the Enneagram personality types and emphasized the importance of leaders developing self-awareness. Exploring one's Enneagram type, which led to the first key competency, knowing one's self, laid the foundation for understanding the other key leadership competencies. Reviewing the variety of leader types also underscored the idea that there is not just one type of personality that is suitable for leadership; anyone can lead as long as they understand their strengths and weaknesses.

Subsequent days were spent exploring the benefits of creating a personal vision as well as an institutional one; the necessity of continually assessing the library profession—and the internal and external developments that affect it, such as technology and public policy—as it evolves; the importance of looking to the future and determining how you want to get there; the need to act with courage, even when you are fearful; the value of embracing change and encouraging those around you to do the same; and methods of developing relationships and increasing your influence to promote your vision. An underlying theme for all of these topics was the idea one could lead from any position. That is, a librarian did not necessarily have to be in a managerial or administrative position in order to be concerned with these issues and to develop leadership skills.

Presentations by Schreiber and Shannon were augmented by informal talks given by the mentors, who provided "Mentor Insights" specifically related to the key leadership competencies and who also spoke more at length in the "My Practice, My Passion" segments. By hearing from the mentors about their real life experiences, successes, challenges, and failures, participants were able to make connections and hear the concepts and ideas applied to actual situations. A culminating event was the opportunity for an individual consultation with the mentor of one's choice.

Taking advantage of the stunning location, the program also balanced the intellectual content with recreational activities. These included star watching on top of a mountain and a guided wildflower walk.

The institute ended after the 2000 meeting. According to Schreiber, there were three main reasons for Snowbird's cessation: several states had started their own leadership institutes, so the need for a national program diminished; the Salt Lake City Public Library, a main organizer of the institute, turned its focus from leadership to community involvement, and no other organization was able to step in to pick up the project; and Snowbird likely reached the end of its natural life cycle (pers.comm.). Despite the end of the Snowbird initiative, Shannon and Schreiber continue to offer library leadership programs utilizing similar content throughout the United States.[8]

Leaving the Nest: Lessons Learned

Because I was not entirely sure if I had the ability to be a leader or if I even wanted to be one, I initially struggled with the Snowbird program. In 1999, I was a mid-level librarian in a fairly hierarchical organization without much authority to initiate change, and I did not think of myself as leader material. Ironically, my Enneagram type was Eight, otherwise known as The Boss or The Leader. It was fortunate Schreiber and Shannon began their program by exploring Enneagram types and the concept of leading from any position because I learned there are many different styles of leadership, and I found I could embrace the idea of leading from behind, regardless of one's type. That particular approach to leadership stayed with me as I moved to a smaller college library with a flattened organizational structure and was able to work directly under the library director. I felt equipped to consciously support her and the success of the library by working behind the scenes. Even now that I am a library director, I continue to live by this philosophy by supporting my direct supervisor, the provost.

While somewhat resistant to what at first seemed like a lot of touchy-feely content, I soon came to appreciate the emphasis nearly everyone—Schreiber and Shannon, the mentors, and the organizers—placed on the emotional aspects of library work. Having grown up in the era of dressing for success and women feeling like they had to behave like men to get ahead, I felt grateful and reassured to hear successful leaders discuss the importance of knowing yourself, of personal relationships, and of recognizing fear but moving through it.[9] The institute's professional approach to and pragmatic advice about being a leader balanced with its acceptance that people's feelings need to be taken into consideration was a tremendous relief. I realized I did not have to be an emotionless leader treating my staff as worker bees. Having been given permission by Snowbird to address emotions in the workplace and later finding a position in a library with less administrative hierarchy, I was able to develop into a library director who acknowledges and addresses the emotional context of what happens in my library.

Other lessons of Snowbird took a little longer to emerge, mostly because I needed to find the right combination of institution and position for them to come to fruition. It was not until I started working at my current institution that I was able to more fully apply what I had learned at Snowbird. One significant lesson was the importance of self-awareness. I have come to believe that knowing who you are is absolutely essential for working with people, developing relationships, and achieving one's vision. When I first became a library director, I revisited my Snowbird notes and found the Enneagram description of my type, including the "vices and virtues," to be very helpful in reminding me what strengths and weaknesses I needed to beware of as I began to exercise my leadership muscles.

I also learned

- the difference between managing and leading and how to balance both,
- the importance of collaboration,
- how to embrace change and encourage others to do so as well, and
- how to do things that are outside my comfort zone.

Perhaps the best thing I learned from Snowbird is that I *could* be a leader. Even if I was not necessarily ready to lead when I attended the program, the fact that people believed I had the ability and potential to become a leader planted a seed that eventually bore fruit.

The Theoretical Foundation of Snowbird

When asked what, if any, leadership theory Schreiber Shannon Associates used to form the underpinnings of the Snowbird program, Schreiber stated,

> We have combined many writings over the years to come up with our own approach, which is experiential and team oriented. We see leadership as involving all the stakeholders to assess the situation, establish a plan, implement the plan, evaluate its success, and adjust as needed... Some of the theorists who have influenced us are Warren Bennis, David A. Kolb, Peter Vaill, and Peter Senge. There are so many more, but we wouldn't say we are adherents of any one theorist.[10]

While Schreiber and Shannon have developed their own system based on Bennis's more democratic, adaptive approach to leadership; Kolb's experiential learning model; Vaill's descriptions of the organizational excellence movement; and Senge's vision of the learning organization, the theory that seems to most accurately describe the foundation underlying Snowbird's content is the shared leadership theory.[11]

Although there are many definitions of shared leadership, Craig L. Pearce and Henry P. Sims, researchers in the field of leadership theory, state, "Whereas vertical leadership entails the process of one individual projecting downward influence on individuals, shared leadership entails the process of shared influence between and among individuals."[12] France St. Hilaire summarizes their definition of shared leadership as

> a dynamic, interactive influence process among individuals in groups for which the objective is to lead one another to the achievement of group or organization goals or both. This influence process often involves peer, or lateral, influence and at other times involves upward or downward hierarchical influence. The key distinction between shared leadership and traditional models of leadership is that the influence process involves more than just downward influence on subordinates by an elected leader.[13]

Joyce K. Fletcher and Katrin Kaufer identify three paradigm shifts inherent in shared leadership. They say it is

- distributed and interdependent [in that it] acknowledge[s] the interdependent nature of leadership and signal[s] a shift away from individual achievement... toward a focus on collective achievement, share responsibility, and the importance of teamwork;

- embedded in social action [because, instead of focusing] on the leaders' effect on followers, the followers are understood to be playing a role in influencing and creating leadership; [and]

- depend[ent] not only on an individual's ability to learn, question assumptions, and understand concepts... for oneself, but also on the ability to create conditions.... where collective learning can occur.[14]

Fletcher and Kaufer conclude their description of shared leadership by stating,

> Models of shared leadership reenvision the *who* and *where* of leadership by focusing on the need to distribute the tasks and responsibilities of leadership up, down, and across the hierarchy. They reenvision the *what* of leadership by articulating leadership as a social process that occurs in and through social interactions, and they articulate the *hows* of leadership by focusing on the skills and ability required to create conditions in which collective learning can occur.[15]

With its emphasis on knowing oneself, leading from behind, building relationships, and creating an environment that promotes individual empowerment, Snowbird's approach to leadership can be said to have been grounded in the shared leadership model. Throughout the program, Schreiber and Shannon consistently stressed the importance of understanding one's leadership style, strengths, and weaknesses in order to be able to effectively interact with and inspire people. This approach aligns with Fletcher and Kaufer's description of the skills and abilities needed to encourage collective learning, including self-awareness and other "relational practices and skills such as authenticity, openness, vulnerability, and the ability to anticipate the responses and learning needs of others."[16]

Additionally, Snowbird reinforced the need to involve stakeholders in creating a shared vision for the future and establishing a collaborative, team-oriented environment where all members are empowered to influence the direction of the organization. This echoes Pearce and Sims when they write about "the process of shared influence" and the idea "that the influence process involves more than just downward influence on subordinates by an elected leader."[17]

While not explicitly addressed, the importance of emotional intelligence (EI) in the workplace was implicit in much of the content Schreiber and Shannon developed for Snowbird.[18] Peter J. Jordan, Neal M. Ashkanasy, and Kaylene W. Ascough summarize one definition of EI as "the ability to be aware of emotions in self and others, and the ability to modify our reactions to situations accordingly."[19] In their book, *What We Know about Emotional Intelligence*, which seeks to summarize current research, results, and conclusions about EI, Moshe Zeidner, Gerald Matthews, and Richard D. Roberts define it simply as "a generic competence in perceiving emotions (both in oneself and in others)."[20] Analyzing the results of research concerning the correlation between EI and leadership skills, they state,

> EI research on organizational management and leadership has focused on a set of leadership qualities subsumed under the umbrella term of *transformational* style of leadership.... Transformational leadership is characterized by the following attributes: (1) charisma and articulation of a vision of the future—the leader transmits a sense of mission that is effectively articulated, instills pride, faith, and respect, and has a gift of seeing what is really important; (2) intellectually stimulating—arouses followers to think in new ways and emphasizes problem solving and the use of reasoning before taking action; (3) individualized consideration—the leader pays attention to individual differences among peers and subordinates, delegates projects to stimulate learning experiences, provides coaching and teaching, and treats each follower as a respected individual.[21]

Although they never discussed the need for leaders to have the intangible quality of charisma that transformational leadership seems to demand, Schreiber and Shannon did encourage Snowbird participants to develop several of the skills included in the definition of transformational leadership.[22] They stressed that a leader must have a vision and be able to both articulate that vision and convince others to buy into it. In addition, their focus on including all stakeholders when developing, implementing, and assessing plans corresponds to the attributes of problem solving, delegation, and treating staff as individuals.

By being willing to acknowledge the emotional aspects of the work environment, the facilitators and mentors at Snowbird implicitly accepted the significance of EI as a leadership skill, allowing participants to embrace it as well. It appears they were on to something. Zeidner, Matthews, and Roberts closely examined studies investigating transformational leadership and EI, and although research on this topic has produced limited and sometimes contradictory results, they conclude, "High EI has also been linked to effective leadership, especially transformational leadership dependent on charisma and inspiration."[23]

Even though Schreiber and Shannon did not associate their Snowbird program with a particular leadership style, it seems clear it contained elements of shared leadership, emotional intelligence, and transformational leadership theories.

Literature Review

Much of the literature available about Snowbird either describes the program or is a participant's personal reflection on his or her experience. In "Library Leadership 2000 and Beyond," Summers and Summers recount how Snowbird was created, summarize the major topics covered, and describe the program schedule.[24] They ask "Will it work?" and answer "It is too early to tell in any real sense. Yet it is obvious from the evaluations that participants go away feeling very strongly that the institute has been a very important event in their lives."[25] C. Allen Nichols, Jennifer E. Chilcoat, and Sandy Brooks describe their experiences attending Snowbird in, respectively, "Leaders: Born or Bred: Confessions from a Leadership Training Junkie," "Report from Snowbird Leadership Institute," and "Library Leadership Institute at Snowbird." Nichols writes, "The clarity I gained resonates in my day-to-day actions even now. I came home better prepared to deal with work and life."[26] He answers his own question about whether he would have been as successful in his career without attending Snowbird by saying, "I might have muddled through. I would not have had the polished vision for my involvement in the profession, the insight gained from participating with other 'young leaders,' and a solid network of mentors and colleagues."[27] Chilcoat states, "Simply getting selected to go was an enormous confidence builder, and the lessons I learned about myself and about working with other people have already changed the way I approach my work and my life."[28] Brooks lists the highlights of what she learned at Snowbird, including, "know your personality type," "teams can work," and "a true leader can lead from anywhere in the organization."[29]

Even though these personal reports anecdotally speak to the value of Snowbird, they do not provide conclusive evidence that the institute created leaders. However, Teresa Y. Neely and Mark D. Winston have written two articles that attempt to measure the impact of Snowbird on participants' career development.[30] In both articles, Neely and Winston surveyed librarians who attended Snowbird between 1990 and 1998, asking them about their career progression, involvement in leadership activities (as defined by the authors), and their perceptions of the impact of the Snowbird experience on their careers. They sent surveys to 213 individuals and received 150 usable responses for a response rate of 70 percent.[31]

Neely and Winston looked at the career progression of the respondents, along with "leadership activities," which they defined as "research (i.e., publications and presentations) and service, including participation in committees and professional/scholarly associations."[32] Responses to questions about career changes and advancement seemed to indicate that survey respondents did, in general, progress from entry level or mid-level positions to jobs with more administrative responsibility. At the time they attended Snowbird, nearly 50 percent of responding librarians were working in public or technical services, and 38 percent had administrative positions such as department or branch head, assistant dean or director, or dean or director; the remainder served in other areas of the profession.[33] Following Snowbird, only 27 percent still had positions in public or technical services, and 52 percent had obtained administrative positions.[34]

When asked if they felt their Snowbird experience had any influence on them obtaining subsequent positions, 59 percent of respondents indicated that the institute was influential to a great extent or somewhat.[35] In a related question about career progression, almost half (49 percent) answered that they thought their career paths would have been different had they not attended Snowbird.[36] Forty-two percent said it would not have been different.[37]

Neely and Winston concluded that, following their attendance at Snowbird, participants increased their involvement in professional development activities, such as attending and presenting at conferences. They also published more, from a total of 104 publications before Snowbird to 170 after.[38] Neely and Winston state,

> It is difficult to identify a direct relationship between participation in the Snowbird Leadership Institute and career

progression and greater participation in leadership activities. However it is clear that the respondents report an increased level of activity in a number of different categories of leadership activity. In addition, their perceptions regarding the value of the Institute with regard to their career progression are largely positive and reflect that many of their career paths would have been different had they not had the Snowbird experience.[39]

Soaring with the Wind: Life after Snowbird

Intrigued by Neely and Winston's findings, I decided to conduct my own mini-survey of Snowbird graduates. Neely and Winston were able to contact 213 former Snowbird participants using a list kept at the institute's Salt Lake City offices at the time they conducted their research. Because the program is no longer operational and the once active Snowbird listserv is defunct, I did not have access to a wide range of participants. In fact, the only Snowbird people I was able contact were those who attended with me in 1999 and a friend who attended in 2000. After developing a survey instrument similar to Neely and Winston's but shorter and more focused on the attendees' perceptions of their experience and its impact (see Appendix 14.1 for the survey instrument); obtaining permission from my institution's IRB to conduct research using human subjects; and locating current e-mail addresses for 24 of the 32 people in my year by using the participants list from 1999, in December 2012 I sent out the survey to those 24 people, plus my friend from the 2000 class.

I received sixteen responses, a 64 percent response rate. While the small sample size and limited diversity of the respondents, along with the self-selective nature of the responses (perhaps those who did not enjoy their Snowbird experience or who are not particularly happy with their career progression chose not to complete the survey) may lessen the validity of the conclusions one can draw from the results, it is nonetheless worthwhile and perhaps, ultimately, revealing about the Snowbird impact, to consider the responses.

As Neely and Winston found in their research, librarians working in public institutions made up the largest number of Snowbird participants and survey respondents, with academic librarians coming in second. This was also reflected in my survey respondents, with 44 percent (7) being librarians employed in public libraries and 31 percent (5) in academic libraries. As for career development, two (12 percent) are in the same position at the same institution as when they attended Snowbird and four (25 percent) are in a different position at the same institution. Nine (56 percent) have different jobs altogether, and one is not working in a library. While the more recent survey is not statistically valid, it is interesting to compare these data in table 14.1 to the numbers described in the Neely and Winston studies. They found that 39 percent of respondents were in the same position at the same institution, 25 percent were in a different position at the same institutions, and 28 percent were at a different institution.[40] These numbers are not altogether similar to the data in the recent survey, though there are most likely many reasons for this such as small sample size, self-selection of respondents, and length of time between Snowbird attendance and the follow-up survey chief among them.

TABLE 14.1. Comparison of Career Development Responses		
	Neely and Winston 1999 Responses*	2012 Survey Responses
Same position at the same institution	58 (38%)	2 (13%)
Different position at the same institution	37 (24%)	4 (25%)
Different institution	43 (28%)	9 (56%)
Not working in a library	12 (10%)	1 (6%)
Note: *Some respondents selected more than one category in response to this question.		

Plain numbers, however, do not reveal much about Snowbird's influence on the respondents decisions to stay in their jobs, move on to other jobs, or leave the professional altogether. Nor, perhaps, does data on positions held and promotions achieved or number of publications and conference presentations made speak to leadership ability. Possibly more illuminating are the respondents' comments as they reflect on their Snowbird experience and its impact on their lives 14 years later.

When asked in 2012 if their involvement in Snowbird contributed to obtaining subsequent positions, only three (20 percent) of the 15 people who answered the question said Snowbird had no impact. The other twelve

(80 percent) described the ways in which the institute influenced their career path, with the most frequent comments involving the networking opportunities; a direct connection between participation and job offers; a sense that the experience was influential as a whole; and a belief that Snowbird was confidence building, both professionally and personally. A sample of responses from the 2012 survey included

- I think [Snowbird contributed to my obtaining subsequent positions] a fair amount in considering the experiences, perspectives, and interpersonal awareness and skills that results from Snowbird participation
- Snowbird opened my eyes to my own potential.
- Subsequent to my Snowbird attendance, I was offered a deputy director position within my library. I used my knowledge and experience from Snowbird in the position.... I feel that my Snowbird experience and leadership ability contributed to my being assigned to be a committee member during the design and development of our new... Archives Building.
- It was due to my experience at Snowbird that I sought my next position.... I learned a great deal in this position and I think the lessons from Snowbird prepared me to be open to those lessons.
- Snowbird did come up in a meeting with the search committee when I applied for the Systems Librarian position.... The one member who was familiar with Snowbird asked about my participation and I had the opportunity to describe the great experience and the leadership lessons I received there. I think it helped me to get that position.
- Attending Snowbird was a great networking and confidence building experience for me.
- I think participating in Snowbird helped boost my confidence.
- Snowbird Leadership Institute gave me the confidence to pursue positions in which I had the experience or qualifications necessary to ably perform the positions.
- Snowbird Leadership Institute encouraged me to be willing to go outside of my comfort zone.
- Snowbird extended my network of seasoned and peer professionals in the industry. [It] gave me the courage to "lead from any position" in the organization.

Asked to consider if their career path would have been different if they had not attended Snowbird, 60 percent (9) said it would have been different, 13 percent (2) said it would not have been different, and 27 percent (4) were not really sure. Those who felt that attending Snowbird affected their careers were very clear about the ways in which the institute influenced their career progression:

- The core of Snowbird for me was getting a new perspective of myself and my leadership abilities. It is an intensely personal experience! I came away strengthened in conviction in trying to improve library service to rural communities. If I had not attended Snowbird I may have remained stuck in an untenable position longer than I was.

- I believe my Snowbird participation put me in a position to be recognized for leadership opportunities that I might not have been offered otherwise.

- There are some experiences at Snowbird that still stick with me and remind me that I have talents and skills in the area of leadership that I have a responsibility to use. Snowbird also reinforced for me the belief that you do not need to be in a senior administrative position to be a leader, that we need good leaders throughout an organization. The move from my coordinator role… to a more traditional management role… was a direct result of the experience at Snowbird. I likely would not have sought that position if I had not gone to Snowbird. That position had a significant and positive impact on my career since, so yes, Snowbird made a difference.

- I may not have had the confidence/understanding to move from managing a branch to administration [if I had not attended Snowbird].

- Possibly. I might have stayed in public library practice instead of returning to school.

- I think that I may have been more content to stay in current positions rather than have the confidence to seek new experiences and challenges.

- I know it would have been different, yes. I needed Snowbird to solidify my self-awareness and my commitment to growth and development as a leader. I continue to rely on my Snowbird experiences as the foundation for building my work.

- My career path took an unexpected but fulfilling direction for 2 years. The path was not in libraries, but was a result of my training and growth at Snowbird. I ran for and was elected to the County Council—the legislative body for [my state]. I used the decision-making exercises I learned at Snowbird to decide to run.

Ninety-three percent of the respondents (14) felt that Snowbird helped them develop leadership skills, while one person (7 percent) said it did not (and one person did not answer). Respondents described learning to broaden and expand their ideas about leadership and being changed by the experience, both personally and professionally.

- At Snowbird I came to realize where I fit into the leadership pecking order so to speak. I am an excellent mid-level leader. I identified the niche I best fit and proceeded from there. Snowbird focused my own vision to be clearer and more concrete. Not only did this refocusing happen in my professional life but carried into my personal life.
- Snowbird was a great stepping-stone!
- Snowbird was certainly one of the experiences I have had which have helped me to become a better leader. I do not think one week-long experience alone can make someone a leader. Good leaders are continuing to grow and learn, throughout their careers. I aspire to be such a leader. Snowbird was a very important milestone in setting me up for what I hope to be life-long growth in personal discovery and leadership skill development.
- Not only did the week at the institute make a difference but it helped me network and find other opportunities for learning and mentoring.
- I believe attending Snowbird opened the door for me to learn more about library leadership, which grew my desire to do and be more. My interest in leadership grew more because of Snowbird.
- I think participating helped me realize that I have intrinsic qualities and character traits that I cannot deny and that I need to consider whenever deciding about what to do in professional situations. I now recognize myself as a reluctant but competent leader. I prefer to work as a team member or as second to a dynamic and thoughtful leader.

- Snowbird showed me that most people are capable of leading, but they need confidence, a clear vision, and the ability to share ideas and help gather necessary support from others.
- Snowbird changed the way I viewed myself and the way I interact with people when it comes to decision making and group dynamics. Snowbird had everything to do with how I proceeded to determine the risk to reward aspects of a run for political office—something soooo far outside my comfort zone. I decided, yes, this was way out of my comfort zone, but I would do it anyway—BECAUSE OF SNOWBIRD. I would never had thought of it or done it otherwise.

Respondents had an opportunity to include additional comments in the survey. They said,

- Snowbird helped introduce [me] to various leadership and management concepts, helped broaden my understanding and awareness of various dynamics around libraries, library management/leadership/strategy/service. Snowbird also prompted and catalyzed growth in personal awareness of my own gifts, traits, preferences, weaknesses, and interpersonal and organizational capabilities.
- One could say that I wasted the Snowbird experience because within 15 months of my attendance I left the library profession. However, I would disagree. Although I took a long break from working in the profession, eventually I returned. I matured at Snowbird and throughout the years because of how my mind was opened to thinking and evaluating things differently.… There is a certain sense of security and assuredness that I ultimately developed out of the Snowbird experience.
- Although it has been almost 14 years since my participation, I still look back at Snowbird as an awesome opportunity to develop my leadership skills and to connect with peers and mentors from the program.
- The Snowbird experience is something I draw on regularly. Too bad it was discontinued as I think some fabulous library leadership came out of this Institute.
- I think it was a good institute, but would be better aimed towards someone in library school rather than librarians already working or in management positions.

- When I am faced with challenging situations, I often reflect back to lessons learned at the Snowbird Institute and find the strength and vision to forge ahead.
- Because of Snowbird, so many opportunities opened up to me and remain open to me.

While it may not be possible to quantify the affect that the Snowbird Library Leadership Institute has had on the library profession, especially given the small sample size of this study, the reflections offered by the librarians who attended Snowbird indicate that, for most of them, the experience was beneficial. Even if they did not necessarily advance in their careers, which could be a result of many factors, most attendees seemed to gain something positive from the experience they could apply to their careers and even their personal lives. Whatever it was, this survey suggests that Snowbird was perceived to have had an important and affirmative influence on many librarians who attended it and contributed to their career development, if not career advancement.

Flying Off into the Sunset: Final Reflections on Snowbird

When looking at Neely and Winston's research along with the published personal reflections about the Snowbird experience and the responses to the 2012 survey, it appears that Snowbird had an effect on those who attended the program. The question of whether it is possible to impart leadership skills and create leaders in a five-day program has not been answered. It seems evident that Snowbird opened participants' minds and hearts to the possibilities of the different ways they could become leaders and many of them made a choice to pursue that career path.

Because assessing the benefits and influence of Snowbird has relied on self-selected survey respondents, it is difficult to conclusively determine what elements of the program were most helpful to participants. Snowbird's emphasis on self-awareness, shared leadership, and emotional intelligence resonated with me and formed the underpinnings of my evolution as a leader. That approach may not have been effective with every participant just as every leadership development program may not be appropriate for every personality type, but Neely and Winston's and my survey results reflect that it inspired quite a few librarians to look for opportunities to become leaders in their organizations. If other leadership institutes do not stress these elements, perhaps more need to.

Schreiber indicated that Snowbird had reached the end of its natural life and that was one of the reasons it ceased operations. Nonetheless, as revealed in the surveys, such leadership training encourages potential leaders, however reluctant, to develop their potential and act as positive influences on their organizations, colleagues, and patrons. This can only enhance the profession. While some leaders are able to continuously develop their skills independently, others can benefit from attending leadership programs, and not just at the beginning of their careers. Programs that address the needs of mid-career leaders should be established if they do not already exist, building on the content of earlier workshops participants may have attended and introducing them to new ideas in the field. Mid-career programs might also have the added advantage of rejuvenating professionals.

One model for early and mid-career leadership development could be the Eureka! Leadership Institute, a program developed by Schreiber and Shannon and sponsored by the California State Library. Although similar to Snowbird in size and curriculum, Eureka has a different goal and a longer reach. According to the Eureka Institute website:

> The Institute is an intensive six-day residential leadership training program for California libraries. It is similar to the Aurora Leadership Institute (Australia) [which itself is based on Snowbird] but incorporates a project component similar to the Urban Libraries Council's Executive Leadership Program....The Institute is designed to be most beneficial for those with MLS degrees who have between 3 and 10 years of professional experience.... Each person admitted to the Institute must, in consultation with their library administration, select a significant project to work on over the course of the year following the Institute. The project should be something that makes the library more responsive to community needs, and must fall within California LSTA guidelines. The California State Library provides grant awards of up to $5,000 to support the projects.

The Institute is designed to be a transformational experience. Each segment of the multi-day curriculum builds to make a final impact on the last day. The emphasis on small group work will involve a very high level of intensity, group bonding, and risk-taking unlike traditional multi-day trainings or conferences. The project requirement, grant support for the projects, the monthly webinars, and the Encore and Anniversary events insure continued interaction among the members of the group and also with the mentors, Institute facilitators, and Infopeople staff.[41]

With its focus on developing and implementing a specific long-term project, ongoing support, and follow-up events, Eureka is a different approach to leadership programs that could provide valuable training and experience to leaders beyond the state of California (participants are limited to employees of California libraries).

Quantifying the success of any leadership program is a challenge. The survey results only revealed part of the picture, and more research needs to be done to determine what, if any, effect attending a leadership institute has on participants. A comparative study of several programs may reveal if certain practices and curricula were more effective than others in resulting in measurable leadership results. Researchers could expand this study's scope by surveying attendees of other leadership programs 15 or more years after their participation to measure the long-term impact of those programs and compare results to Snowbird. Researchers would need to surmount the problem of self-selection if surveys are used. Locating participants is also a potential difficulty. However, in this era of data-driven decision making, the results of such research could be very revealing and might even help improve existing programs.

I am unclear about what exactly the Wayne State University library and information science program director saw in me, but I am grateful I had the opportunity to attend the Snowbird Library Leadership Institute. I may not have been seeing leadership potential in myself at the time or been ready to pursue leadership positions beyond "leading from behind," but the lessons I learned at Snowbird, along with knowing *someone* had confidence in my abilities, planted a seed that enabled me to bloom into a leader when the opportunity arose.

Appendix 14.1.Snowbird Survey Questions

1. What type of library did you work in at the time you attended the Snowbird Library Leadership Institute?
2. What was your job title when you attended Snowbird?
3. Which category describes your current job situation with regards to your Snowbird participation? In the same position at the same institution? In a different position at the same institution? Neither?
4. What type of library do you work in now?
5. What is your current job title?
6. Do you think your participation in Snowbird helped you get other jobs?
7. Do you think Snowbird had an effect on your career development/progression?
8. Do you think your participation in Snowbird helped you develop leadership skills and/or become a leader?
9. Do you have any other comments concerning the influence of Snowbird on your career?

Notes

1. Summers and Summers, "Library Leadership 2000," 38.
2. Horton, "It All Began over Dinner."
3. Summers and Summers, "Library Leadership 2000," 38; for more information about ALA, see http://www.ala.org.
4. Schreiber and Shannon, "Developing Library," 39.
5. Summers and Summers, "Library Leadership 2000," 38.
6. Schreiber and Shannon, "Key Leadership Competencies."
7. See http://www.keirsey.com/ for more information about this measure; see http://www.enneagraminstitute.com/ for more information about this survey.
8. Schreiber and Shannon, "Leadership Institutes & Consulting."
9. This is a reference to a book by John T. Molloy, *Dress for Success,* published in 1975, which touted the effect of clothing on a person's success in the workplace. Molloy, a scientific image consultant, currently hosts a blog where you can continue to find his perspective on dress and success at http://www.thedressforsuccesscolumn.com/.
10. Ibid.

11. "Warren Bennis," *Wikipedia*; David A. Kolb," *Wikipedia*; "Peter B. Vaill," Harvard Business School Bulletin Online; "Peter Senge and the Learning Organization," Infed.
12. Pearce and Sims, "Shared Leadership," 116.
13. St. Hilaire, "Leadership Theories," 35.
14. Fletcher and Kaufer, "Shared Leadership," 22–24.
15. Ibid., 24.
16. Ibid.
17. Pearce and Sims, "Shared Leadership," 116.
18. *Emotional intelligence* is a term popularized by Daniel Goleman in his 1995 work *Emotional Intelligence*.
19. Jordan, Ashkanasy, and Ascough, "Emotional Intelligence," 358.
20. Zeidner, Matthews, and Roberts, *What We Know about Emotional Intelligence*, 3.
21. Ibid., 269.
22. Ibid., 280.
23. Ibid.
24. Summers and Summers, "Library Leadership 2000."
25. Ibid., 41.
26. Nichols, "Leaders: Born or Bred."
27. Ibid.
28. Chilcoat, "Report from Snowbird."
29. Brooks, "Library Leadership Institute at Snowbird."
30. Neely and Winston. "Snowbird Leadership Institute"; Winston and Neely, "Leadership Development and Public Libraries."
31. Neely and Winston. "Snowbird Leadership Institute," 415.
32. Ibid.
33. Ibid., 418.
34. Ibid.
35. Ibid., 421.
36. Ibid., 422.
37. Ibid.
38. Ibid., 420.
39. Ibid., 424.
40. Ibid., 424.
41. Hinman, "Eureka!"

Bibliography

Brooks, Sandy. "Library Leadership Institute at Snowbird." *New England Libraries* 33, no. 1 (2001): 2–3. http://www.nela2.org/files/nel1_01.pdf.

Chilcoat, Jennifer E. "Report from Snowbird Leadership Institute." *Arkansas Libraries* 49, no. 5 (1992): 31.

Fletcher, Joyce K., and Katrin Kaufer. "Shared Leadership: Paradox and Possibility." In *Shared Leadership: Reframing the Hows and Whys of Leadership*, edited by Craig L. Pearce and Jay A. Conger, 21–47. Thousand Oaks, CA: Sage Publications, 2003.

Goleman, Daniel. *Emotional Intelligence*. New York: Bantam Books, 1995.

Harvard Business School Bulletin Online. "Peter B. Vaill." Accessed June 23, 2015. https://web.archive.org/web/20130425014954/http://www.alumni.hbs.edu/bulletin/1999/april/spirit3.html.

Hinman, Holly. "Eureka! Leadership Institute Frequently Asked Questions." *Eureka Leadership Institute*. Accessed April 9, 2013. http://eurekaleadership.org/institute/faq.

Horton, Warren. "It All Began over Dinner." *Australian Library Journal* 45, no. 1 (1996): 12–16.

Infed. "Peter Senge and the Learning Organization." Accessed January 19, 2013. http://www.infed.org/thinkers/senge.htm.

Jordan, Peter J., Neal M. Ashkanasy, and Kaylene W. Ascough. "Emotional Intelligence in Organizational Behavior and Industrial-Organizational Psychology." In *the Science of Emotional Intelligence: Knowns and Unknowns*, edited by Gerald Matthews, Moshe Zeidner, and Richard D. Roberts, 356–75. Oxford: Oxford University Press.

Neely, Teresa Y., and Mark D. Winston. "Snowbird Leadership Institute: Leadership Development in the Profession." *College & Research Libraries* 60, no. 5 (1999): 412–25. http://crl.acrl.org/content/60/5/412.full.pdf+html.

Nichols, C. Allen. "Leaders: Born or Bred; Confessions from a Leadership Training Junkie." *Library Journal* (August 2002): 38–40.

Pearce, Craig L., and Henry P. Sims. "Shared Leadership: Toward a Multi-Level Theory of Leadership." In *Team Development*, edited by Michael M. Beyerlein, Douglas A. Johnson, and Susan T. Beyerlein, vol. 7, 115–39. Amsterdam, NY: JAI, 2000.

———. "Vertical Versus Shared Leadership as Predictors of the Effectiveness of Change Management Teams: An Examination of Aversive, Directive, Transactional, Transformational, and Empowering Leader Behaviors." *Group Dynamics: Theory, Research, and Practice* 6, no. 2 (2002): 172–97.

Schreiber, Becky, and John Shannon. "Key Leadership Competencies: Focus Questions for the Institute." *Library Leadership Institute at Snowbird Program Materials*. Schreiber Shannon Associates (1999).

———. "Developing Library Leaders for the 21st Century." *Journal of Library Administration* 32, no. 3/4 (2001): 37–60.

———. "Leadership Institutes & Consulting." Schreiber Shannon Associates. Accessed January 15, 2013. http://schreibershannon.com/Schreiber_Shannon_Associates/Leadership.html.

St. Hilaire, France. "Leadership Theories: Toward a Relational Model." Retrospective exam, Universite Laval, 2008. http://www.college-risquespsychosociaux-travail.fr/site/exam_retrospectif_final_fsth.pdf.

Summers, F. William, and Lorraine D. Summers. "Library Leadership 2000 and Beyond: Snowbird Leadership Institute." *Wilson Library Bulletin* 66 (1991): 38–41.

Wikipedia, "David A. Kolb." Accessed February 27, 2013,

———. "Warren Bennis." Accessed March 15, 2013.

Winston, Mark D., and Teresa Y. Neely. "Leadership Development and Public Libraries." *Public Library Quarterly* 19, no. 3 (2001): 15–32.

Zeidner, Moshe, Gerald Matthews, and Richard D. Roberts. *What We Know about Emotional Intelligence: How it Affects Learning, Work, Relationships, and Our Mental Health*. Cambridge, MA: MIT Press, 2009.

CHAPTER 15

Riding Tall:
Experiences with the TALL Texans Leadership Institute

Martha Rinn

THE TEXAS LIBRARY Association's TALL Texans Leadership Institute started over 20 years ago. Its primary mission is the development and promotion of leadership skills in mid-career library professionals and laypersons. This chapter provides an overview of the association's overall leadership program, recaps past participants' experiences and views of how the institute affected them as library managers and leaders, and investigates evaluation opportunities for the program.

Program History
In August 1991, Texas Library Association (TLA) President Cynthia Gray appointed an Ad Hoc TLA Leadership Development Program Committee to "investigate the feasibility of establishing a leadership development program to benefit the Texas library community."[1] This committee consisted of seven appointed members, six ex-officio members, and four members from the Texas State Library and the Texas Education Agency. The committee subsequently submitted a proposal to TLA's executive board recommending the TLA form the Texas Accelerated Library Leaders (TALL) program, which would feature an annual institute.

The ad hoc committee reviewed seven other leadership development programs that were in existence at the time. The review included both library-based programs and non-library programs connected to a chamber of commerce, a university faculty, and a Junior League chapter.[2] In its recommendation to found a leadership program, the ad hoc committee suggested the program's goal be "to provide ongoing, multifaceted leadership education opportunities for the TLA membership."[3]

The committee's proposal set out the following guiding principles in their recommendation for a TLA-based leadership program:

The program should accommodate a variety of participants and learning styles;

- the institute should be aimed at mid-career TLA members (both professional and paraprofessional) with at least five years experience in libraries;
- the program should strive for cultural diversity in content and participation; and
- the institute should be self-supporting, with the possibility of generating revenue in the future.[4]

The TALL Texans Leadership Development Program would consist of two to four leadership education opportunities per year plus an annual institute. The committee's proposal included a lengthy discussion of the budgetary philosophy of the program and a sample annual budget.[5]

The purposes of the annual institute included "instruction, mentoring, networking, and experiential learning."[6] The institute was fee-based and ran for five days. Participants included 25–30 attendees and four to six instructors and mentors. The proposal outlined characteristics of possible retreat centers or other locations for the institute and provided a list of possible locations. Attendees were expected to develop a personal action agenda including two to four leadership development opportunities per year for TLA members. Attendees were also expected to engage in at least two years of follow-up activities and meetings. This structure essentially set up a sustainable model for member involvement in creating leadership-training opportunities. The cycle of leadership education began with a limited number of participants at the institute, and then transferred to leadership opportunities for the TLA membership at large.[7]

The committee's proposal included discussion of key elements and requirements of establishing a vital, active program. Budgetary support as well as member involvement and commitment were cited as essential. The committee stated that an annual institute alone could not be the sole opportunity for leadership education offered by TLA. The importance of diversity in the program was stressed; not only must the program be inclusive of all types of libraries, but cultural diversity must also be honored and purposely supported. The networking piece of the program was seen as extremely important. To reinforce and support this facet, the committee urged that reunions of cohorts attending the institute be organized. The support of Texas's three American Library Association-accredited library schools was seen as vital. The committee also recognized the involvement of other organizations such as the Texas State Library and the Texas Education Agency as important to the success of the program. Recommendations for committees and councils to sustain and support the program were included in the committee's proposal.[8]

The committee's proposal made two additional recommendations to TLA leadership:

- TALL Texans Institute attendees should receive continuing education units for their participation, and
- TALL Texans Institute attendees should become eligible to earn graduate credit from one of Texas's accredited library schools for their participation.[9]

The program and institute continue to this day with very few adjustments to the original structure and goals proposed by the 1992 ad hoc committee.

TALL Texans Institute Curriculum

The program proposal set forth a detailed curriculum for the TALL Texans Leadership Development Institute. Six original objectives were assigned to the goal of "[fostering] leadership capabilities of attendees."[10] While the curriculum has naturally changed over the years to encompass new materials, the basic outline set forth in the proposal is essentially intact. Table 15.1 includes a recap of curriculum topics found in the proposal.

TABLE 15.1. Objectives and Curriculum of TALL Texans Institute	
Objective	Topics
Assess knowledge of and define ways to enhance personal leadership style and capabilities.	Leadership, vision, motivation, self-esteem
Learn tools, techniques, and interpersonal skills to enhance leadership capabilities.	Communication styles, communication assessment, team building, mentoring, networking
Learn to understand and apply political processes and decision-making alternatives to professional environment.	Political assessment and behavior, power, conflict management
Learn risk-assessment and problem-solving techniques to enhance professional risk-taking abilities.	Risk-taking behaviors, risk assessment, risk management
Develop a change-agent framework from which to approach professional leadership responsibilities.	Change agent behavior, leadership responsibilities
Clarify ethics issues affecting leadership behavior.	Personal world view, workplace values
Source: Ad Hoc TLA Leadership Development Program Committee, *Proposal to the Texas Library Association*, 7–9.	

The institute runs for four days in June, beginning on Monday afternoon and running through lunch on Friday. Each participant receives a set of comprehensive readings and working papers, which also includes bibliographies of works that are intended to be useful after the institute ends. The format of the program is a combination of discussion, lecture, group and individual work, testing, and free time.

Until recently the location of the institute was Harambe Oaks Ranch near the small town of Fisher in the Texas Hill Country. When this property changed hands, the institute moved to the Montserrat Retreat Center near Lake Dallas. The importance of locating the institute at an accessible retreat center with well-developed facilities was thoroughly described and researched in the original proposal.[11]

Jack Siggins and Maureen Sullivan have been the institute's instructors and facilitators for most of the program. Sullivan is a library consultant, active with many leadership educational institutes and institutions, and the 2012–2013 American Library Association president. Siggins has held library leadership positions at Yale, George Washington University, and other prestigious institutions. These two well-known and highly respected library leaders provide a significant draw for applicants and make acceptance to the institute viewed as a coveted accomplishment.

Literature Review

A 10-YEAR INTERNAL REVIEW

In late 2001, a subcommittee of the TLA Executive Board was formed for the purpose of assessing the TALL Texans Program. This subcommittee, in collaboration with the TLA Leadership Development Committee chair, conducted a focus group of TALL Texans past participants and posted questions to the TALL Texans listserv. Anecdotal evidence was also gathered in informal discussions between subcommittee members and TLA members at large. The results of these assessments were submitted to the executive board in April of 2003.[12] This 10-year review showed that the program was flourishing. At the time of the report the structure of TALL was very active, and leadership training opportunities related to the program had grown significantly.

Results of surveys and interviews indicated members were generally happy with the program and wanted to see it continue, but also had suggestions for future changes. Some questioned whether the application requirement of five years of experience in libraries was ideal. There was overall satisfaction with the trainers and general satisfaction with the curriculum. Some curriculum changes were suggested by members, including specific topics as well as the desire to be more intentional and careful about how the program strives to develop TLA leaders. Respondents felt that the process of applying to the TALL Texans Institute could be simplified and that the program should be promoted to library directors so that they could encourage staff to participate. Members did not see the need to open the program to out-of-state mentors, although some felt TALL Texan alumni might be invited to mentor even if currently living out of state. Others stated that TLA needed a much wider variety of leadership training opportunities, including advanced programs or programs aimed at directors. There was also a perception that TALL alumni should be utilized more heavily, including an idea for sharing of online action plans via "study circles."[13]

TEXAS LIBRARY JOURNAL AND TALL TEXANS

Texas Library Journal (*TLJ*), the in-house publication of TLA, has included many articles over the years about the program, the institute, and the individuals who participate in the annual institute cohorts. In all, 13 articles about various aspects of the TALL Texans Program have appeared in *TLJ* since the program began.[14]

The Winter 1999 issue of *TLJ* was dedicated to leadership stories. The issue showcased the TALL program and institute in four articles. It also included a reprint of an article by Pat Hawthorne entitled, "Leadership in the Lone Star State: The TALL Texans Leadership Development Institute." Originally published in *The Southeastern Librarian* in 1998, it provided an overview of the program and institute.[15] The Winter 1999 *TLJ* issue also included articles by 1999 institute attendees Tish Mulkey (mentor) and Tina Oswald (participant).[16] One article included e-mail interviews with five of the original persons involved in the creation and inception of the program. Interviewees included Dale Cluff, Bonnie Juergens, Mary Lankford, James Stewart, and June Kahler Berry.[17] In this article all agreed that the institute was producing library leaders for the state of Texas. There was also agreement that institute graduates generally showed enhanced leadership skills and greater involvement in leadership roles in TLA and at their home institutions. There was a call for more formal efforts to map TLA participation and leadership to institute attendance. There was also agreement that funding for the institute could be problematic. Interviewees noted that it was an annual struggle to try to gather funding from TLA unit contributions, outside sources such as vendors and corporations, and the relatively modest fee charged to participants. Berry, who was the project manager for the institute at the time of the interviews, wrote that once these sources were fully tapped, TLA made up the difference to complete funding. She saw this as evidence of the association's commitment to leadership development within its own ranks. Bonnie Juergens wrote that she would like to see an endowment established that would underwrite the institute and ensure that it could continue into the future.[18]

OTHER PUBLICATIONS

In library literature, TALL is often cited as an exemplary leadership program. Florence M. Mason and Louella V. Wetherbee included the TALL Texans program in a 2004 article that analyzed library leadership programs.[19] The authors state that TALL Texans is one of several program that use mentors, which the authors characterize as "effective development tools."[20] The authors state that mentors are also used by the UCLA Fellows Program, the Aurora Leadership Institute, the Northern Exposure to Leadership Program, and the Snowbird Institute. Mason and Wetherbee write that the TALL Texans' personal action agenda is a personal growth device that can "help participants to develop self-understanding through an exploration of their personal values and interests."[21] Other programs using such devices are Outward Bound and the ACRL/Harvard Program. TALL Texans is also characterized as one of several programs that "foster networking with other colleagues and extending personal development through activities beyond the classroom."[22] The authors name UCLA Fellows and the Snowbird Institute as two other examples of programs that include post-institute activities.[23]

The TALL Texans Leadership Development Institute is included on the American Library Association's "Library Leadership Training Resources" page.[24] In 2002, Berry wrote an article about the institute for *Interface*, a publication of the Association of Specialized & Cooperative Library Agencies.[25] Susan E. Cleyle and Louise M. McGillis describe the program and categorize it as "successfully identifying and fulfilling a continuing education need."[26] The institute also appears in a variety of books containing lists of library leadership programs, including *Continuing Professional Development* by Ann Ritchie; *Librarian's Career Guidebook*, Priscilla K. Schontz, ed.; *LIS Career Sourcebook* by G. Kim Dority; *Middle Management in Academic and Public Libraries* by Tom Diamond; and *Leadership in the Library and Information Sciences*, Mark D. Winston, ed.[27]

Online references to TALL Texans show that the institute is an important milestone in many individuals' careers. Eric Frierson states that the institute is "the most valuable experience I have had."[28] Lonnie Beene also writes of a positive experience at the 1999 institute, describing it as "a high point of what continues to be a very satisfying career."[29]

Personal Experiences with the TALL Institute

THE AUTHOR'S EXPERIENCE

Over the years I heard very good things about the institute and the overall program. My first library supervisor, who was a director at a public library, was heavily involved with TLA. Through her I was exposed to many aspects of the state association. She also encouraged me to get involved professionally and remain active in the profession after I obtained my library master's degree in 1990. When I became an academic library director in 2002, I felt the time was right for me to apply to attend the TALL Texans Institute. With the encouragement of my dean and my provost, I was accepted for the 2003 institute.

The curriculum, instructors, and mentors were highly engaging, and the institute was structured to accommodate a variety of learning styles. I had taken a library administration class in graduate school, but it was an introductory course that did not particularly concentrate on leadership. Learning about the differences between management and leadership was eye opening to me. The curriculum explored a variety of management styles and included exercises that allowed us to learn about these styles and see how they might apply in our own lives. The institute was all I expected and more; a recap of the institute agenda for my cohort is included in table 15.2.

TABLE 15.2. Agenda, 2003 TALL Texans Leadership Development Institute

Day	Agenda Element
Day 1	Introduction and overview
	Purpose and goals; schedule and activities review; and learning approach and resources
	Introduction of mentors and participants
	"Leadership in Libraries Today: Challenges and Opportunities"
	Mentor Discussion: Our Careers
Day 2	Community Review
	Understanding Your Work and Leadership Styles
	Situational leadership theory; Assessing your style and preferences; and Improving your effectiveness as a leader
	Inter
	Key components for effective communication; Basic skills and techniques; and Skill practice: active listening and feedback
	Using Power and Influence
	Understanding personal power and styles of influence
	TLA: An Overview of the Structure
	Mentor Discussion: Power and Influence in TLA

TABLE 15.2. Agenda, 2003 TALL Texans Leadership Development Institute

Day	Agenda Element
Day 3	Community Review
	Risk Taking
	Factors in risk taking; A process for making risky decisions
	Managing Differences
	Diagnosing sources of conflict and disagreement; Individual responses to conflict; and Negotiating skills
	Working with Groups and Teams
	Stages of group development; Characteristics of effective teams; and Consensus decision making
	Introduction to Personal Action Agenda
	Zephering and Other Activities
	Free time to enjoy the retreat center (hike, swim, read, relax) or to begin work on the Personal Action Agenda
Day 4	Community Review
	Transforming Libraries: Creating a Culture of Commitment and High Performance
	Key elements in a culture of commitment; The organization as a system; and Building trust
	Creating a Shared Vision
	Developing Others; Understanding motivation; and Coaching and mentoring
	Mentor Discussions: Topics of Interest
Day 5	Community Review
	Achieving Your Potential: Personal Planning
	Developing commitment to change; and Planning your development
	Guidelines for Continuing Your Leadership Development
	Summary and Closure

Source: Siggins and Sullivan, "TALL Texans Leadership Development Institute Agenda."

The curriculum devoted a significant amount of time to helping us identify our own preferred leadership styles. All attendees completed a DiSC personality profile assessment.[30] The results of this assessment were used to help us understand our own strengths, tendencies, and preferences. It was very helpful to receive confirmation of my own strengths and to get affirmation that there is no one right way to lead. Conversely, it was just as beneficial to learn about areas in which I was not as strong, and it was encouraging to be given tools to assist in my personal development of these areas. I found my DiSC results to be in alignment with my results from an earlier Myers-Briggs assessment, which for me reinforced the validity of the results of the DiSC profile assessment.[31] DiSC results were used as a reference for each attendee as the remainder of the curriculum unfolded.

One of the leadership models included in the curriculum was the situational model, which I found to be a most useful and pragmatic means of approaching leadership.[32] As I have moved into positions of increasing responsibility and leadership I have had many opportunities to lead groups of people and to follow other leaders. My experiences have shown me that every team or group has its own personality, some of which can be attributed to what Paul Hersey and Kenneth Blanchard called follower readiness.[33] The ability to map this readiness to a particular leadership style is very useful. I feel that the utilization of a situational leadership model is a very good choice for the TALL Texans curriculum.

The sections on interpersonal communication and managing differences and conflict were especially helpful to me. After attending the institute I went home with a personal plan for how I would develop my own skills in these areas, which I felt were somewhat weak. Intentional development of my communication and conflict management skills has been very useful to me as the leader of a variety of faculty committees at my institution and in leadership positions within and outside of the profession. I find it interesting that developing these specific skills has also helped me in my roles as undergraduate professor and academic advisor. The actual practice sessions we conducted on active listening, providing constructive feedback, and diagnosing and negotiating conflict were valuable learning experiences for me.

I especially enjoyed and benefited from the section on risk taking. I am naturally a risk-averse person, so learning to see risk taking as potentially beneficial was enlightening. The institute even provided some tools to use in processing risky decisions and making good choices in such situations. I have used these skills often in negotiating quickly evolving library landscapes. For example, some situations where I have applied the risk-taking lessons have been when called upon to lead an orderly migration to electronic resources. I am also a team leader responsible for planning and implementing a strategic move to a more holistic learning environment in the library. This new environment actively embraces and integrates what many would consider non-library academic support services.

One requirement of attending the institute that may seem minor to some was quite daunting to me. The dormitory-style housing at the institute required each attendee to room together with two others. As a 51-year-old who had not lived in a group setting for nearly 30 years, the prospect of living in one room with two strangers for four days was uncomfortable. However, after getting settled in and beginning actual sessions I almost immediately saw the reasoning and logic behind forcing us to bond with our cohort in this manner. I was matched with a school librarian and a public librarian; this method of pairing was very effective since it facilitated the exchange of ideas and allowed me to gain valuable insights from my non-academic library colleagues. One of the strengths of the institute and the overall program is the fact that it serves all types of libraries. The lesson I took away from this feature of the institute was to be open-minded and ready to learn from others who might be in different settings from my own.

The long-term effect of the institute was to empower me to remain very active in the library profession. I have served on TLA conference program and local arrangements committees, presented papers at conferences, served on library software user group boards, served as a regional consortium president, served on statewide library working groups and task forces, and participated in many other professional activities that benefit the profession and my institution. When called upon, I also served as an accreditation team member for our regional accrediting body, the Southern Association of Colleges and Schools Commission on Colleges. I truly believe that the TALL Texans Institute equipped me with the unique tools I needed to stay on track and productive in the library profession and in my position at an academic library.

OTHERS' EXPERIENCES

I conducted an informal survey of 10 individuals who were institute alumni and mentors and one current officer of the TALL Texans Round Table unit of TLA.[34] All respondents had participated in the institute at various times from 1997 through 2007. Some remain active in the Round Table.

As a whole, the respondents found their experiences to be very positive. All could describe their post-institute action plan and report whether it was implemented. All reported continued involvement with TLA including various leadership roles at some point after the institute. Every responding participant reported that knowledge gained at the institute had helped them advance in their own professional careers. Some cited personal growth that was a result of insights gained through the institute. Others described maintaining relationships with mentors and pursuing additional advanced degrees due to their experience at the institute. Still others talked about how the institute allowed them to advance at work, in some cases even to the surprise of skeptical supervisors who eventually became supporters after seeing the effects of the institute on the participant.

The survey participants did not have suggestions for major changes to the institute. However, three of the alumni who had attended 10 years or more in the past commented that they had begun to feel somewhat isolated from the program and the TALL Round Table that functions within TLA. These respondents wanted to see more outreach to institute alumni.

Leadership Theories and TALL Texans

In their 2004 article "Learning to Lead," Mason and Wetherbee describe a shift in thinking about leadership that began in the 1970s and 1980s. Good leaders began to be viewed as fulfilling visionary, inspirational roles rather than strict, top-down managerial roles.[35] Mason and Wetherbee described some differences between management and leadership:

> Leaders are more than managers… Management is about *what* things get done, while leadership is about *how* things get done. Management involves accomplishing tasks, while leadership involves influencing and guiding a course of action. Management is usually understood as a skill set that includes planning, organizing, directing, and managing workers and work activities. Leadership, on the other hand, includes the ability to create a vision of the future, engage others in the cocreation and/or perfection of that

vision, describe it in a compelling and powerful manner, and create an environment where stakeholders inside and outside the organization work together productively and effectively to implement the vision successfully.[36]

This new way of thinking about leadership began to take hold. Increased interest in library leadership programs followed in the 1990s, which is the time TALL Texans was created. TALL Texans embraces behavioral, transformative, and transactional leadership models and styles. First and foremost, TALL Texans is grounded in the behavioral theory of leadership, which states that leadership ability is not necessarily an innate talent. This grounding is not unique to TALL Texans; it would be a rare leadership development program that is not rooted in the belief that leadership skills can be acquired and learned.

The TALL Texans curriculum and institute structure actively facilitate the pragmatic application of behavioral leadership theory. Institute participants are introduced early on to the situational leadership model developed by Hersey and Blanchard. Situational leadership theory posits that a leader must employ a variety of leadership styles as he or she adapts to different situations and groups of followers. Situational leadership depends on a team's readiness to perform a given set of tasks and on the leader's ability to be flexible in using the best style for each specific situation. The act of increasing team members' readiness levels can even be part of the situational model as the leader finds ways to support followers in pursuing their own development. This model of leadership encourages a leader to move away from what Hersey and Blanchard call "task behavior," which is managerial and supervisory, to the preferred method of "relationship behavior," which casts the leader as facilitator and coach and encourages autonomy and responsibility in subordinates.[37]

Hersey and Blanchard created a tool that leaders can use to assess the appropriate leadership style for a given situation. This tool features a "follower readiness" continuum that a leader aligns with one of four specific styles or approaches arranged in a bell curve. Follower readiness can range from low (immature) to high (mature). Leadership styles include directing or telling (low readiness); selling or coaching (moderately low readiness); participating or supporting (moderately high readiness); or delegating (high readiness).[38]

Transformational leadership theory also finds a place in the TALL Texans program. Bernard M. Bass described transformational leadership as

> Superior leadership performance—transformational leadership—occurs when leaders broaden and elevate the interests of their employees, when they generate awareness and acceptance of the purposes and mission of the group, and when they stir their employees to look beyond their own self-interest for the good of the group.[39]

Mason and Wetherbee state that "transformational leaders lead by motivating others and by appealing to higher ideals and moral values."[40] They add that "key transformational skills for leaders are long-term vision, empowerment, and coaching" as well as the ability to create trust.[41]

The TALL Texans curriculum heavily emphasizes the attainment of skills meant to assist participants in moving toward the kind of transformational leadership style described by Bass and Mason and Wetherbee. Curriculum elements dealing with understanding interpersonal communication, building trust, developing others, coaching or mentoring, negotiating, managing conflict, recognizing and honoring differences, and engaging in consensus decision making move participants toward a transformational leadership model.

The TALL Texans curriculum also uses Fran Rees's L.E.A.D. model, which embodies aspects of Hersey and Blanchard's situational leadership theory.[42] Rees's model focuses more specifically on the leader's attributes and does not stress the follower readiness continuum found in Hersey and Blanchard's theory. The title acronym (L.E.A.D.) stands for *lead* with a clear purpose, *empower* to participate, *aim* for consensus, and *direct* the process. Rees states that "styles of leadership can be placed on a continuum, with a *controlling* style at one end and a *facilitating* style at the other."[43] Rees makes the following observation:

> In many organizations... the trend is away from controlling leadership and toward facilitative leadership, in which leaders and subordinates share the responsibilities of making decisions, planning to implement decisions, and

carrying out those plans. The reason for the trend is that today's organizations, with their emphases on teamwork, challenge, and motivation, have found that employees are more motivated and productive if they are allowed to share in the plans and decisions that affect them and their work.[44]

Rees commends the facilitative style of leadership as bringing about superlative results because followers become stakeholders as they buy into a shared vision and goals. Rees describes a facilitative leader's activities as listen, question, direct process, coach, teach, build consensus, share in goal setting and decision making, and empower others.[45] The TALL Texans curriculum intentionally and deeply addresses most of these roles with units on communication, active listening and feedback, consensus in decision making, cultures of commitment, trust building, creating shared vision, understanding motivation, and coaching and mentoring.

TALL Texans in the Context of Other Programs

The Ad Hoc TLA Leadership Development Program Committee was strongly committed to an immersion-style institute. In fact, all of the library leadership programs that were reviewed by the committee were residential in nature.[46] The importance the committee placed on an immersion, residential experience can be seen in their proposal, which goes into great detail describing the location and requirements of the retreat setting.

An immersion experience continues to be a hallmark of many library leadership programs. Teresa Y. Neely reported that "the residential nature is a big plus for participants" at many of the institutes she included in her research on the Association of Research Libraries (ARL) Leadership and Career Development Program (LCDP).[47] In 2004, Mason and Wetherbee identified 31 existing library leadership programs and reported on the programs' attributes. Of these 31 programs, 28 were identified with a program mode of "residential" while only three were classified as "workshop."[48]

Library leadership programs are not alone in utilizing immersion as a delivery technique. While language programs might be the best-known users of immersion learning, other disciplines also value this mode of delivery.[49] From business to education, the virtues of an immersion program as an educational tool are widely embraced. In 2006, Dan Gjelten and Teresa

Fishel provided an overview of their experiences at the ACRL/Harvard Institute and the Frye Institute. Speaking of the opportunity for networking and building relationships with other participants, they stated that "both programs are 'immersion experiences' and provide the opportunity to reflect on these issues away from the daily operational grind of the office."[50] They add that "because the Frye Institute is a longer immersion (two weeks as opposed to one week for ACRL/Harvard), one is likely to develop closer connections with fellow participants."[51] Gjelten and Fishel make an additional observation about the result of participating in these institutes, "We have redefined ourselves in a growing sense of our role: from 'I'm a reference librarian' to 'I'm a librarian' to 'I'm an educator in support of the academic enterprise.' This movement *away* from specialization has brought us closer to the larger vision of the world in which we work."[52]

Anthony Andenoro and Adrian Popa have raised questions about the viability of immersion programs in a time when governmental funding is decreasing. Although they are specifically writing about immersion programs related to global studies, this same question can be asked about library leadership immersion programs. Andenoro and Popa call on the providers of immersion experiences to utilize new methodologies and innovative approaches to bring participants together outside of a full immersion.[53] While technological or other methods could be employed to supplement the TALL Texans Institute experience or improve outreach activities, the TALL Texans Institute was intentionally set up as an immersion experience. Given the program's continued ability to recruit participants as well as the continued use of an immersion model by other library leadership programs, for the present the benefits of immersion appear to outweigh potential costs.

Conclusion

PROGRAM IMPROVEMENTS AND VIABILITY

The TALL Texans Leadership Development Program appears to be robust and there is evidence that it continues to meet its original objectives. The alumni, mentors, and officers contacted for this study expressed contentment with the program and institute. Informal survey results revealed a desire among long-term alumni for more connection and contact with the program. The institute itself is considered a desirable activity for Texas library staff and supporters. However, one gets the sense that many Texas librarians believe that TLA's leadership program is limited to participation in the institute. The TALL Texans Round Table while quite active and regularly sponsors programming and events at TLA's Annual Conferences, may benefit from more intentional engagement of alumni to enhance these efforts and raise the profile of the overall program for non-Round Table members. After this many years of successful institutes, TLA has a pool of potential alumni mentors. It is not financially feasible to bring equal numbers of mentors and participants to the institute each summer. However, there has been positive movement in this direction in the form of a one-day reunion of TALL Texans alumni, which is scheduled to take place the day before the current institute. The reunions are held at the institute locale and include programming and an opportunity for alumni to stay overnight at the retreat center. Perhaps additional less formal mentoring opportunities could be set up to utilize the skills of alumni outside of attending the actual institute.

Another recommendation noted earlier in this article was the possible formation of an endowment to support the program. A scholarship endowment has been established in memory of June Kahler Berry, coordinator of the TALL Texans Institute from 1994–2003. Alumni of the institute led the efforts to raise funds to create this endowment. The proceeds from this endowment are distributed annually to selected institute attendees in the form of scholarships. Officers of the TALL Texans Round Table and the current institute coordinator distribute these funds based on need as identified from information acquired through the application process. There is usually enough money to provide one or more scholarships to pay a portion of the institute fee. However, the endowment is not large enough to underwrite all costs of the institute (Ted Wanner, pers. comm.).[54] The TALL Texans Program webpage states that the "budget for the entire program is approximately $45,000, with some variation year to year. TLA member unit contributions support 60 percent of the expenses, with individual registrations 33 percent, and the remainder from DEMCO [sic] corporate sponsor."[55] As recommended in the original leadership program proposal, the TALL Program continues to intentionally keep participants' costs at a low, stable level. This bolsters the program's goal of diversity by making the institute more affordable for a wide variety of individuals from all types of libraries. As of 2013, the program is very fortunate to enjoy loyal support from corporate sponsor Demco, but in an uncertain economy such sponsorships sometimes become unsustainable. An endowment could form a reliable under-pinning that would allow the institute to continue to function at its current level even in lean times. This suggestion may carry extra weight if funding becomes an insurmountable issue for prospective participants.

A potential challenge might come about if long-time instructors Siggins and Sullivan are no longer available to facilitate the institute. A succession plan for such an eventuality would be advisable.

RESEARCH OPPORTUNITIES

Mary Jo Romaniuk and Ken Haycock point out that leadership programs must have specific goals and objectives if their success is to be evaluated in meaningful ways.[56] Fortunately, the founders of TALL Texans were insightful enough to lay out clear goals, objectives, and strategies in the original proposal to create the program. However, Romaniuk and Haycock go on to state that even when programs have good theoretical bases, "the library sector has had difficulty establishing whether leadership development interventions have made a sustained difference to the organizations and the library community."[57] It appears that the only attempt so far to evaluate the effectiveness of the TALL Texans program, the ten-year follow-up "TALL Review," also might have fallen short of proving the program's effect on change.[58] For the "Tall Review," surveys, focus groups, and anecdotal comments were used to assess the success of the program at the 10-year mark. However, some assumptions of causality were erroneously made in the study. For example, at the 2002 TLA Annual Assembly a focus group was convened. The review states that 85 percent of the 100 focus group attendees were TALL Texans or mentors, while 15 percent were interested in applying or mentoring. The review uses these statistics as indications of the program's success. However, while this nice-sized turnout shows continued interest in TALL Texans, it does not measure or prove change that might have occurred as a result of the TALL Texans Institute. No studies have been performed to prove a causal connection between participation and later activities and successes within TLA or the participants' professional lives.

TALL Texans is far from alone in proving the direct effects of its leadership institute on post-participation actions. Romaniuk and Haycock state that "unfortunately, only one of the library leadership programs, Executive Leadership Institute of the Urban Libraries Council in the USA, has demonstrated any long term community or organizational impacts."[59] They observe that "many leadership programs do not currently provide mechanism for ongoing evaluation, thus program objectives matched to outcomes are not evidenced across the discipline" and conclude their article by saying that "this paper proposes research-based program foundations to support successful outcomes."[60]

Given the fact that TALL Texans has solid, established goals, the program is well positioned to carry out just this kind of research. TLA may consider replicating and expanding the survey conducted by Neely in her 2007 study of the ARL program. Neely used a survey instrument developed for evaluation of the Snowbird Leadership Institute. This same survey has been used in multiple studies, allowing for comparisons with other programs. While the survey concentrates on participants' perceptions, it also includes some revealing demographic data with regard to participants' rise into higher-level positions. The survey asked participants to report their job titles at the time of participating in LCDP and at the time of the survey. Results revealed "a significant decrease in the number of positions with titles categorized by the researcher as 'librarian' (58 percent), and 'coordinator'; (67 percent), and a marked increase in the number of position titles categorized as 'department or branch head' (83 percent), 'assistant or associate dean or director' (200 percent) and 'dean or director' (500 percent)."[61] However, Neely adds that

> without further more individualized inquiry, it is difficult to directly correlate participation in LCDP to these findings. We could assume that program participants would have attained higher position levels without program participation; however, this shift in the number of participants reporting higher level position titles is remarkable and should not be discounted.[62]

Neely goes on to report that 42 percent of respondents said that their own professional progress would have been "different" if they had not participated in the program.[63] TLA could take this research a step further by conducting the survey but following up with the "individualized inquiries" noted by Neely in an attempt to prove that participation in the TALL Texans Institute impacted participants' career paths.[64]

The TALL Texans Leadership Development Program continues to be a popular, vibrant program that develops Texas library leaders. The TALL

Texans Round Table is well established, and as a successful unit of TLA, it continues to provide structure and leadership for the program and institute. The prospects for continued existence of this acclaimed and highly useful program are good. The Texas library community should continue to enjoy the benefits of this program for many years to come. Deeper, more formal research should be conducted to prove that the established goals of the TALL Texans Institute are being met.

Notes

1. Ad Hoc TLA Leadership Development Program Committee, *Proposal to the Texas Library Association*, 3.
2. Ibid., Appendix I.
3. Ibid., 3.
4. Ibid.
5. Ibid., 15.
6. Ibid., 4.
7. Ibid., 13, Appendix II.
8. Ibid., 5.
9. Ibid., 4–6, 10.
10. Ibid., 6.
11. Ibid., 13.
12. TLA Executive Board Subcommittee, "TALL Review."
13. Ibid., 14.
14. "2005 TALL Texans Leadership Development Institute," 124; Cleyle and McGillis, "Conversation with TALL Texans Pioneers"; Cunningham, "Report on the TALL Texans"; Homick, "Library Leadership Training Texas Style"; Moore, "In the Land of Giants"; Mulkey, "A Week out of Time"; Oswald, "TALL Texans"; Perry and Brannon, "TALL Texans Leadership Institute"; Schill, "Sowing the Seeds of Leadership"; "Tall Texans Class of 2010"; Trost, "Under the Oaks"; Vera, "TALL Texans Leadership Conference"; and Wanner, "Montserrat Retreat Center."
15. Hawthorne, "Leadership in the Lone Star State."
16. Mulkey, "A Week Out of Time"; Oswald, "TALL Texans."
17. Cleyle and McGillis, "Conversation with TALL Texans Pioneers."
18. Ibid., 167–68.
19. Mason and Wetherbee, "Learning to Lead," 206.
20. Ibid.
21. Ibid.
22. Ibid., 206–07.

23. Ibid.
24. "Library Leadership Training Resources," American Library Association.
25. Berry, "Texas-Sized Leadership."
26. Cleyle and McGillis, *Last One Out Turn Off the Lights,* 186–87.
27. See "Sources Consulted" in these books.
28. Frierson, "Leading With Heart."
29. Beene, "Learning Resource Center Director," 169.
30. Goodman, "The Everything DiSC Profile vs. DiSC Classic Profiles."
31. Myers-Briggs Type Indicator (MBTI) is a personality inventory instrument. More information may be found at http://www.myersbriggs.org/my-mbti-personality-type/mbti-basics/.
32. The situational leadership model was developed by Paul Hersey and Kenneth Blanchard. It refers to the leader adapting their style to their followers. For more information see Hersey and Blanchard, "Situational Leadership."
33. Hersey and Blanchard, "Situational Leadership."
34. This survey received IRB approval from the Texas Lutheran University Institutional Review Board.
35. Mason and Wetherbee, "Learning to Lead," 189–90.
36. Ibid., 190
37. Hersey and Blanchard, "Situational Leadership."
38. Ibid.
39. Bass, "From Transactional to Transformational Leadership."
40. Mason and Wetherbee, "Learning to Lead," 190.
41. Ibid.
42. Rees, "From Controlling to Facilitating."
43. Ibid., 213.
44. Ibid.
45. Ibid., 214.
46. Ad Hoc TLA Leadership Development Committee, *Proposal to the Texas Library Association,* Appendix I. Library leadership programs reviewed by the committee included the Michigan Library Association Leadership Academy (seven-day residential), the New Jersey Library Leadership Institute (five-day residential), the Snowbird Leadership Institute (six-day residential), and the UCLA Fellows Program (three-week residential).
47. Neely, "Assessing Diversity Initiatives," 831.
48. Mason and Wetherbee, "Learning To Lead," 197–202.
49. Examples located in a general Internet search included the Harvard Business School's Field Immersion Experiences for Leadership Development; John Carroll University's multidisciplinary Immersion Experience Program; the American Management Association's Course for Presidents & CEOs; the

Center for Creative Leadership's Leadership at the Pea; the Association of
College & Research Libraries' Information Literacy Immersion Program;
and the more general Dale Carnegie Immersion Program in Effective Leadership and Communication.

50. Gjelten and Fishel, "Developing Leaders and Transforming Libraries."
51. Ibid., 411.
52. Ibid., 412.
53. Andenoro and Popa, "Introduction," 87.
54. "June Kahler Berry Endowment," Texas Library Association.
55. "TALL Texans Program," Texas Library Association.
56. Romaniuk and Haycock, "Designing and Evaluating Library Leadership Programs," 36.
57. Ibid., 33.
58. TLA Executive Board Subcommittee, "TALL Review."
59. Romaniuk and Haycock, "Designing and Evaluating Library Leadership Programs," 33.
60. Ibid., 37–38.
61. Neely, "Assessing Diversity Initiatives," 14.
62. Ibid.
63. Ibid.
64. Ibid.

Bibliography

"2005 TALL Texans Leadership Development Institute." *Texas Library Journal* 80, no. 3 (2004): 124.

Ad Hoc TLA Leadership Development Program Committee. "Proposal to the Texas Library Association Executive Board Concerning Development of a TLA Leadership Development Program." Austin, TX: Texas Library Association, 1992.

American Library Association. Library Leadership Training Resources. Accessed January 22, 2013. http://www.ala.org/offices/hrdr/abouthrdr/hrdrliaison-comm/otld/leadershiptraining

Beene, Lonnie. "Learning Resources Center Director." In A *Day in the Life: Career Options in Library and Information Science*, edited by Priscilla K. Shontz and Richard A Murray, 167–70. Westport, CT: Libraries Unlimited, 2007.

Berry, June Kahler. "Texas Accelerated Library Leaders: TALL Texans." *Public Libraries* 39, no. 6 (2000): 311–13.

———. "Texas-Sized Leadership." *Interface* 24, no. 1 (2002).

Cleyle, Susan E., and Louise M. McGillis. *Last One Out Turn Off the Lights: Is This the Future of American and Canadian Libraries?* Lanham, MD: Scarecrow Press, 2005.

Cunningham, Nancy. "Report on the TALL Texans Leadership Development Institute, Harambe Oaks." *Texas Library Journal* 73, no. 3 (1997): 123–24.

Diamond, Tom, ed. *Middle Management in Academic and Public Libraries.* Santa Barbara, CA: ABC-CLIO, 2011.

Dority, G. Kim. *LIS Career Sourcebook: Managing and Maximizing Every Step of Your Career.* San Barbara, CA: Libraries Unlimited, 2012.

Frierson, Eric. "Leading with Heart." *In the Library with the Lead Pipe.* August 10, 2011. http://www.inthelibrarywiththeleadpipe.org/2011/leading-with-heart/.

Goodman, John C. "The Everything DiSC Profile vs. DiSC Classic Profiles." Access March 4, 2013. http://www.internalchange.com/what-is-disc.htm.

Hawthorne, Pat. "Leadership in the Lone Star State: the TALL Texans Leadership Development Institute." *Southeastern Librarian* 47, no. 4 (1998): 27–29.

Hersey, Paul, and Kenneth H. Blanchard. "Situational Leadership: A Summary." SSPC. 2011. Accessed June 22, 2015. http://www.researchgate.net/publictopics.PublicPostFileLoader.html?id=5389104cd4c-11879228b4685&key=60b7d5389104c56e57.

Homick, Ron. "Library Leadership Training Texas Style: TALL Texans." *Texas Library Journal* 69 (1993): 121–24.

Mason, Florence M., and Louella V. Wetherbee. "Learning to Lead: An Analysis of Current Training Programs for Library Leadership." *Library Trends* 53, no. 1 (2004): 187–217.

Moore, JoAnne. "In the Land of Giants: A Mentor's Experience With TALL Texans." *Texas Library Journal* 73, no. 3 (1997): 125.

Mulkey, Tish. "A Week Out of Time: A Mentor's Reflection on the TALL Texans Institute 1999." *Texas Library Journal* 75, no. 4 (1999): 160–62.

Neely, Teresa Y. "Assessing Diversity Initiatives: The ARL Library Leadership and Career Development Program." *Journal of Library Administration* 49, no. 8 (2009): 811–35.

Oswald, Tina. "TALL Texans: It's a Kick!" *Texas Library Journal* 75, no. 4 (1999): 164–65.

Perry, Beth, and Sian Brannon. "TALL Texans Leadership Institute." *Texas Library Journal* 81, no. 3 (2005): 110–13.

Ritchie, Ann. *Continuing Professional Development: Pathways to Leadership in the Library and Information World.* Munich: K. G. Sauer, 2007.

Schill, Victor. "Sowing the Seeds of Leadership." *Texas Library Journal* 73, no. 3 (Fall 1997): 122–23.

Schontz, Priscilla K., ed. *Librarian's Career Guidebook*. Lanham, MD: Scarecrow Press, 2004.

Siggins, Jack, and Maureen Sullivan. "TALL Texans Leadership Development Institute Agenda." June 2003. "TALL Texans Class of 2010." *Texas Library Journal* 86, no. 1 (2010): 36.

Texas Library Association. "June Kahler Berry Endowment." Accessed June 23, 2015. http://www.txla.org/sites/tla/files/CE/docs/June_Kahler_Berry_Endowment.doc.

———. TALL Texans Program. Last modified April 14, 2011. http://www.txla.org/talltexansprogram.

TLA Executive Board Subcommittee. "TALL Review... Ten Years of So of TALL." Austin, TX: Texas Library Association, April 2003.

Trost, Tess. "Under the Oaks." *Texas Library Journal* 73, no. 3 (1997): 124–25.

Vera, Pat. "TALL Texans Leadership Conference at Harambe Oaks." *Texas Library Journal* 72 (1996): 192–93.

Wanner, Ted. "Montserrat Retreat Center to Welcome TALL Texans Again in 2010." *Texas Library Journal* 85, no. 3 (2009): 98–99.

Winston, Mark D., ed. *Leadership in the Library and Information Sciences: Theory and Practice*. New York: Haworth Press, 2001.

PART 5

Programs that Include Librarians among the Participants

CHAPTER 16

The Women's Leadership Institute:
Developing Library Leaders

Carolyn Carpan

I HAD THE opportunity to participate in the third annual Women's Leadership Institute, cosponsored by the Association of College and Research Libraries (ACRL) along with six other organizations in December 2008.[1] The purpose of the Women's Leadership Institute "is to give women in managerial positions in higher education the opportunity to explore the factors that influence their effectiveness at home and at work."[2] The institute hosts women from professional associations across many functional areas in higher education.

A description of the institute states,

> The Women's Leadership Institute is the premier program for women leaders across campus. The program is held at a resort-style location to maximize learning and minimize distractions, and is designed for women who aspire to new leadership positions on campus. The institute features a curriculum with an overall focus on building the next generation of leaders in higher education administra-

tion and student affairs. This is a wonderful program for women of all ages to come together to learn and network with one another, forming bonds that will last a lifetime.[3]

The institute opened with a keynote address, followed by two full days of educational seminars, with each session offered twice during the day. Programs focused on mentoring and coaching, reframing power and influence, leadership for change, thinking strategically, life-work balance, men and women at work, and advancing your career. Evening learning activities and speakers were available and a closing keynote wrapped up the event.

The Women's Leadership Institute Program

The program began with a keynote address, "Women and the Power of Negotiation: Learning to Ask," by Sara Laschever, coauthor of the book *Women Don't Ask*.[4] Laschever stated that women are much less likely than men to use negotiation as a tool to improve their circumstances at work, and the result for women is often lost wages and delayed career advancement. We received copies of *Women Don't Ask*. To learn more about negotiation techniques, I bought Linda Babcock and Laschever's follow-up book titled *Ask For It*, which provides women with strategies for negotiating what they want and need in their personal and professional lives. Babcock and Laschever outline several negotiation strategies including best alternative to a negotiated agreement (BATNA), reservation value (RV) or bottom line, contract zone or difference between each negotiator's bottom line, and target value or aspiration value.[5] I have used the negotiation strategies in *Ask For It* to negotiate salary utilizing both the reservation and target value strategies, and I found the reservation value to be more successful. I have also obtained opportunities for professional development simply by asking and letting my supervisors know I am open to learning new ways to do my work. I also used the BATNA strategy to determine that it was time to leave a position and obtain a new and similar position in a larger organization that offered me more opportunities. I often reread Babcock and Laschever's books, and I have recommended them to colleagues and direct reports.

Kathryn Deiss, content strategist for the Association of College and Research Libraries, introduced me to the concept of coaching in her program titled "Mentoring and Coaching: Critical Power Relationships." While I understood mentoring as a concept, the idea that as a leader I should also be a coach was new for me. Mentors take an interest in someone else's growth and development and provide guidance based on their experience, while coaches focus on helping others achieve long-term excellent performance, self-correction, and self-generation through conversations focused on changing behaviors.

Lynn M. Gangone, dean of The Women's College of the University of Denver, presented a session on reframing power and influence. Gangone noted that the ways in which women act, think, look, sound, respond, and market themselves as well as their refusal to "play the game" like men, holds them back from achieving the power and influence they wish to have in their organizations. Gangone introduced me to Lee G. Bolman and Terrence E. Deal's four frames leadership model: structural, human resource, political, and symbolic.[6] The structural frame focuses on alignment of structure with goals and environment, the human resource frame focuses on the fit between the individual and the organization, the political frame focuses on getting and using power and managing conflict to get things done, and the symbolic frame focuses on building culture. Gangone had participants do Bolman and Deal's Leadership Orientations test to determine our strengths and weaknesses within these frames.[7]

Melanie Hawks, learning and development coordinator at the University of Utah's J. Willard Marriott Library, presented a session focused on life-work balance. Hawks reviewed a set of negative assumptions about how we think about our time that constrain us, and she introduced a set of counter-assumptions that can help put us back in control of our work and our personal time. She recommended four scientifically proven ways to deal with stress: exercise, meditation, serving others, and nurturing relationships. More details about the counter assumptions and how to deal with stress can be found in Hawks' workbook *Life-Work Balance.*[8]

Marsha Herman-Betzen, the executive director of the Association of College Unions International, presented a session about gender and communication titled, "Men and Women at Work." Herman-Betzen noted that men and women have different conversational styles. Men exchange information, make decisions, solve problems, negotiate position, and preserve independence. Women create connections, share feelings, build community, preserve intimacy, and avoid isolation. This presentation was full of activities to help us think about how women communicate. This workshop ended with a review of traditional leadership traits of men and women. Leadership traits of men typically include focus on the bottom line, encourage competition, use command and control style, focus on goals, exchange rewards for services, and issue punishment for inadequate performance. Leadership traits of women, on the other hand, typically focus on process as well as the bottom line; concern for how actions will affect others and the community; value diversity; draw on personal experience; are more concerned about keeping good relationships; and perceive power coming from charisma, interpersonal skills, hard work, and personal contact.[9] Herman-Betzen noted that men and women can borrow from each other's traits to achieve balance and effectiveness as leaders.

Louise Sandmeyer, executive director of the Office of Planning and Institutional Advancement at the Pennsylvania State University, conducted a session on change leadership. She began with the following question, "How must I change if I want *them* to be different?" Sandmeyer discussed the challenge of resisting change and how our individual and organizational responses to change matter. She presented the three states of change as detailed in the Richard Beckhard and Rueben T. Harris's transition model, which describes the existing state as comfortable and familiar; the transition state as uncontrollable and unpredictable; and the new state, with new roles and new work, as risky and unfamiliar.[10] Sandmeyer presented John P. Kotter's eight steps for leading organizational change: establish a sense of urgency, create a guiding coalition, develop a vision and a strategy, communicate the vision and the strategy, empower broad based action, generate short term wins, consolidate gains and produce more change, and anchor new ways in the culture.[11] Sandmeyer also included guidelines for leading change, phases of change and what leaders should do at each phase, and reasons why change efforts fail. She noted it is helpful to have an "elevator speech" that enables us to "clearly and simply state the need for change and describe the future state in a compelling way that is essential for rallying the support and commitment of key constituents."[12]

During an evening session, we had the opportunity to review the reports of our Clifton StrengthsQuest test, which we had filled out prior to the institute.[13] Melissa Hinrichs, from the Gallup Organization Higher Education Division, informed us of our top five strengths and she gave us exercises designed to help us understand what we learned about ourselves from the test. Another evening session titled "Lessons Learned by Women Executives" featured a panel of women working in various sections of higher education, including Herman-Betzen, executive director of the Association of College Unions International; Teri Bump, vice president of university relations and student development at American Campus Communities; Ellen Heffernan, a partner in Spelman & Johnson Group; and Susan Jurow, senior vice president of professional development and communications at the National Association of College and University Business Officers. Lessons shared by these leaders in higher education focused on familiar themes at the institute, including life-work balance, career planning, and the range of opportunities for women in higher education.

The closing keynote address was given by S. Georgia Nugent, president of Kenyon College, who shared with us the story of her career path from professor to college president.

Evaluation of the Women's Leadership Institute

The Women's Leadership Institute has grown since 2008. In 2009–2010, the cosponsoring organizations experimented by offering two sessions annually, one on the east coast and one on the west coast of the United States. Currently the location alternates between the west coast and the east coast with one event per year. The curriculum has grown, with new learning outcomes and a new curriculum offered in 2013. Learning outcomes include building a stronger community of practice among women in the college and university environment, personal and professional growth through reflection and both general and concurrent sessions, team building and leadership development, and empowerment for women to pursue higher-level positions in their respective fields. Current curriculum topics include gender communication, negotiating salary, techniques for good supervision, life-work balance, conducting quality searches, mentoring, financial competency, and career mapping. Participants can join a Facebook group to meet colleagues prior to attending the institute and to continue learning about leadership with their colleagues after their session ends.[14]

The growth of the Women's Leadership Institute points to a desire for a leadership program specifically for women working in higher education. The Association of College Unions International's publication *The Bulletin* reports women's experiences of the institute: "[The Women's Leadership Institute] has been by far the most valuable, transformational, and useful professional or personal development experience of my career " and "the culture of the Women's Leadership Institute [based on] inclusivity, authenticity, and mutual support … incredible."[15] In addition to the professional development opportunities and the positive educational environment, participants also described the experience as "refreshing" and "renewing."[16] One respondent said she would "recommend this program to others as an opportunity to refocus yourself and [your] career path."[17]

Evaluation indicates the program is strong and beneficial for participants:

> Assessment of the 2011 program showed that 97 percent of the respondents believed the program met or exceeded their expectations, and 99 percent would recommend the Women's Leadership Institute to a friend or colleague. In terms of the content of the program, 88 percent of the respondents believed the topics covered by the institute faculty were "excellent"—a 3 percent increase from the respondents of the 2010 Women's Leadership Institute evaluation. Overall, 84 percent of the 2011 respondents believed the learning objectives were met, and 91 percent thought the value of the program was "excellent."[18]

Experience and Application of the Women's Leadership Institute

The Women's Leadership Institute developed my skills and knowledge by introducing me to several ideas. First, Deiss's session introduced me to the concept of coaching. I had not considered my role as manager and leader to include coaching, and since the institute, I've been able to provide coaching to direct and indirect reports in my organizations to work more effectively in their roles, help them take on new roles, advance their careers, and pursue further studies. One example is a librarian who, after several coaching sessions, tackled her liaison librarian role with renewed enthusiasm and more confidence. She was able to take a new approach with faculty and students that was well received. I was also able to mentor a staff member who decided to pursue graduate studies in library and information science. I think coaching is a method that works well and enables professional librarians to feel empowered in their work and in their organizations. I have learned that there must be trust in the relationship before someone can be coached, and I would highly recommend Stephen M. R. Covey's book *The Speed of Trust* to anyone taking on a coaching role.[19] Covey describes 13 behaviors for building trust, including talking straight, demonstrating respect, creating transparency, righting wrongs, showing loyalty, delivering results, getting better, confronting reality, clarifying expectations, practicing accountability, listening first, keeping commitments, and extending trust.[20] If we master these behaviors, we will have relationships with colleagues and direct reports who are open to being coached in their work. In her session on coaching at the Women's Leadership Institute, Deiss noted that one unconscious "de-railer" for women as mentor and coach is often the need to be liked. This idea struck a chord with me, and I try to be conscious of my need to be liked when it gets in the way of getting my job done.

Second, Sandmeyer informed me that if I want others to change and to be a change agent in my organization, I have to be open to changing myself and how I approach my work. I have to be the model of change. This notion was reinforced by the ACRL Harvard Leadership Institute for Academic Librarians. This has been the most important lesson I have learned in my professional development. My growth and development is always ongoing. I need to take the time to do my professional development and then bring what I've learned back to the organization and be ready to help lead change in the organization.

Third, Gangone's session on reframing power and influence introduced me to Bolman and Deal's four frames of leadership. The structural, human resource, political, and symbolic frames can be used as a model of change leadership. The structural frame allows us to organize around goals and objectives and to address problems and performance gaps through analysis and restructuring. The human resource frame puts people at the center of our organizations, which exist to serve human needs. When the balance between the needs of the organization and the needs of the human resources fit well, people "find meaningful and satisfying work, and organizations get the talent and energy they need to succeed."[21] Politics is defined as the "process of making decisions and allocating resources in a context of scarcity and divergent interests."[22] In the political frame, organizations are coalitions of individuals and interest groups and goals and decisions are made via bargaining or negotiating for scarce resources. Finally, the symbolic frame focuses on how people make sense of the world using symbols. The symbolic frame assumes that meaning is more important than what happens and people create symbols to help make meaning. Leaders using the symbolic frame to create healthy organizational cultures by uniting people around shared values and beliefs.

In doing Bolman and Deal's Leadership Orientations test, I learned I was strong on the structural and political frames and weaker in the human resource and symbolic frames. I encountered Bolman and Deal's four frames leadership model again at the ACRL Harvard Leadership Institute for Academic Librarians in 2011. Again I scored the same on the Leadership Orientations test. I was surprised to learn from Joan V. Gallos, coauthor of *Reframing Academic Leadership*, that my score on the test should be shifting if I was growing.[23] I was relieved to learn that skills in all the frames can be learned and this has helped me to understand where I need to focus my professional development. I am making an effort to strengthen my skills where I am weaker and also to rely on others in the organization whose strengths are different from my own. Gallos emphasized that as library leaders, we need to learn how to use all the frames and apply them at the right times for the situation at hand. For instance, one can learn to utilize the symbolic frame by becoming more charismatic and telling stories that resonate with people. Library leaders and librarians aspiring to leadership positions may find it useful to read *Reframing Organizations* and librarians in academia, *Reframing Academic Leadership*, in order to understand how to apply the four frames leadership model.

Fourth, as I reach the middle of my career, I remember and draw upon Hawks' work on life-work balance. I've found an organization that encourages this balance, and I've tried out some of Hawks' suggestions, including exercise and meditation, to relieve stress and find balance. I would also add yoga, which I have been practicing for two years, to this list. When my supervisor recently commended me for the work I was doing to improve my leadership in our organization, I attributed some of my success to my recent professional development efforts, but I also realized that my recent practice of yoga and meditation were showing up in my job in a positive way. I realize that I need down time to be able to do my job more effectively. I've also discovered that traveling on vacations helps me recharge. I recognize that emotional intelligence, the capacity to regulate one's emotions, and mindfulness, the capacity to be fully aware of all that one experiences and the ability to be attentive to the people, environment, and events around us, are both important for mindful leadership.[24] Taking time for myself allows me to recharge so I can practice emotional intelligence and mindful leadership on the job.

Finally, my career was also affected by the informal networking that took place at the institute. During one of the meals, I met another academic librarian who lived in my area and who offered to be a mentor for me. She remains a mentor for me today, despite the fact that we have both moved on to new positions and I have moved to a new state.

Conclusion

The Women's Leadership Institute introduced me to the change leadership theories of Kotter, who distinguishes between change management and change leadership. Change management focuses on a set of basic tools or structures intended to keep change efforts under control, while change leadership focuses on urgency, big visions, and empowering people to make things happen. Kotter notes that organizations are good at change management, but change leadership is more difficult to do because of "the bigger leaps we have to make, associated with windows of opportunity that are coming at us faster, staying open less time, [and] bigger hazards and bullets coming at us faster."[25] Change leadership is a challenge that leaders in higher education must master in order to take the bigger leaps, find the windows of opportunity, and be ready for the hazards we will encounter as we continue to support our institutions of higher education in a fast changing world. The Women's Leadership Institute was the beginning of my leadership development, and Kotter's change leadership theories and Bolman and Deal's four frames model for change leadership have both remained central in my work.

Finally, I would recommend that organizers of the institute provide the opportunity for people to attend all the sessions offered, since I felt like I missed several important workshops. It was not possible to do all the sessions due to the way the program was structured. I would suggest more cohesive themes, maybe day to day, which might help participants make better connections between the materials presented. It would also be helpful if the institute could tie theory to practice more closely, enabling participants to see how change leadership can go from theory to practice. It would be helpful to have more opportunities to think and talk about how to put leadership theory into practice before returning to the library.

Notes

1. The other six organizations are the American College Personnel Association (ACPA), Association of College Unions International (ACUI), APPA: Leadership in Education Facilities, National Association of College and University Business Officers (NACUBO), National Assessment of Educational Progress (NAEP), and NASPA: Student Affairs Administrators in Higher Education. Today the institute is coproduced by members of the Council of Higher Education Management Associations.
2. Association of College Unions International, *Women's Leadership Institute Materials.*
3. Association of College Unions International, "Women's Leadership Institute."
4. Babcock and Laschever, *Women Don't Ask.*
5. Babcock and Laschever, *Ask For It,* 75–87.
6. Bolman and Deal, *Reframing Organizations.*
7. Bolman and Deal, *Leadership Orientations.*
8. Hawks, *Life-Work Balance.*
9. Herman-Betzen, "Men and Women at Work."
10. Beckhard and Harris, *Organizational Transitions.*
11. Kotter, *Leading Change.*
12. Sandmeyer, "Leadership for Change."
13. The Gallup Organization, *StrengthsQuest.*
14. Facebook, Women's Leadership Institute for Higher Education.
15. Association of College Unions International, "Women's Leadership Institute."
16. Ibid.
17. Ibid.
18. Ibid.
19. Covey and Merrill, *The Speed of Trust.*
20. Ibid., 125–229.
21. Bolman and Deal, *Reframing Organizations,* 115.
22. Ibid., 181.
23. Bolman and Gallos, *Reframing Academic Leadership.*
24. Boyatzis and McKee, *Resonant Leadership.*
25. Kotter, "Change Management vs. Change Leadership."

Bibliography

Association of College Unions International. *Women's Leadership Institute Materials.* December 7–10, 2008, Amelia Island, FL: Association of College Unions International, 2008.

———. "Women's Leadership Institute Seeks to Replicate 2011Success with Two Locations." *The Bulletin* 80, no. 5 (2012). http://www.acui.org/publications/bulletin/article.aspx?issue=36082&id=18859&terms=women%27s%20leadership.

———. "Women's Leadership Institute." Last modified October 10, 2012. Accessed February 13, 2013. http://www.acui.org/wli/.

Babcock, Linda, and Laschever, Sara. *Women Don't Ask: The High Cost of Avoiding Negotiation and Positive Strategies for Change.* New York: Bantam Books, 2007.

———. *Ask for It: How Women Can Use the Power of Negotiation to Get What They Really Want.* New York: Bantam Books, 2008.

Beckhard, Richard, and Reuben T. Harris. *Organizational Transitions: Managing Complex Change.* Reading, MA: Addison Wesley, 1977.

Bolman, Lee G., and Terrence E. Deal. "Leadership Orientations." Leadership Frameworks, 440 Boylston Street, Brookline, Massachusetts, 02146, 1988.

———. *Reframing Organizations: Artistry, Choice, and Leadership.* 3rd ed. San Francisco: John Wiley & Sons, Inc., 2003.

Bolman, Lee G., and Joan V. Gallos. *Reframing Academic Leadership.* San Francisco: Jossey-Bass, 2011.

Boyatzis, Richard, and Annie McKee. *Resonant Leadership: Renewing Yourself and Connecting with Others through Mindfulness, Hope, and Compassion.* Boston: Harvard Business School Press, 2007.

Covey, Stephen M. R., and Rebecca R. Merrill. *The Speed of Trust.* New York: Free Press, 2006.

Facebook. Women's Leadership Institute for Higher Education. http://www.facebook.com/pages/Womens-Leadership-Institute-for-Higher-Education/208133019221133.

Gallup Organization. *StrengthsQuest.* Princeton, NJ: The Gallup Organization, 2000.

Hawks, Melanie. *Life-Work Balance.* Chicago: Association of College and Research Libraries, 2008.

Herman-Betzen, Marsha. "Men and Women at Work." Paper presented at the Association of College Unions International Women's Leadership Institute, Amelia Island, FL, December 2008.

Kotter, John P. "Change Management vs. Change Leadership: What's the Difference?" *Forbes,* July 7, 2011. http://www.forbes.com/sites/johnkot-

ter/2011/07/12/change-management-vs-change-leadership-whats-the-dif-
ference/.

———. *Leading Change*. Boston: Harvard Business School Press, 1996.

Sandmeyer, Louise. "Leadership for Change." Paper presented at the Association
of College Unions International Women's Leadership Institute, Amelia
Island, FL, December 2008.

CHAPTER 17

"Playing at the Big Table":
Betting on Transformative Change and Collaboration at the Frye Leadership Institute

Adriene Lim, Vivian Lewis, and Neal Baker

THE FRYE LEADERSHIP Institute was a premier continuing-education opportunity offered to key leaders in higher education between 2000 and 2012. Over its 12-year run, Frye enhanced the leadership development of over 500 chief information officers, librarians, faculty, IT professionals, and other administrators. The institute was cosponsored by the Council of Library and Information Resources (CLIR), Emory University, and EDU-CAUSE, with partial funding from the Robert W. Woodruff Foundation. After a period of assessment and experimentation, Frye was reborn in 2012 as the Leading Change Institute.[1]

The origins of the institute stemmed from conversations between CLIR and Emory University starting in 1995. Key leaders at both institutions were deeply concerned about the intense challenges associated with managing change in higher education, particularly as that change affected the roles of librarians and technologists. The original concept of a digital leadership institute was proposed to prepare individuals holding (or about to hold) positions "responsible for transforming the management of scholarly information in the higher education community."[2] When implemented, the planned institute was renamed in honor of Billy E. Frye, former CLIR board member and chancellor of Emory University.

Participation in Frye was highly competitive. Prospective candidates were required to submit personal statements, curricula vitae, and proposals for individual research projects. Applications were vetted by the Frye Leadership Council. The majority of participants came from the United States, but cohorts typically included at least a small number of individuals from other countries. The targets of the institute were academic librarians, disciplinary faculty, and educational technologists who aspired to improve their administrative leadership skills in higher education and libraries. Typical cohorts came from all types and sizes of academic organizations. The purpose of the institute was to "effect fundamental change in the way universities manage their information resources in the new digital era… instilling new methods and practices and creating a new information culture."[3] Frye believed its target participants to be typically at mid-career and from "libraries, administrative staffs, computer centers, and information-technology divisions, and faculties."[4]

The physical location at a relatively isolated conference center affiliated with Emory University reduced potential distractions for participants and facilitated a strong focus on the institute's content. The group lived, worked, and played together for the two-week period—in most cases, including a layover weekend in the middle. Participants, who were also referred to as "fellows," were strongly discouraged from contacting their home institutions. They were encouraged to focus on their own personal leadership development over the course of the residential program.

Through the years, Frye faculty honed a carefully crafted format. The 10-day, face-to-face institute was supplemented by personal practicum projects and an e-mail distribution list for ongoing conversations. The days were rigorous and demanding. High-level speakers were brought in from across the US higher education landscape. Provosts, presidents, chief information officers (CIOs), chief financial officers (CFOs), and prominent library leaders took turns revealing their personal leadership stories—often divulging difficult challenges and personal sacrifices. Guest speakers were interspersed with group exercises. Participants were clustered into small groups to work through their practicum projects and to take on challenging tasks. The days were long, but routinely ended with the cohort members gathering together late at night to continue the conversations.

Literature Review

Despite the popularity and prestigious reputation of the Frye Leadership Institute in its heyday during the 2000s, little was published about the institute in the literatures of higher education, and library and information science. Annual reports, overviews, and lists of participants were released by the program's sponsors on a regular basis, but no in-depth reviews or studies were conducted to explore the institute's features or its impact on participants' leadership practice or careers.[5] Some of the publications during this period addressed Frye in the context of summarizing leadership development programs available for librarians or professionals in higher education, while others provided participants' reflections about the curriculum and their experiences at Frye.[6] For example, Pattie Orr attributed the successful redesign of technological training at Wellesley College in part to her 2000 Frye practicum project, where she was inspired to "take advantage of partnerships, packages, and new technological tools."[7]

Authors typically described the impact of Frye on participants' leadership development as very positive. Medaline Philbert perceived that participants came "away from Frye exuberant with hope and strength to affect change."[8] Susan Rosenblatt provided a summary of a program about Frye at the 2000 EDUCAUSE Annual Conference where panelists "testified that the Frye Institute exceeded their expectations and provided a unique learning experience."[9] In an editorial in *Information Technology and Libraries*, Dan Marmion remarked that "what we really took away from Atlanta the summer of 2002 was enlightenment, a sense that we can see the big picture, and we can lead the way."[10] Deanna B. Marcum and Brian L. Hawkins, heads of CLIR and EDUCAUSE respectively, shared participant-evaluation comments from the inaugural institute that included such accolades as "I left Atlanta forever changed," "the best professional-development event I have ever attended," "meaningful," "powerful," and "delightful, amazing, and transforming."[11]

Frye took place during an era when the creation of CIOs and the mergers of academic libraries and campus computing operations were being discussed as a continuing if not increasing trend in higher education.[12] The creation of CIO positions and mergers of libraries and IT were seen by advocates to be logical steps for academe to take in order to leverage the transformative power of digital information and technology. Referring to Frye as a proponent of this trend, Carla J. Stoffle and others noted,

The Frye Leadership Institute has been created to "train" future leaders of such combined organizations. CLIR is sending newsletters on information and digital library issues to our presidents and provosts; these newsletters are filled with thinly veiled suggestions that we need and must be preparing for such a position. The individuals being groomed see themselves as senior leadership—CIO (Chief Information Officers)—at the vice-presidential level. The implications for our libraries are unclear at this time. However, we cannot sit on the sidelines aloof from this discussion, pretending it could never happen at our institutions.... What are the implications for the traditional library values of access, intellectual freedom, individual privacy and equity of service, regardless of ability to pay, in merged organizations? It is too late to address the necessary issues when the president of your university decides to create such a position.[13]

The participants of the inaugural institute did not agree with this perception that Frye focused on mergers, but instead felt the program presented a balanced approach. They explained,

The issue of merged library/IT organizations arose in the course of the institute, along with many other issues, but no effort was made to advocate any organizational approach by the institute's sponsors ... A primary outcome for us was to embrace the need to work seamlessly with colleagues across organizational silos because this shared expertise is critical to the mission of higher education.[14]

Stoffle responded by pointing out that CLIR recommended "some campus leader must exercise or be given authority to bring together relevant parties to evaluate electronic-information needs and developments."[15] She stated, "It appeared that CLIR was advocating a CIO position, and the Frye Institute was a vehicle for preparing people for these positions."[16]

In 2010, the sponsors of the institute used a one-year hiatus to "assess and articulate the depth and consequence of changes that had taken place in the field of higher education since the Institute's conception."[17] According to George F. Claffey Jr. and others this reassessment led to a reinvigorated version of the program, which they dubbed the Frye Leadership Institute 2.0.[18] The new version of the institute was characterized by several changes in the general design and curriculum, such as a shortened time span from 10 days to six, and more focus on collaborative learning and student projects that were purported to "advance higher education as a whole."[19] Eventually, in 2012, this new version of Frye was renamed the Leading Change Institute, and relocated from Emory University in Atlanta to Washington, DC, where it continues to be held.

Key Themes and Features of the Frye Leadership Institute

THE CORE VALUE PROPOSITION

Unlike some other leadership programs, the Frye Leadership Institute was not built explicitly on any single leadership or management text or theoretical framework, nor did it use the analysis of case studies to convey its lessons. Instead, Frye provided an experiential venue where established leaders shared their perspectives on the changes occurring in higher education. It espoused a core value proposition: the power of collaboration among libraries, campus technology units, and disciplinary faculty. The message was persuasive and repeated by speaker after speaker throughout the institute.[20]

Frye's model forced participants to acknowledge the silo-based approach typically in play on university campuses. It placed a heightened value on the importance of deep collaboration. The recognition of equal partnership with other educators and colleagues was self-affirming, subverting an outmoded traditional approach of treating disciplinary faculty and administrators as "users" or "customers." This realization encouraged some participants to articulate stronger roles for their library faculty and staff when implementing new collaborations rather than reinforcing old models.

However, entering into deep partnerships needs careful consideration. With extreme collaborations, there may be a risk of loss of control over the respective units' core functions. The political and programmatic advantages may be great, but they may also come bundled with new burdens, culture clashes, and the risk of dilution of specialized roles and functions.

"PLAYING AT THE BIG TABLE": A CAMPUS-WIDE PERSPECTIVE ON LEADERSHIP

"Playing at the big table" captures a core principle espoused by the Frye faculty. Participants were encouraged to rethink their assigned roles and professional identities in service of a new paradigm of collaborative leadership that would seek transformation of old models deemed less effective in the digital age. Librarian participants in particular were asked to consider relinquishing their identities as "librarians" and instead to embrace their identities as "leaders" and "partners" with technologists in the educational enterprise. This change in identity and focus would sometimes require them to act against the immediate interests of their home units in favor of the common vision or mission.

For some participants, this precept became the single most critical message delivered at the institute. In the five years since we attended the Frye Institute, the need to adopt a campus-wide—rather than a strictly library-focused—perspective on critical issues has happened repeatedly. Taking the bigger view sometimes garnered internal resistance. The organizational rewards were not always self-evident. Over the longer term, however, the benefits were clear, not just personally (i.e., committee appointments, promotions, etc.), but also organizationally. Clearly, taking the larger view and working to advance the university as a whole reflected well on the library.

"CHIN UP!"—THE NEED FOR CONFIDENCE AND ATTENTIVENESS

The institute's motto stressed the need for strategic leaders to consistently look ahead and above their operational functions and daily tasks in order to gain new perspectives about the issues affecting higher education. Frye participants were encouraged to "chin up." The effective leader, the cohort was told, was confident and courageous. Part of this strategy was to maintain a sense of optimism and persevere in difficult times. As the idiom also suggests, the strategic leader is attentive to surroundings and kept well informed of events within and outside his or her organizations.

LEADING FROM THE MIDDLE

Emphasis was placed on the abilities of all participants, no matter where they were situated in their respective institutional hierarchies, to serve as change agents and transformational leaders in their organizations. Frye faculty espoused the principle that leaders can be found and groomed at all levels. The concept recognized and affirmed a broad spectrum of contributions. During our 2008 cohort, Allegheny College's Rick Holmgren reinforced the *leading from the middle* notion while relating his decades-long history at a small, single institution in western Pennsylvania, inspiring the cohort to see power potential throughout the workplace. This type of lesson offered alternative ways to perceive leadership and career development that did not necessarily involve verticality or a single-minded focus on competitive career advancement in the workplace.

"MULTILINGUAL" APPROACH

One Frye dean's concept of taking a multilingual approach to learning was particularly powerful for some participants. This dean noted that librarians spent a lot of time preoccupied with other librarians and libraries, even though leading for change and innovation might better arise from listening to voices outside the profession and reading everything from Plato, a morning online newspaper in Japanese, a novel, or the sports page. The dean encouraged multilingual leaders to read widely and then *zig* instead of *zag* across disciplines and divisions at opportune moments. The concept is akin to the colloquial hockey adage *skate to where the puck is going to be, not where it is.*

HIGH-IMPACT SPEAKERS

A group of prominent leaders were brought in from across the US higher education landscape to speak and interact with the cohort. Provosts, presidents, leaders of libraries, executives from educational associations, CIOs, and CFOs all took their turns revealing their perspectives about the state of higher education and their personal leadership stories—often sharing the daunting challenges they overcame and the personal sacrifices they made along the way. They delivered powerful messages, always with a high-altitude view of leadership and the academy. Topics ranged from financial challenges and change management to public policy, technological innovative and disruption, and scholarly communication. A smaller portion of time was dedicated to learning about teacher/scholar and student responses to current challenges in higher education.

The institute provided an impressive group of speakers, but the messages conveyed by those individuals were decidedly homogeneous. The speakers presenting to the 2008 cohort were relatively diverse in terms of racial background and came from different kinds of institutions (large and small, public and private), but they also seemed to share a similar leadership style and approach to work and life. Their personal successes were impressive. Yet, the participants may have benefited from hearing more about the political pitfalls, lessons learned from failures, and self-doubts that inevitably hinder forward progress at some point in most people's careers and at many institutions.

WORK-LIFE BALANCE

Based on the anecdotal reactions of participants at the time, many fellows found the institute's philosophies about work-life balance to be troubling. The Frye faculty and invited speakers expressed opinions that clearly accepted as inevitable the need to de-emphasize the importance of one's own personal life if one were to serve with distinction in any senior leadership position within academe. Many speakers seemed to take great pride in the long hours they worked and suggested that this approach was critical to success. During the course of the institute, participants sometimes questioned aloud whether other equally successful approaches existed, but this seemed to be outside of the personal experiences and philosophies of the institute's organizers.

SELF-KNOWLEDGE: THE POWER OF PERSONALITY

The institute offered participants several opportunities to engage in significant amounts of self-reflection, including the chance to complete Myers-Briggs Type Indicator (MBTI) testing and to discuss the results together. According to John A. Edwards, Kevin Lanning, and Karen Hooker, the MBTI is "certainly one of the best known personality inventories used among non-psychologists (if not the best known)" and measures Carl Jung's three personality dimensions of Introversion (I)—Extroversion (E); Sensing (S)—Intuition (N); and Thinking (T)—Feeling (F); and a fourth dimension, Judgment (J)—Perception (P).[21] For many cohort members, the focus on personality types became very powerful on a personal level. While some participants had completed similar tests before, the large community setting of the institute put the results into a much broader context and enhanced a sense of self-awareness through the interaction with others sharing the same profile. Participants discovered that, in many cases, they shared more with colleagues from other professional realms than they did with their own.

The experience was particularly powerful for those who measured on the "introverted" end of the personality spectrum—a characteristic not traditionally identified with leadership. The exercise illustrated that introverted leaders can be very effective, especially when they leverage their listening and contemplation skills. Introverted people can capitalize on their gifts to advance the objectives of their organization.

HYPOTHETICAL INSTITUTIONS EXERCISE

Several of the speakers focused on the wide-ranging issues facing higher education and the need for leaders to be well versed in all aspects of an institution's functions and operations. Special attention was also given to the sobering fiscal realities confronting higher education, in terms of declining government investment and increasing costs, and the hope that new financial models would enable institutions to overcome these challenges. Efficiency and effectiveness measures, technology innovation, restructuring of employee benefits, and the consolidation of operations and activities were addressed as ways to achieve higher-impact results and cost restructuring. To reinforce these points, Frye fellows were instructed to form small groups and explore the creation of hypothetical institutions—universities named and planned "from scratch" by the groups, for which the low endowment levels and limited revenue streams available, as determined by the parameters of the assignment, were expected to be balanced with the usual high operational costs. As Philbert remarked about this particular exercise,

Balancing revenue and expense for the hypothetical institutions was an eye opener for me, because it revealed how enrollment, retention, employment can adversely affect the sustainability of an institution. A slight percentage change in either direction for one of these areas had a huge impact on the financial health of the institution. I gained new respect for administrators who have to deal with these issues on a daily basis. Leadership from the top is essential because it sets the tone.[22]

NETWORKING

The networking opportunities were an important component of the institute. As groups of participants joined Frye, they became members of an exclusive cohort where lasting personal connections could be made across different universities, countries, and professions. Strong personal connections were also encouraged by the institute organizers through the use of two weeks' worth of meals enjoyed as a community, ample scheduled "downtime" for socialization, and informal communications via institute-sponsored e-mail distribution lists before, during, and after the sessions were over.

PRACTICUM PROJECTS

All Frye applicants were required to submit a practicum project that they undertook after the institute. The projects were expected to advance the goals of the applicant's home institution, such as magnifying library-writing center collaboration or developing information-literacy lessons plans, resources, and assessment activities for a distance education venture focusing on first-generation students. Frye deans were available throughout the institute to converse informally about the potential of any project, but the projects themselves were not a formal component of the curriculum.

Personal Reflections

In the following sections, we share our experiences as former Frye fellows in the 2008 cohort and reflect on the general influence the program has had on our careers over the intervening five-year period.

BAKER

The Frye Leadership Institute was a vital learning experience. My perspectives on Frye might be construed as atypical, and if that is the case, they largely stem from deep ambivalence about whether to apply in the first place. The institute's reputation conjured up images of a self-important, exclusive club replete with private receptions at conferences. I also had conflicting emotions about the discourse I associated with EDUCAUSE, one of the institute's partners. It seemed to me—perhaps uncharitably—that higher education's most influential IT professional association had vested interests in promoting a potent mix of technology triumphalism and crisis rhetoric. While my own analysis of academe, IT, and libraries likewise oscillated between Cassandra and digital nirvana, I was suspicious of both EDUCAUSE's corporate sponsorship and a seeming "We will bury you!" stance à la Nikita Khrushchev to Western diplomats circa 1956.[23] Despite such misgivings, or because of them, I decided to apply to Frye and was accepted. I arrived at the institute full of career angst, trying to figure out what I could or wanted to be in the context of a changing profession and a higher education sector under duress.

Upon arrival in Atlanta, I quickly learned to appreciate a Frye cohort filled with wonderful, compassionate individuals who had the courage and integrity to articulate their ambitions, both personal and professional. While some participants evinced confidence and drive, others expressed doubts about their situation in life vis-à-vis career choice, workplace prospects, and work-life balance. Despite the diversity, everyone was encouraging and empathetic. It was the cohort that made the institute such a remarkable event.

Given my educational background and employment history at places like Carleton College, Dickinson College, and Earlham, Hawkins's insight about "multilingual learning" made me appreciate the liberal arts even more than before. Looking back over my career, I have been best served by wide-ranging personal interests and addiction to reading a variety of materials such that I am part geek, part humanities "scholar" who has published several peer-reviewed essays on the science fiction/fantasy genres, part jock, and part administrator. I obtain more credibility in certain circles for serving as a senior bibliographer for the *MLA International Bibliography* than I do for management moxie or how much I know about librarianship. A second key insight learned from Hawkins and others at Frye was that of leading from the middle. This is now a management adage that I attempt to honor, recognizing and affirming the ability to achieve momentum with contributions from everyone and not just a "visionary" at the helm.

A third related insight debunked stereotypes I had of leadership. Namely, by dint of the MBTI exercise, I learned that introverts and quiet folks could be leaders. Granted, such participants were the Frye minority, but the exercise underlined that people have different gifts and can adjust accordingly. More recently, Susan Cain's bestseller, *Quiet: The Power of In-*

troverts in a World That Can't Stop Talking, spotlights what can be accomplished by contemplation, listening, and other behaviors not usually associated with workplace leadership.[24] Both the Frye exercise and Cain offered suggestions for how introverts might capitalize on their innate strengths by working with, and through, extroverted colleagues to advance organizational objectives. Looking in the mirror, I cannot imagine "selling" the Earlham Libraries without direct reports to supply the lion's share of the charm in contrast to my own unprepossessing efforts.

Finally, and most importantly, I learned to keep the big picture in mind at Frye, such that I am not just a librarian but instead a servant of the institution. My ultimate job is to contribute to the mission of the college, not necessarily the libraries per se. This has me always on the lookout for ways to connect the libraries to overall college priorities. For example, I recently worked with two vice presidents at our college to implement a personal research librarian initiative that targets at-risk students, directly addressing institutional concerns about admissions yield and undergraduate retention. At the same time, the program addressed information literacy outcomes in the context of a weekly discussion circle with a librarian and the use of iPad Minis. This approach directly furthered library goals.

From an even broader vantage, I left Frye with an indelible epigram courtesy of Emory University's provost and executive vice president, Earl Lewis, who spoke to our cohort near the conclusion of the institute. While I neglected to write down the exact words, Lewis at one point asserted that if a college education does not help 18–22 year-old students to think they can change the world, then we have failed. Lewis's assertion might come across as righteous and carefully scripted, but it was delivered humbly. Regardless, in the biggest, most absolute terms, my mission is to foster change not via libraries or IT but at the level of student hearts and minds. Frye, via Lewis, gave me an inviolate precept and an inspiration that still sustains me as academe and its various support structures lurch onward against an increasingly dire backdrop of MOOCs, accountability demands, and spiraling cost. I cannot thank Frye enough.

LEWIS

At the point I embarked on the Frye experience, I was at a pivotal juncture in my career. I had been an associate university librarian for a few years and was starting to think about next steps. Like many mid-career professionals, I had aspirations, but also some concerns. Did I possess the right mix of strengths and competencies to assume a leadership position? Was my current institution the best fit for my particular skill set and personal goals? Was I willing to accept the work-life challenges typically associated with moving to the next rung? I headed to Atlanta with high expectations and, for the most part, I wasn't disappointed.

The experience was, in many respects, all-consuming. From the point I was first accepted into the program, I felt myself being pulled into a strong community with an established culture. The hearty congratulations from past graduates assured me that I was embarking on a life-changing journey, an experience that would transform me as a leader and as a person. I was forewarned of the intensity of the experience (as well as the air conditioning in the conference center).

The actual content delivered during the program was generally rich and always well delivered. I must acknowledge that as a non-American some of the specific topics were less pertinent to me than, I'm sure, to others in the room. For instance, the focus on copyright and financing of higher education was interesting at an academic level, but it was presented with a purely US focus. Some of the key concepts (positional leadership, collaboration between library and IT, etc.) have stuck with me over the years and definitely influenced some of the decisions I have made during my leadership journey. When times are hard, some of the mantras ("chin up," etc.) regularly come to mind.

As with any professional development experience, the true impact can't be felt until months, or even years, after the event. While some of the content has, of course, faded from memory, many of the experiential aspects of the program remain present in my memory. I found the focus on personality types to be very powerful on a personal level. Like many participants, I had taken similar tests before, but the large community setting put the results into a much broader context. I met colleagues from many different work settings with similar profiles to mine. I believe that I understood myself better by seeing the same (or sometimes more exaggerated) results in others. I also gained a better understanding and respect for those who come to leadership with a more introverted disposition. In the years following my participation in Frye, I believe I've become more conscious of the need to make space in the conversation for the quieter voices. This lesson has served my organization and I well.

The hypothetical institutions exercise was as powerful as it was preposterous. My team struggled during the first meeting to find a common voice: The mixture of librarians and IT and instructional skills professionals felt awkward at first. How could we possibly formulate a plan for a completely new institution over the course of a few harried meetings? As the days wore on, we discovered the value of our collective expertise. The sum was truly better than the parts—especially in the late hours of the night before group presentations with imminent public humiliation in the wings. The experiential aspect of the assignment was critical: I learned from my peers in a way I could not from a textbook or lecture. The spirit with which we approached the task was compelling. Have I been called upon to build a new university in the last five years? Certainly not. But I have been asked to create new services and approaches from scratch in a ridiculously short period of time. I believe Frye prepared me well for this.

The brand value of the experience cannot be overstated. The sheer power of the Frye name became very clear to me over the intervening years when meeting with new colleagues, applying for new positions, or even filling in grant applications. Being a Frye fellow opened some important doors for me in the intervening years. The name holds value with colleagues across the academy.

Was the Frye the "life-changing" experience some of my predecessors promised it to be? No. The program did, however, have a tremendous and very positive impact on my leadership journey. The opportunity to retreat from the operational grind and reflect on my strengths and weaknesses as a leader, all in the company of like-minded professionals, was an extraordinary experience.

LIM

When I attended Frye, I had just been promoted from a middle-management position to a senior-level position, so sitting at the "big table" at a large library was new to me, let alone considering the "big table" at the university level. During the hypothetical institutions exercise, I learned more about how endowment levels, revenue streams, and research expenditures differentiate institutions in ways that are often hidden to the general public and even to some of us in academia. For example, while there are articles that talk generally about library endowment levels, there are no sources that provide librarians with ready data about library-specific endowment levels. One academic library I contacted later, for example, enjoyed the benefits of several endowed librarian positions and their corpus generated over a million dollars a year in discretionary funding. This was in contrast to other libraries I came to know that had much more modest endowments, skeletal staffing, and relatively little to no discretionary funding, and yet these under-resourced libraries seemed to be thriving relative to the institutional investments that sustained them. It reinforced my own belief that optimism and perseverance and a strategic mindset were keys to a leader's success in these fiscally stressed environments. Because of this one exercise in the Frye program, I became exceedingly curious about these and many other aspects of higher education funding, categorization, and ratings, and this curiosity continues to serve me well now that I have played at more "big tables" in my career. It has also made me more acutely aware of the need for libraries to devise high-impact strategies, achieve effective performance, and implement cost-containment measures if we are to be successful as educational partners.

I recall being intrigued but also disturbed by the Frye program's insistence that we needed to give up our librarian identities in order to break down silos between IT and library-related functions and initiatives. I identify with and feel quite passionately about library-specific roles, their unique relevance and importance in the quality of education for students, and I was already engaged in endeavors that leveraged cross-campus IT partnerships at the time, so I did not embrace unreservedly the espoused idea that one had to overcome or break down one's professional identity to accomplish transformative change. I think that our librarian identities were already evolving admirably and continue to evolve in anticipation of and reaction to technological change, but the librarian-specific roles and functions we embodied—teaching of research strategies, organizing knowledge, providing access to shared information, and offering integrated services in technology-rich learning environments—were crucial to the whole enterprise and needed specialization and advocacy on their own. My feeling was that we indeed needed to focus on technological opportunities and disruptions, but that we would risk diminishing our unique, still-important roles by doing so too single-mindedly. This concern was validated later when one industry leader made the provocative statement that he would no longer hire librarians in the future but would only hire post-docs and technologists instead. I was surprised to see this statement later quoted by a higher-education association in a presentation to university provosts, along with the claim that even librarians questioned their own future relevance in the academy. I felt then and continue to believe that we are stronger collaborators when we are well versed and proudly confident in the library and information science specializations we offer and bring to the table. If strong identities as librarians foster that, then to my mind, more power to us—as long as we allow those identities and specializations to expand our possibilities, rather than let them isolate and limit us.

For me, the coverage of scholarly communication, copyright, and other information policy issues was the weakest part of Frye content and affirmed my belief that our librarian roles were important. This was because the content, while valuable, was obviously intended more for the non-librarians in the room who might not have been as familiar with these issues as the librarians. By virtue of our library and information science disciplines and specializations, I would argue, most of us were already steeped in these developments and trends.

I remember being struck by some of the teacher-scholar responses to changes in libraries. One of the disciplinary faculty members who spoke to us mentioned her suspicion that librarians now hated books. If I am remembering this correctly, she was reacting to her library's desire to decommission large numbers of stacks and move materials to storage. This seemed, to me, to be evidence of either too much overzealousness on our part or perhaps an illustration of a gap in relationship building, communication, and marketing within some of our campuses. All the libraries in which I have worked have been transforming spaces to make way for more learning and study, but we had been doing this in a discipline-specific and responsible way. I came away from Frye with a good understanding of the pitfalls that could be encountered if one did not cover the aspects of communication and collaborative planning with stakeholders' input in an adequate way.

Doing more with less and the impression of endless fiscal pressures and crises were concerns mentioned quite frequently throughout the program, and yet, in retrospect, for many of us, those were flush financial days compared to now. As the institute focused so much on technological change and innovation, I remember sitting in the audience thinking to myself, "We can hardly keep our current high-demand services running with our declining resources, and now we were also failing if we do not move into multiple other initiatives requiring new technology staffing and expertise." I sometimes felt that the joint library-IT-faculty nature of Frye lent itself to downplaying many of the unique challenges that libraries were facing in their desires to transform themselves. Extremely flat or diminishing budgets, reduced staffing levels, legacy print operations that were still in heavy demand on some of our campuses, problems wherein our roles were increasingly perceived as more expendable by university administrators (reports from 2009 show that institutional allocations for academic libraries had fallen for the 14th year in a row to below 2 percent from highs of around 7 percent), and the fact that librarians were considered expendable even by some leaders within our own ranks—well, these realities and more just had to be dealt with somehow in still more creative, innovative ways, practical realities aside.[25] Most leaders know that a critical function of theirs is to keep hope alive and that determination and creativity often win the day, but at some junctures, I believe it is important to ask ourselves about the downsides of continuing to do ever more with less.

The emphasis on collaboration across silos at Frye helped me to strengthen my own resolve that librarians are partners in the academy, not just supporters and suppliers of information. I gained my early experiences as a librarian in the mid-1990s when the popular service paradigms of the day turned library users into "customers" and librarians into "customer service providers," not educational partners in the true sense of that word. By participating in Frye, I realized the importance of the partnership model and this inspired me to work across organizational boundaries on many collaborative initiatives. It also has helped me raise my library faculty members' and staff's aspirations and performance when we've implemented new models of engagement and integration, models that I feel strengthen our core roles. For those reasons alone, I feel honored and grateful to have been part of the Frye experience, especially at that specific point in time in the evolution of academic libraries. Those were very heady, exciting days indeed!

Survey of the 2008 Frye Cohort

Although a post-institute evaluation form was sent to graduates immediately following their two-week participation, the results of the Frye Leadership Institute have never been addressed formally in the literature of library and information science. No study has examined the use that Frye graduates have made of the conceptual material presented in the program and whether they maintained professional relationships with cohort members from the institute during their later careers. For this reason, we wanted to explore the impact of the program on other participants' leadership practice and networking over time, so that their own experiences could be situated into a larger context.

Based upon the evaluation methods of other leadership programs and loosely based upon a survey instrument developed by researchers who evaluated a different library and information science leadership development program, Baker and Lim conducted an online survey to learn about the perceptions of the institute's graduates regarding whether and to what degree their leadership capacity had changed as a result of their participation in the 2008 institute.[26]

METHODOLOGY

The survey was web-based and was conducted in early 2013, with the primary method of distribution achieved through direct e-mail messages to 47 individuals in the subject population. The subject population was comprised of all but one of the 48 participants who graduated from the 2008 institute.[27]

The first 12 questions asked respondents to indicate the extent to which general Frye themes and specific components from the curriculum had changed their leadership capacities. The possible answers were set on a five-point scale (i.e., no change, not much change, some change, great change, very great change). The next question asked respondents to select from a list of 12 Frye features any that seemed to have the most important and enduring influence on their leadership practice. Another set of questions asked participants to indicate the number of Frye cohort members with which they remained in contact and the types of advice and support they received from these colleagues. Finally, an optional free-text comment box was provided so that respondents could communicate any unstructured information about their participation in the institute and its impact on their leadership practice or career.

FINDINGS

Twenty-five valid responses were obtained from the population of 47 Frye fellows, yielding a 53 percent response rate. Among those surveyed, 13 of the 25 respondents (78.26 percent) indicated that they had held either a librarian or library administrator role at the time of the 2008 Frye Institute. The remaining participants identified themselves as technologists (13.04 percent) and academic staff/professionals (8.70 percent).

Ranked in tabular form based on the magnitude of change, respondents indicated that several features of the institute had led to either "great change" or "very great change" in their leadership capacity and practices. The four features receiving the highest ratings were

- "Gaining a broader perspective about finances, policies, and strategic challenges in higher education as conveyed during the institute" (72 percent);
- "Challenges in higher education, academic and financial perspectives, presentations/discussions" (60 percent);
- "Taking advantage of the opportunities to use professional networks more effectively, as a result of [one's] participation in the institute" (52 percent); and
- "Leadership and change management presentations/discussions" (50 percent).

Seven of the 12 features garnered mixed results. One item in particular, "information and IT policy, presentations/discussion," received an almost even distribution of votes, with 36 percent indicating "some change" and the rest indicating great or very great changes (32 percent), or little to no change (32 percent). The remaining six features were all given "some change" ratings by the majority of participants as shown below:

- "Understanding the critical components of effective leadership in managing higher education information resources in the digital era" (56 percent);
- MBTI Exercise (52 percent);
- Hypothetical Institutes Exercise (48 percent);
- "Clarifying and taking advantage of the relationships among stakeholders in library, IT, and/or faculty groups within [one's] institution, using the methods taught at the institute" (44 percent);
- "Creating a learning environment that is conducive to personal reflection and enhancing your personal abilities as a leader, as a result of [one's] experiences at the institute" (44 percent); and
- Practicum project (44 percent).

A majority of participants (56 percent) rated only one Frye feature, "copyright and scholarly communication presentations/discussions," as having little to no change on their leadership philosophies or practices. Although not in the majority, a large group of respondents (40 percent) also gave "Personal Practicum Project" low ratings.

In order to obtain other general impressions, the survey asked participants, "What have been the most important and enduring effects of the 2008 Frye Leadership Institute on your leadership practice?" The survey provided a list of 12 features from which respondents could choose. Of the 12 features, one was selected as a top choice along with the next most frequently chosen items as shown below:

- "Self-awareness, especially of my personal strengths/barriers to change" (92 percent);
- "Strategic planning" (68 percent);
- "Strategic leadership on campus" (56 percent);
- "Effective leadership of transformational change" (56 percent); and
- "Establishing new leadership goals for [one's self] (52 percent).

See figure 17.1 for a graph showing respondents' selection rates for all 12 features.

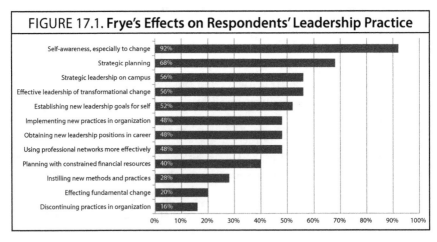

FIGURE 17.1. **Frye's Effects on Respondents' Leadership Practice**

The survey posted three questions set on a six-point scale, asking respondents to describe the extent to which the institute led to ongoing networking relationships with their cohort members. A majority (44 percent) indicated that they remained in contact with four to 10 peers from the institute. A great number of participants agreed or strongly agreed that they exchanged leadership advice (84 percent) and career advice (64 percent) with their Frye peers, more so than they shared library-related advice (44 percent). All but a few (84 percent) perceived that valuable professional support was provided by the cohort. Overall, the results showed that the Frye experience led to a cohort with a number of continuing professional relationships.

There were 14 general comments submitted by respondents. All but two were extremely positive, with superlatives used such as "unmatched," "phenomenal," "incomparable," "transformative," and "profound." One individual highlighted as valuable the "self-awareness" gained and the lessons learned about the "high-level pressures faced by higher education," while another mentioned a belief that the program had provided "insight into leadership and institutional change." Other respondents stressed the important impact of Frye on participants' leadership styles and careers and the continuing benefits of networking with the Frye community.

The networking opportunities were noted by several respondents as one of the most important component of the institute. Years after the face-to-face experience, some cohort members remained connected. For some, these points of personal connection were mentioned as invaluable throughout their careers. "I really value the Frye community," said one participant, while another commented, "I think the greatest gift out of the whole Frye experience has been the support from our cohort; it has been phenomenal."[28] But one person dissented on this point about networking, writing that the experience "has not resulted in many enduring relationships for provision of long-term support."

Two persons submitted contrasting comments about the lack of balance between library-specific and IT-specific topics in the Frye experience; one found it to be "very library-centric," while another noted that many discussions were "more IT-focused than is relevant for my position." Notwithstanding these few criticisms, the grateful tone of many respondents' comments was represented in the following response, "Frye helped me to take a giant career leap, from running a smallish IT shop to a managing the finances, facilities, and human resources for a graduate school. This was an unanticipated move, but the opportunity arose, and Frye had given me perspective and faith in my own ability to play at the next level."[29]

Discussion

The responses of survey participants matched well with many of our own reflections about Frye in regard to the institute's positive impact on career advancement, networking benefits, and content related to the challenges of leading change in academe. The Frye fellows generally agreed with the proposition that one of the most memorable elements about Frye was its ability to convey a broader perspective about finances, policies, and strategic challenges in higher education. In the "personal reflections" section, we noted our initial ambivalence about transitioning to senior-level positions—with one of us having just been promoted to a new position, one stating she had been at a "pivotal point" in her career, and one pondering whether he could fit into the prevailing leadership culture—and how our Frye experiences gave us the chance to reflect on our strengths and weaknesses and gain confidence in our abilities to serve in higher capacities. These reactions coincide with the survey respondents' identification of Frye's self-awareness theme as very effective, specifically that fellows came to know their personal strengths and the barriers to change and that this feature had the most important and enduring effect on their leadership practice through the years.

Interestingly, however, the arguably mission-critical features of the institute, ones that addressed libraries and IT collaboration and scholarly communication and copyright were rated lower in terms of their value and enduring impact. Cross-campus collaborations were mentioned by us and some respondents, but features related to library and campus IT collaborations were not rated as highly as other parts of the institute. Evidence of familiar library-IT boundaries also occurred when two participants submitted conflicting perceptions about Frye alternately being too library-centric and too technology-centric. Another participant criticized our survey instrument as being focused mainly on libraries, and yet there was only one survey question that addressed libraries alone in an explicit way. The question asked respondents to indicate whether they agreed or disagreed with the statement, "I exchange library-related advice with my Frye peers." All other questions mentioned both the "library" and "IT" as units.

These mixed results suggest that Frye was highly effective in its general training and development of aspirational leaders, yet perhaps was not as successful in its signature aim to develop leaders who would institute "fundamental change in the way universities manage their information resources in the new digital era" or leaders who would create "a new information culture."[30] The organizational roles and identities of librarians, along with those of academic technologists and disciplinary faculty, had seemingly remained intact in the participants' worlds, even if individual participants were reportedly more collaborative and fully developed as change agents/leaders than they were pre-Frye.

Frye occurred during an era when mergers of libraries and campus technology organizations occurred on several campuses with great fanfare. By the end of the Frye 1.0 phase, these organizational convergences were no longer a highly visible trend, and in fact, some combined units had been de-merged.[31] In many ways, since the days when CLIR, Emory University, and EDUCAUSE first conceived of Frye, the scholarly communication realm, libraries, and campus technology units had all seen significant shifts and innovations (e.g., the expansion of the open access movement, the proliferation of institutional repositories, the implementation of large-scale digital libraries, etc.) but had not changed as drastically as one might have posited in earlier days. Some overarching practices related to scholarly communication have remained fairly consistent and resistant to change.[32] Print materials and their attendant operations did not disappear entirely. Academic libraries and their institutional technology counterparts did not merge at many universities. These dynamics, coupled with ongoing political and fiscal pressures, have created greater demands and complexities for transformative library and IT leadership than before, even if the units remained differentiated and apart in their different cultures. In fact, their continued separation in large numbers calls for more collaborative efforts and the formation of virtual teams. Frye fellows overwhelmingly reported that the institute was successful in exposing them to the concepts and resources that would help them grapple with these difficult challenges, even if the information services culture ahead is far different than the original founders of Frye imagined.

Conclusion

The Frye Leadership Institute, at least as it existed in its original two-week format, made a significant and positive contribution to the library profession. Over its 15-year run, 500 CIOs, librarians, and IT professionals were given an extraordinary opportunity to reflect on their strengths and weaknesses as leaders and learn from some of the best theorists and practitioners in the academy. The traditions surrounding Frye became legendary: Cohort after cohort of carefully chosen candidates headed to Atlanta fully anticipating to be transformed. For many, the expectation became a self-fulfilling prophecy. Some of the profession's most prominent and future-driven librarians list the Frye as a critical component of their leadership journey.

To date, very little research had been done to determine the influence of the Frye Leadership Institute on participants' professional practice and career trajectories. The literature review uncovered many personal reflections on the Frye experience as well as articles comparing Frye to other professional development programs. These various contributions are helpful from an anecdotal perspective but lack the rigor necessary to form strong conclusions about Frye. Future research on Frye and its successor, the Leading Change Institute, could attempt to move beyond this study's analysis of participants' perspectives and instead delve deeper into actual leadership changes that were experienced after participation in the programs, perhaps through case studies examining members' leadership results at their respective institutions.

The survey conducted as part of this research suggests that, at least for one particular cohort, Frye was attributed by the participants as meeting its primary objective of preparing leaders to transform their organizations. In this respect, although Frye was not based on any explicitly named leadership or management text or theory, its results most closely resembled features associated with transformational leadership. Respondents from the 2008 cohort clearly felt an enhanced sense of self-awareness. They perceived that Frye had improved their strategic planning skills and gave them a better, more balanced approach to strategic leadership on campus. The mantras around preparedness ("chin up"), taking an enterprise-wide approach to leadership ("playing at the big table"), and broadening their universe of information sources (being "multilingual") stayed with graduates long after leaving the Emory Conference Center. These findings were echoed by our own personal reflections.

Where Frye might arguably have been less successful was in conveying a preferred vision of what that transformed organization would look like. Admittedly, whether Frye organizers fully intended to project a preferred image is open to debate. Librarian participants gained a better understanding of their campus IT colleagues and were forced to come face to face with the silos they themselves helped create and sustain. The concept of deep collaboration between library and campus IT makes perfect sense, but the precise shape of that collaboration varies tremendously from campus to campus. Blending is painfully hard to achieve and even more difficult to maintain in real organizations over an extended period of time.

The succession of deans organizing and leading the Frye Leadership Institute made a singular contribution to the profession. The fact that certain components of the Frye experience (the practicum project, the hypothetical institutions exercise, the formal leadership style assessment tools, etc.) had less perceived sticking power than other components is not surprising. As was seen during the Frye experience itself, the deans fully intended to challenge the participants, to present them with uncomfortable realities and new lenses with which to view their organizations. In doing so, the deans forced the fellows, even for a few short weeks, to suspend their disbelief and rethink the boundaries of their profession. Graduates of the program returned from Atlanta to many different kinds of organizations and many different kinds of roles. Perhaps they did not come back transformed, but they did come back with a broader vision of the academy, a richer network of colleagues, and a larger set of tools with which to lead change.

Notes

1. According to its website at http://www.clir.org/, the Council of Library and Information Resources (CLIR) is an organization that "forges strategies to enhance research, teaching, and learning environments in collaboration with libraries, cultural institutions, and communities of higher learning." EDUCAUSE is a nonprofit association of information technology leaders and professionals committed to advancing higher education. EDUCAUSE was created through the merger of two professional associations in the higher-education information technology community, CAUSE and Educom. More information about all of these organizations can be found at the EDUCAUSE website at http://www.educause.edu/about/mission-and-organization/roots-educause.
2. Leading Change Institute, "History of the Leading Change Institute."
3. Ibid.
4. Ibid.
5. For example, see Council on Library and Information Resources, *Council on Library and Information*; Rosenblatt, "EDUCAUSE Organizational Update."

6. For example, see Gjelten and Fishel, "Developing Leaders and Transforming Libraries"; Matthews, "Becoming a Chief Librarian"; Leger-Hornby, "The 2003 Frye Leadership Institute"; Maloy, "Creativity as a Leadership Strategy"; Marmion, "Editorial: Chin Up!"; Orr, "Transforming Technology Training"; Philbert, "Frye Leadership Institute"; Philbert, "Frye Leadership Institute—A Report."

7. Orr, "Transforming Technology Training," 16.

8. Philbert, "Frye Leadership Institute."

9. Rosenblatt, "EDUCAUSE Organizational Update."

10. Marmion, "Editorial: Chin Up!"

11. Marcum and Hawkins, "The Frye Leadership Institute."

12. For example, see Snyder, "CIOs and Academic Research Libraries"; West and Smith, "Library and Computing Merger."

13. Stoffle et al., "Continuing to Build the Future."

14. Agee et al., "Letter to the Editor."

15. Council on Library and Information Resources, "CLIRinghouse Number 1."

16. Stoffle, "Letter to the Editor."

17. Leading Change Institute, "History of the Leading Change Institute."

18. Claffey Jr. et al., "Frye Leadership Institute 2.0."

19. Ibid.,10.

20. Although Frye did not use a specific leadership theory in its curriculum, its key themes and features exhibited many of the same components associated with transformational leadership and change leadership. According to Peter G. Northouse in his book *Leadership: Theory and Practice*, transformational leadership is "the process whereby a person engages with others and creates a connection that raises the level of motivation and morality in both the leader and the follower" (186). In a 2011 *Forbes* magazine article entitled "Change Management vs. Change Leadership—What's the Difference?," John P. Kotter noted that change leadership "concerns the driving forces, visions and processes that fuel large-scale transformation" (n.p.).

21. Edwards, Lanning, and Hooker, "The MBTI and Social Information Processing."

22. Philbert, "Frye Leadership Institute—A Report."

23. "We Will Bury You!," *Time*, November 26, 1956, 24.

24. Cain, *Quiet*.

25. Kolowich, "Library Budgets Continue to Shrink."

26. Barney, "Evaluation of the Impact of the 2003 Aurora Leadership Institute"; Phelan, "Creating Leaders"; Zauha, "Turned On and Tuned In?"; Casey et al., "Leadership Development Program Survey."

27. One well-respected and loved Frye fellow passed away in the intervening five years since the cohort was formed.
28. "Leadership Development Program Survey," respondents 2013.
29. Ibid.
30. Leading Change Institute, "History of the Leading Change Institute."
31. For example, see Massis, "Academic Libraries and Information Technology"; Neff, "Merging the Library and the Computer Center."
32. For example, see Ithaka S+R, *Faculty Survey Series.*

Bibliography

Agee, Anne, Bruce Aarsvold, Lois Brooks, Jo Ann Carr, Patricia Cutright, Barbara Dewey, Renee Drabier et al. Letter to the Editor. *portal: Libraries and the Academy* 4, no. 2, (2004): 311–15. http://muse.jhu.edu/journals/portal_libraries_and_the_academy/v004/4.2letters.html.

Barney, Kay. "Evaluation of the Impact of the 2003 Aurora Leadership Institute—The Gift That Keeps on Giving." *The Australian Library Journal* 53, no. 4 (2004): 337–48.

Cain, Susan. *Quiet: The Power of Introverts in a World That Can't Stop Talking.* New York: Crown Publishers, 2012.

Casey, Anne, Jon Cawthorne, Kathleen DeLong, Irene Herold, and Adriene Lim. "Leadership Development Program Survey Instrument." Unpublished manuscript, Simmons College, 2010. Microsoft Word file.

Claffey, Jr., George F., Katherine Furlong, Amy Badertscher, Julie Kane, and Gentry Holbert. "Frye Leadership Institute 2.0: Educating, Incubating, and Innovating Change." *EDUCAUSE Review* 46 no. 6 (2011): 10–11. http://www.educause.edu/ero/article/frye-leadership-institute-20-educating-incubating-and-innovating-change.

Council on Library and Information Resources. "CLIRinghouse Number 1." August 2001. http://www.clir.org/pubs/archives/cliringhouse/house.html/house01.html.

———. *Council on Library and Information Resources Annual Report 2001–2002.* 2002. http://www.clir.org/pubs/annual/previous-annual-reports/annrpt2001/leadership.html.

Edwards, John A., Kevin Lanning, and Karen Hooker. "The MBTI and Social Information Processing: An Incremental Validity Study." *Journal of Personality Assessment* 78, 3 (2002): 432–50. doi: 10.1207/S15327752JPA7803_04.

"Frye Leadership Institute Participants Named." *CLIR Issues* 61 (2008). http://www.clir.org/pubs/issues/issues61.html/#frye.

Gjelten, Dan, and Teresa Fishel. "Developing Leaders and Transforming Libraries: Leadership Institutes for Librarians." *College & Research Libraries News*
67, no. 7 (2006): 409–12.

Ithaka S+R. *Faculty Survey Series*. Accessed September 29, 2013, http://www.
sr.ithaka.org/research-publications/faculty-survey-series.

Kolowich, Steve. "Library Budgets Continue to Shrink Relative to University
Spending." *Inside Higher Ed*. February 21, 2012. http://www.insidehigh-
ered.com/news/2012/02/21/library-budgets-continue-shrink-relative-uni-
versity-spending.

Leading Change Institute. "History of the Leading Change Institute." Accessed
September 26, 2013. http://www.leadingchangeinstitute.org/histo-
ry-of-the-leading-change-institute.

Leger-Hornby, Tracey. "The 2003 Frye Leadership Institute: A Recap." *Library Hi
Tech News* 20, no. 8 (2003): 36.

Maloy, Frances. "Creativity as a Leadership Strategy in Times of Change." *College
& Research Libraries News 65, no.* 8 (2004): 444–69.

Marcum, Deanna B., and Brian L. Hawkins. "The Frye Leadership Institute: A
Unique Opportunity for a Unique Problem." *EDUCAUSE review 35, no.* 6
(2000): 8–9. http://net.educause.edu/ir/library/pdf/erm0066.pdf.

Marmion, Dan. "Editorial: Chin Up!" *Information Technology and Libraries* 21,
no. 2 (2002): 99. http://www.ala.org/lita/ital/21/3/editorial.

Massis, Bruce E. "Academic Libraries and Information Technology," *New Library
World* 112, no. 1/2 (2011): 86–89.

Matthews, Catherine J. "Becoming a Chief Librarian: An Analysis of Transition
Stages in Academic Library Leadership." *Library Trends* 40, no. 4 (2002):
578–602.

Neff, Raymond K. "Merging the Library and the Computer Center: Indications
and Contraindications." In *Books, Bytes, and Bridges: Libraries and Computer Centers in Academic Institutions*, edited by Larry Hardesty, 38–45.
Chicago: American Library Association, 2000.

Northouse, Peter G. *Leadership: Theory and Practice*. 6th ed. Thousand Oaks, CA:
Sage Publications, 2013.

Orr, Pattie. "Transforming Technology Training: Partnerships, Packages, and
Policies: The Lone Ranger Doesn't Work Here Any More!" In *Leadership,
Higher Education, and the Information Page: A New Era for Information
Technology and Libraries*, edited by Carrie E. Regenstein and Barbara I.
Dewey, 115–42. New York: Neal-Schuman, 2003.

Phelan, Daniel. "Creating Leaders: The Impact of Leadership Training Programs
on the Subsequent Leadership Behaviour of Librarians." Presentation at

the OLA Super Conference 2005, Toronto, Ontario, Canada, February 3, 2005. http://www.accessola.com/superconference2005/thurs/100.html.

Philbert, Medaline. "Frye Leadership Institute." *The Information Edge—Library Newsletter* (Fall 2005). http://digitalcommons.pace.edu/lib_bulletin/2.

———. "Frye Leadership Institute—A Report." October 10, 2007. http://digital-commons.pace.edu/dc_library_staff_publications/5.

Rosenblatt, Susan. "EDUCAUSE Organizational Update: The Frye Leadership Institute." *Library Hi Tech News* 18, no. 1 (2001): 30.

Snyder, Carolyn A. "CIOs and Academic Research Libraries." *Library Administration & Management* 20, no. 2 (2006): 72–74.

Stoffle, Carla J. Letter to the Editor. *portal: Libraries and the Academy* 4, no. 2 (2004): 311–15. http://muse.jhu.edu/journals/portal_libraries_and_the_academy/v004/4.2letters.html.

Stoffle, Carla J., Barbara Allen, David Morden, and Krisellen Maloney. "Continuing to Build the Future: Academic Libraries and their Challenges." *portal: Libraries and the Academic* 3, no. 3 (2003): 363–80. http://muse.jhu.edu/journals/pla/summary/v003/3.3stoffle.html.

West, Sharon M., and Steven L. Smith. "Library and Computing Merger: Clash of Titans or Golden Opportunity." In *The Proceedings of the 1995 Cause Annual Conference: Realizing the Potential of Information Resources: Information, Technology, and Services* (1995): 881–89. http://net.educause.edu/ir/library/pdf/CNC9564.pdf.

Zauha, Janelle M. "Turned On and Tuned In? Professional Side Effects of Library Leadership Institution." *PNLA Quarterly* 71, no. 3 (2007): 6–11.

CHAPTER 18

The HERS Institute Experience:
Designing the Path Forward

Lois K. Merry

ATTENDING THE HIGHER Education Resource Services (HERS) Institute gave me networking opportunities, career mapping and leadership strategies, and a wider view of the context of academic institutions, including my own. The experience also gave me the confidence to pursue career advancement through promotion and publication. HERS was the first leadership program of its kind, but today there are many others, and they have increased the number of women leaders in academe.

The HERS Institute

HERS Institute is a management institute for academic women.[1] While held in multiple locations and different formats, I attended the institute at Wellesley College in Wellesley, Massachusetts. HERS began when a 1972 gathering of academic women at Brown University discovered that women were underrepresented in the ranks of college and university administrators and decided there ought to be a leadership program designed to increase the number of women holding those positions. They named themselves the "Committee for the Concerns of Women in New England Colleges and Universities." Besides improving the status of women in academe they sought to help colleges and universities implement Title IX, the new law that made gender discrimination illegal in educational institutions receiving federal funds. With support from the Ford Foundation, HERS founder Cynthia Secor launched HERS Mid-Atlantic at the University of Pennsylvania in 1974. In 1976, the foundation also provided funds for the first HERS Summer Institute held at Bryn Mawr College. Two years later, the summer institutes became self-supporting. HERS moved to Wellesley College in 1976, becoming HERS New England. HERS Mid-Atlantic migrated to the University of Denver in 1983, changing its name to HERS Mid-America. Recent program initiatives included the Institute for Administrative Advancement, intended for women coaches and athletic administrators, which began in the 1990s, and HERS South Africa, based in Cape Town, which started in 2000 and is an independent chapter of HERS Mid-America.[2] Today there are more than 4,300 alumnae of the HERS program.[3]

The three HERS Institutes (HERS Wellesley Institute, Bryn Mawr Summer Institute, and HERS Denver Summer Institute), each a total of 12 days long, individually serve a diverse group of approximately 70 women who learn from guest speakers and HERS faculty and alumnae in four three-day seminars at Wellesley or attend immersive two-week programs at Bryn Mawr and Denver. Seminars include presentations and group work supplemented by assignments to be completed outside of the sessions. Most institutions assist their chosen participants financially.[4]

Content of Current HERS Institutes

The HERS website (www.hersnet.org) features the HERS New England curriculum, which follows five basic themes: understanding the higher education environment, planning and leading change in the academy, managing and investing strategic resources, engaging individual and institutional diversity, and mapping your own leadership development. (Each of these themes will be explained in more detail later in this chapter.)

The HERS New England experience incorporates assignments to be completed outside its four weekend sessions. Assignments include a comprehensive resource portfolio developed by the participants that includes the mission statements and strategic priorities of their institutions and of their own units. Each participant also adds her own personal mission statement and strategic plan as well as completes questionnaires about her local institutional demographics, organizational chart, and budget and financial statements. The HERS leadership project requires participants, having identified a challenging conflict in their home institutions, to develop and lead a plan for changing it.

SEMINAR 1

Participants are introduced to the current state of higher education through presentations, small group exercises, and large group discussion. They learn about the elements of organizational culture and values. Chief academic officers and chief financial officers present their perspectives on finance, budgeting, and advancement as well as the environments of accreditation and the impact of information and communication technology. Participants are introduced to the leadership project for which they identify a challenging conflict in their home institution and plan a remedy.

SEMINAR 2

Participants evaluate the results of their personal Myers-Briggs Type Inventory (MBTI) and engage in discussions about negotiating strategies based on their own leadership style as revealed by the MBTI. They learn about institutional advancement, leading and managing change, conflict management, the search process, designing a curriculum vita or resume, and drafting an executive summary. They engage in coaching and mentoring role-play.

SEMINAR 3

Participants continue learning about institutional finance, budgeting, and planning. Lessons and strategies for planning and leading change are presented and work proceeds on their career mapping exercises in small peer groups. They also develop cover letters and learn about the interview process and negotiation techniques.

SEMINAR 4

Participants get information about today's college students and the anticipated characteristics of future students. They hear about student affairs and developing strategies for helping students achieve success. Speakers discuss legal issues pertaining to institutions, organizational cultures, and diversity in higher education. Participants report on their leadership projects. The institute concludes with a presidential panel and graduation ceremony.

Literature Review

Searching for scholarship on leadership programs for women yields relatively little, but there are two recent articles about HERS. One by Estella Lopez, published in 2011 in *On Campus with Women*, describes the current HERS curriculum, emphasizing the importance for women of leading change in an institution.[5] Lopez notes that HERS doesn't provide a leadership toolkit, but a way for women to develop their own unique skills within the context of their home institution. Rather than being handed a ready-made set of tools, participants are expected to construct their own, a more personalized, albeit more difficult, approach. Another recent article by Judith White, published in 2012 in *Advances in Developing Human Resources*, gives an overview of HERS history and current developments.[6] White notes that since 2006 the HERS program has sought feedback from its alumnae and adjusted both its structure and curriculum in response.

In the book *Women in Higher Education Administration*, published in 1984 and part of the New Directions for Higher Education series, three chapters explore HERS. In the chapter "The Administrative Skills Program: What Have We Learned?," Jean Speizer reports on her study measuring the effect of attending the HERS program by comparing a group of HERS participants against a group of nonparticipants to determine which had a higher job promotion rate. She concluded that women who had participated in HERS were promoted faster.[7]

Another chapter, "Career Mapping and the Professional Development Process," Adrian Tinsley explores the HERS curriculum's career mapping and professional development exercises that are designed to address career barriers and assist with career goals through a process of identifying and examining both personal and institutional values and goals and considering those different values in tandem. Tinsley notes that participants in the HERS summer institutes stated they had found this the single most valuable takeaway from the program.[8] Career-based exercises let participants ponder their current situations while providing them the opportunity to set career paths for many years ahead and consider methods they might employ to achieve success. Reviewing each other's career maps within triad groups during HERS seminars provided each woman helpful feedback.

Indeed, the career mapping exercise is intensely personal, and although it commonly results in administrative advancement, Tinsley acknowledges that there exists the possibility that a woman may decide to leave her institution or career altogether and pursue other avenues that more closely align with her personal values.

The third chapter about the HERS summer program, "Preparing the Individual for Institutional Leadership: The Summer Institute," written by HERS founder Cynthia Secor, describes the birth of the HERS program, its original and revised curricula, and the benefit of networking and having associations enhanced by the connections formed during the institute.[9] Secor writes that the original intent of the program was to erode the barriers to administrative advancement encountered by women and minorities.

Among the reasons that the editors state for compiling *Women in Higher Education Administration* is the recognition that individual academic careers always unfold within an institutional context.[10] Thus it is imperative for women to understand the relationship between their own aspirations and their institution's formal and informal agendas. Additionally, the editors believe an understanding of the larger context of higher education will contribute to women's advancement in academe. There is little available in the literature concerning HERS or other women's leadership development programs, so this remains an opportunity for additional scholarship.

My Own HERS Experience

"Institutions make poor lovers" is one statement I have long remembered from my HERS experience. I call those words to mind whenever I encounter a colleague who appears to assume that her career investment must guarantee an equivalent return from her institution. Institutional agendas don't align perfectly with any individual's, and it is imperative for career academics to understand the difference and to know what they can reasonably expect and, even more importantly, what they ought never to expect. For me this is the essence of the HERS program, helping women devise their own means for advancement through an understanding of their personal values as they relate to their institution's values.

I am an academic librarian, and currently by my own choice, my title is Reference and Instruction Librarian, one career step down from my former role as a department head. I was one of two women from Keene State

College selected to attend HERS in 2003–2004. In some sense, I felt like an imposter during my HERS experience because, despite my administrative role, I already knew that I preferred not to advance further at my institution or any other. Nevertheless, I found the HERS experience beneficial and consider it reassuring to know that one potential outcome of attending HERS might be vacating a position or even leaving academe entirely. During my five weekends at Wellesley College, I was inspired by women leaders and also by my classmates from colleges and universities across the country. I enjoyed my association with these successful women, and consequently, I never underestimate the value of role models. For an assignment I interviewed six administrators from my home institution who told me their perceptions of their roles, their frustrations and successes, and personal perspectives on institutional politics and power. HERS was an experience that could not fail to change me and it surely did. The opening words of this paragraph were delivered as a warning never to expect a proportional return on a lifetime investment in academe. If I learned nothing else from my HERS experience, it was that you must find a way to do the work that you love and furthermore that you alone must take responsibility for the direction of your career.

As one of only two librarians in my HERS class, and despite my faculty status, I didn't exactly match my classmates, who were either "regular" faculty or administrators. I understand now that in that somewhat minor way I too brought a bit of diversity to my class. Not able to speak "library" with the other participants as had been my experience whenever I had left campus before, necessarily broadened my knowledge of other aspects of the academic environment. Participating in an all-female program was a unique experience for me because I had never before attended a program led by, intended for, and composed almost entirely of women. What follows is a seminar-by-seminar breakdown of the HERS program as I experienced it.

SEMINAR 1

Prior to my first weekend, I received a packet containing a list of HERS participants including my classmates' application forms, the MBTI to complete, and three professional development assignments, which included a reading on women in educational administration. At the first session, the HERS faculty members distributed their brief biographies. Our orientation to the Wellesley College campus included an evening meeting at the

Wellesley Centers for Women where we were introduced to the materials housed there. Using our MBTI scores and career stage exercises we began determining our personal strengths and preferences and charting our academic path. We learned how temperament affects an individual's response to different leadership styles. HERS faculty member, Reba Keele, described the "internal shifts" in thinking necessary for becoming effective in a leadership role. I was both startled and reassured to hear Keele identify herself as an introvert who functioned effectively as a presenter only because she satisfied her need for at least equivalent time alone to recharge. Having conducted many instruction sessions and several book talks since then, I acknowledge that Keele's disclosure has helped me to recognize the importance of accepting and accommodating my own personality in the workplace. In a similar vein, one of Keele's handouts stated another HERS tenet: Finding an organization matching one's strengths first requires a deep understanding of self.

HERS founder Secor was an active presence at our institute. She introduced the topic of "issues in higher education" during the first evening and presented additional sessions on professional development and managing in organizations. An important theme that weekend was the institutional change process. We considered change as it pertained to our own work units and determined the characteristics of our own positions, including our level of campus visibility and our potential for forming helpful relationships. We completed an exercise intended to determine our current level of career performance on a four-stage scale, beginning with stage one, depending on others, and continuing through stage four, leading through vision.

SEMINAR 2

Assignments for the second session included devising a "cultural diversity profile" and conducting an "issues for women survey" for our own institutions. We began working on the career map exercise that was augmented by a number of value questions posed on a separate sheet. At this seminar, we received our campus interview assignment including a list of potential questions we might use according to our personal preference. The task was to select at least five individuals at the highest administrative levels of our institutions. Some questions pertained to the college president alone and addressed how I might help carry out his agenda for the campus and what steps I could take to lead more effectively. Ideally, we would interview campus officers who could be mentors and provide career connections or advice. I designed my interview list in consultation with my library director, but inadvertently confusing the last names of two women named "Anne," I set up an interview with one woman only to realize that I wanted to interview the other, so in the end I interviewed both. It was an admittedly slipshod selection process that is sensibly eliminated from the current version of the assignment because predetermined positions are specified now rather than leaving their selections up to the participant. I ultimately conducted interviews with six people on my campus: the president, vice president of academic affairs, associate vice president of academic affairs, assistant vice president of finance and planning, director of the Elliot Center (supporting student services), and the head of human resources. I conducted my interview with the president jointly with the other HERS participant from my college to save his time and avoid redundancy. Afterwards, I typed up my handwritten notes, compiling the responses and dropping references to positions and names. At the fourth HERS weekend, participants discussed their interviews in a large group setting.

We also learned about change theories, the change process, and characteristics of teams. On the final day we listened to a dynamic college president who described aspects of her daily work life. She brought with her several administrative case studies for us to examine and discuss. That exercise shed light on the many connections that were possible, likely, or even imperative for leaders to consider when faced with potentially difficult situations. A HERS alumna presented a session on the faculty-staff divide that originates in the culture of the academy and then compared that to the differences and expectations of staff and administrators in the corporate environment. She explained how those two nearly opposite cultures impact careers in each setting. She distributed her own bio statement and three "presentation topics," which served as examples for an assignment that we were to complete later.

SEMINAR 3

This seminar covered planning and fiscal management including institutional advancement and public relations. The professional development component employed exercises on resume building, career mapping, and self-presentation. Having analyzed our current positions, we drafted our personal and professional goals and then our resumes, which we discussed in small groups for the purpose of receiving feedback from peers on the strategies we might use to achieve those goals. One of my group's recommendations for me was to add descriptions of search committee work to my resume and work on broadening my campus involvement. Since then I have done exactly that by serving on the college senate and on a task force charged with examining the general education program prior to its formal program review. I think this sort of campus involvement was instrumental in my promotion to full professor. Further, I was advised by my peers to "toot my own horn" more and to elaborate on my research interests rather than state vaguely that I was "planning to write."

Financial officers from different types of institutions described their experiences and lessons learned through presentations and group discussions. We examined case studies of hypothetical situations that required us to consider planning, budgeting, managing resources, and cultivating good relations with the public.

SEMINAR 4

In this seminar we reviewed and discussed the results of our campus interviews as well as explored the topics of institutional culture, strategic planning, and diversity. One insightful piece of advice from the fourth seminar was the admonition to pay attention to an organization's structure keeping in mind that the money always goes where the importance lies. I also appreciated the perspective I gained from interviewing six administrators on my campus. From the president's interview I learned about the thought process behind his decision to move the college from Division II to Division III in athletics, a change he pursued for its ultimate benefit to the college despite being unpopular among some constituencies. He described the scope of his investigative process and when the change was announced, the resulting campus resistance. I think his decision was sound, but hearing the story behind it convinced me that courage and conviction were as necessary to the success of his leadership in this matter as was his fact-finding process and actually making the decision. The interviewees' responses to the question about whom they considered the most and least powerful constituencies on campus were revealing and insightful and formed a common thread in the other participants' reports. I also found much to ponder in their ideas about which qualities they considered important for leaders.

All in all, the perspective I gained on the culture of my own institution can be traced to these interviews.

Later Keele initiated a group discussion of an article from the *Harvard Business Review* whose authors proposed a new strategy for making the most of diversity initiatives. Although increasing raw numbers of minorities and addressing historical omissions are commendable goals, institutions must make space for fundamental cultural change through what the authors called the "learning and effectiveness paradigm" to implement genuine diversity.[11] Keele emphasized the importance of making sure that our work was central to our institution's mission, valued by the institution and, perhaps most importantly, *known* by the institution.

We had brought six copies of our own resumes, biography statements, and presentation topics to this seminar to share and discuss with our peers. All of us had previously read selected articles from the *Chronicle of Higher Education* about information technology and its impact on the academic environment. Two college presidents led group discussions about institutional consortia. The weekend ended with presentations on information technology, diversity, and a wrap-up on organizational management. We heard a presentation from Diana Walsh, then president of Wellesley College, who imparted lessons on leadership from her 10 years on the job. She listed five qualities of trustworthy leaders, namely those who question self, honor partnerships, avoid use of force, value difference, and build community. Walsh helped us understand that an institutional vision is everyone's work.

SEMINAR 5

Keele and Secor opened the final seminar by summarizing and discussing the year's themes, which were the importance and power of institutional cultures, the value of alliances, access and diversity on campus, and finding new ways to lead. They described their own careers in academe, and we watched a short film about uncommon routes to creativity. We also discussed legal issues in higher education.

The institute presented various leadership theories, some of which I later implemented in my department head role. When I took responsibility for leading a newly formed access services department in the library, staffing and personnel matters posed challenges from the start, and over the course of my more than five years in that role I chaired several search committees. I learned the importance of being as open, communicative, and participative as I could when managing department staff. Whatever progress I made in leading change as a department head is in some way attributable to my HERS experience, but for me, the strongest evidence of what I gained from attending HERS involved writing and publishing a book on women pilots in World War II and my decision to seek promotion to full professor. I also gained confidence in my own perspective, which helped when I joined a campus-wide task force that examined the college's general education program and recommended changes. Looking back over my HERS materials while writing this chapter, I realize that much of this work actually involved leading from the sidelines.

Leadership Theories Presented at HERS

PERSONAL TRAITS AND LEADERSHIP STYLES

The MBTI, although I had taken it before, reminded me of my particular personality traits that may determine the effectiveness (or ineffectiveness) of employing the following leadership styles: laissez-faire (delegating), democratic (supporting), authoritarian (directing), or transactional (coaching).[12] The presentations on career stages and the work of devising my own career path document gave me concrete help in planning the most effective career strategy for me.

INSTITUTIONAL CULTURES

Various presentations and exercises helped me understand the context and culture of my own institution and taught me strategies for working with others based on my personal attributes, their individual styles, and the dynamics of the change process within the institutional setting. As a department head, the issues I struggled with were how to implement an integrated acquisitions system and restore the library faculty's primacy in collection development. I also met staff resistance to my plan to move periodicals records to an online format. Although I addressed these issues incrementally by tailoring my approach to the distinct personalities of the two staff members involved, I regret that I never really achieved full transitions in either case, but there was some progress. I experienced the difficulty of introducing change and learned that resistance can occur even when that change clearly benefits the institution. HERS sessions emphasized the importance of knowing my particular strengths and work preferences as a leader in relation to those of the people I supervised.

Highlights from HERS

CAMPUS INTERVIEWS

Having an assignment to conduct these interviews was the only means for me to benefit from one-on-one time with individuals on my campus whose paths I rarely crossed, such as the president or vice president of academic affairs. Being in a position to ask them questions that were unlikely to arise in informal conversation was invaluable for the insight it yielded into these individuals' opinions and thought processes.

CAREER MAPPING EXERCISE

I still revisit and revise the career mapping document I designed during my HERS experience. It has evolved over time and has helped me when contemplating the next steps in my career.

INSTITUTIONAL ASSESSMENT

Not only closely examining my own institution, but hearing about other colleges and universities from my classmates and guest speakers helped to put my own workplace context into perspective. Without the requirement to consider those aspects of my institution's physical presence and unique character, it is unlikely I would have so closely examined the college where I work.

Program Changes since I Attended

CAMPUS INTERVIEW ASSIGNMENT

When comparing the assignment that I completed with the current one, I notice a definite improvement. Today's version requires participants to interview people in specifically designated positions: the chief academic, financial, information, student affairs, and diversity officers as well as the president (or chancellor or system head). Having these parameters spelled out makes the interviewee selection process clearer and gives participants a better cross-sectional image of their institution while at the same time ensuring consistency when the whole group tallies and compares common issues during the next HERS session. I experienced considerable uncertainty about which individuals I should interview due to the stipulation that I include people in positions of power on my campus that could help further my career goals. For that reason, I think that the revision of the campus interview assignment is a good one.

LEADERSHIP PROJECT ASSIGNMENT

In my HERS program we identified and considered changes that we might make in our own units or home institutions. The expectation was that we would pursue these changes either during our HERS experience or later. The addition of a required leadership project, which is now an assignment, makes identifying an opportunity for leadership mandatory for participants. In the new context, direct implementation of leadership knowledge acquired at HERS is an expectation.

One change I would recommend for the HERS program concerns the leadership project. A recent HERS participant described her leadership project as the least helpful aspect of her own HERS experience (pers. comm.). She considered her chosen issue much too broad, and besides that, she felt that she had received little guidance or support for it. Small group sessions planned for discussion of the assignment were unhelpful because they tended to be dominated by a few individuals. Both design and support were lacking, making the assignment seem tangential. She suggested improving the assignment's design by initiating one-on-one meetings with HERS faculty to discuss the leadership project and ensure adequate follow-up, a recommendation I support. Echoing the improvements made to the campus interview assignment, the leadership project assignment would benefit from more prescriptive directions in the beginning and a more assiduous follow-up.

CONDENSING FIVE WEEKENDS TO FOUR

Considering the time commitment that HERS participants must make, this change is sensible and may make it easier for women to participate. Institutes still consist of twelve days on-site, but now the time is evenly distributed throughout the year, allowing each seminar to be an intensive three-day experience.

Conclusion

HERS was the first national program designed to advance the careers of women and minorities in higher education. Today there are many others. A recent article by Susan R. Madsen, Karen A. Longman, and Jessica R. Daniels lists a sample of several international and national leadership development programs for women in higher education.[13] One of the state-based programs, New Hampshire Women in Higher Education Leadership, a branch of the national organization the American Council on Education (ACE), is available to members of the state's academic community. It appears to consist largely of workshops in personal career development rather than leadership development specifically meant to advance the cause of women in academe.[14] However, its website provides a link to the ACE Spectrum Executive Leadership Program.[15] This national program serves women and administrators of color who aspire to presidential positions. Although more narrowly focused, the ACE program mirrors HERS in its emphasis on leadership training that acknowledges the importance of institutional culture. Similarly, another national program, the Women's Leadership Institute from ACRL is intended for "women who aspire to become senior leaders in higher education."[16] Though it shares the scope of HERS, including leadership skills, campus culture, new developments in academe, and networking, it provides less depth because it is presented in only one four-day session. Participants describe it on the website as a "workshop" or a "conference."

Current research on leadership development programs for women is rare but what exists speaks to their value. An article from the journal *Academic Medicine* states that deans of medical schools, although acknowledging gender inequity, perceived the Executive Leadership in Academic Medicine (ELAM) program for women to have had a beneficial effect on their schools and on the fellows themselves.[17] Assessing the value of the ELAM program, another article cites a study posing the question, "Does the ELAM Program for Women have a positive impact on its participants four to five years after completion of the program?[18] The findings suggest that the ELAM program does provide tangible benefits to its participants in three areas: aspirations to leadership, mastery of leadership competencies, and attainment of leadership roles. Findings from a longitudinal case study of the New Zealand Women in Leadership (NZWIL) program for university women indicate that the NZWIL program was determined effective in increasing participants' self-confidence and networking skills and enabling them to apply for and gain promotions.[19]

Areas for future research might include revisiting the Speizer study on promotion rates for HERS attendees compared to non-attendees. But, beyond counting simple numbers, I think it is important to identify and examine institutions whose administrative personnel mirror the percentages of women and minorities found in the larger society and determine whether those institutional cultures vary in any way from more traditional academic environments. Perhaps it may be possible to assess what the impact of women and minority administrators has been on the overall culture of academe.

Notes

1. For general information about the program, see http://hersnet.org.
2. HERS Higher Education Resource Services, "About HERS, HERS Archives."
3. White, "HERS Institutes," 11.
4. Ibid., 12.
5. Lopez, "HERS."
6. White, "HERS Institutes."
7. Speizer, "The Administrative Skills Program," 42.
8. Tinsley, "Career Mapping," 21.
9. Secor, "Preparing the Individual," 32.
10. Tinsley, Secor, and Kaplan, *Women in Higher Education*, 2.
11. Thomas and Ely, "Making Differences Matter," 80.
12. Northouse, *Leadership*, 90.
13. Madsen, Longman, and Daniels, "Women's Leadership Development," 116.
14. New Hampshire Women in Higher Education Leadership, "News & Events."
15. ACE American Council on Education, Leadership and Advocacy, "Leadership Programs."
16. Association of College and Research Libraries, "Women's Leadership Institute."
17. Dannels et al., "Medical School Deans' Perceptions," 75.
18. Dannels et al., "Evaluating a Leadership Program," 493.
19. Harris and Leberman, "Leadership Development for Women," 28–29.

Bibliography

ACE American Council on Education, Leadership and Advocacy. "Leadership Programs," Accessed April 11, 2013. http://www.acenet.edu/leadership/Pages/default.aspx.

Association of College & Research Libraries. "Women's Leadership Institute." Accessed April 11, 2013. http://www.ala.org/acrl/womensleadership.

Dannels, Sharon A., Hisashi Yamagata, Sharon A. McDade, Yu-Chuan Chuang, Katharine A. Gleason, Jean M. McLaughlin, Rosalyn C. Richman, and Page S. Morahan. "Evaluating a Leadership Program: A Comparative, Longitudinal Study to Assess the Impact of the Executive Leadership in Academic Medicine (ELAM) Program for Women." *Academic Medicine* 83, no. 5 (May 2008): 488–95.

Dannels, Sharon, Jean McLaughlin, Katharine A. Gleason, Sharon A. McDade, Rosalyn Richman, and Page S. Morahan. "Medical School Deans' Perceptions of Organizational Climate: Useful Indicators for Advancement of Women Faculty and Evaluation of a Leadership Program's Impact." *Academic Medicine* 84, no. 1 (2009): 67–79.

Harris, Candice A., and Sarah I. Leberman. "Leadership Development for Women in New Zealand Universities: Learning from the New Zealand Women in Leadership Program." *Advances in Developing Human Resources* 14, no. 1 (2012): 28–44.

HERS Higher Education Resource Services. "About HERS, HERS Archives." Last accessed December 2011. http://www.hersnet.org/HERSHistoryHER-SHigherEducationResourceServices.asp.

Lopez, Estela. "HERS: Drawing New Maps for Institutional Change." *On Campus with Women* 40, no. 1 (2011): 4. http://0-search.ebscohost.com.ksclib.keene.edu/login.aspx?direct=true&db=ehh&AN=65168191&site=ehost-live&scope=site.

Madsen, Susan R., Karen A. Longman, and Jessica R. Daniels. "Women's Leadership Development in Higher Education: Conclusion and Implications for HRD." *Advances in Developing Human Resources* 14, no. 1 (2012): 113–28.

New Hampshire Women in Higher Education Leadership. "News & Events." Accessed April 11, 2013. http://www.nhwhel.org/.

Northouse, Peter G. *Leadership: Theory and Practice.* Thousand Oaks, CA: Sage, 2010.

Secor, Cynthia. "Preparing the Individual for Institutional Leadership: The Summer Institute." In *Women in Higher Education Administration,* edited by Adrian Tinsley, Cynthia Secor, and Sheila Kaplan, 25–34. New Directions for Higher Education, vol. 45. San Francisco: Jossey-Bass, 1984.

Speizer, Jeanne J. "The Administrative Skills Program: What Have We Learned?" In *Women in Higher Education Administration,* edited by Adrian Tinsley, Cynthia Secor, and Sheila Kaplan, 35–45. New Directions for Higher Education, vol. 45. San Francisco: Jossey-Bass, 1984.

Thomas, David A., and Robin J. Ely. "Making Differences Matter: A New Paradigm for Managing Diversity." *Harvard Business Review* (September-October 1996): 79–90.

Tinsley, Adrian. "Career Mapping and the Professional Development Process."
In *Women in Higher Education Administration*, edited by Adrian Tinsley,
Cynthia Secor, and Sheila Kaplan, 17–24. New Directions for Higher Edu-
cation, vol. 45. San Francisco: Jossey-Bass, 1984.

Tinsley, Adrian, Cynthia Secor, and Sheila Kaplan, eds. *Women in Higher Education Administration*. New Directions for Higher Education, vol. 45. San
Francisco: Jossey-Bass, 1984.

White, Judith. "HERS Institutes: Curriculum for Advancing Women Leaders
in Higher Education." *Advances in Developing Human Resources* 14, no.1
(2012): 11–27.

PART 6

Findings and Conclusions

CHAPTER 19

Findings

Irene M.H. Herold

UTILIZING THE 18 programs described in the previous chapters as the data source, they are compared in the following areas:

- formation of the program,
- longevity and size of the program,
- process to enroll in a program,
- structure of the program,
- curriculum content,
- leadership theories, and
- supplied evidence of leadership development.

While this still may not provide evidence of leadership development as a result of attending a leadership development program, which will be discussed in Chapter 20, it provides an environmental scan of these programs, their commonalities and differences, and what program creators thought were essential elements to leadership development. The various organizations and programs are referred to using the abbreviations in table 19.1.

Chapter	Full Program Name	Abbreviation
	TABLE 19.1. Program Abbreviations	
1	ACRL-Harvard's Leadership Institute for Academic Librarians	LIAL
2	American Theological Library Association's Creating the Leaders of Tomorrow Program	CLTP

TABLE 19.1. **Program Abbreviations**		
Chapter	Full Program Name	Abbreviation
3	College Library Directors' Mentor Program	CLDMP
4	Historically Black Colleges and Universities Library Alliance Leadership Institutes	HBCU
5	NLM/AAHSL Leadership Fellows Program	LFP
6	ARL's Leadership Career Development Program for Underrepresented Mid-Career Librarians	LCDP
7	Library of Congress Leadership Development Program	LC
8	ARL's Research Libraries' Leadership Fellows	RLLF
9	UCLA Senior Fellows Program	Sr. Fellows
10	The Sunshine State Library Leadership Institute	Sunshine
11	The Stanford Institute	Stanford
12	Minnesota Institute for Early Career Librarians from Traditionally Underrepresented Groups	MNTIEL
13	Rochester Regional Library Council and the Monroe County Library System's Accepting the Leadership Challenge: A Library Leadership Institute	Rochester
14	Snowbird Library Leadership Institute	Snowbird
15	Texas Accelerated Library Leaders Program	TALL
16	Women's Leadership Institute	WLI
17	Frye Leadership Institute	Frye
18	Higher Education Resource Services Institute	HERS

Formation of the Program

Each of the 18 programs had different drivers for its formation (see table 19.2). Nine programs had an individual or small group who identified the need for a leadership program. Eight of the programs had an association identify the need. One program had the need identified by the state government. Eleven of the programs initially worked with a funder, whether a foundation, grant, or association. There was no consistency for the process of forming the leadership programs as some worked with a consultant, others a committee that surveyed the environment of the organization and/or leadership programs, and still others, such as MNTIEL and HERS, formed through a group of academics at a single university who identified a need and then created a committee and program to address that need.

Of the five programs that are now defunct, on hiatus, or morphed into a different program (HBCU, Stanford, Rochester, Snowbird, and Frye), all had initial outside funding support and never changed to self-sustaining support. Three of the five defunct programs cited funding (HBCU, Stanford, and Rochester); three of the five said the program had reached end-of-life/market saturation (Rochester, Snowbird, and Frye); and in Frye's case, at least in that format, as reasons for cessation.

TABLE 19.2. **How Programs Formed**			
Program	Who Identified the Need	Work Done to Decide What Kind of Program to Create	Initial Outside Funder
LIAL	Harvard librarian	Worked with a consultant	None
CLTP	Association	Worked with a consultant	Association
CLDMP	CLS members	Formed committee	Foundation
HBCU	Association	Did an assessment and worked with regional consortia	Foundation
LFP	AAHSL	Data analysis and environmental scan	Association
LCDP	ARL	Survey of member institutions	None
LC	Head of LC	Inspired by General Colin Powell	Foundation
RLLF	Head of ARL	Head of ARL with association	None
Sr. Fellows	CLR president and advisory committee on university libraries	Advisory committee report	Foundation and university
Sunshine	State of Florida	Needs assessment	LSTA
Stanford	University librarian and state librarian	Worked with a consultant	Government grant funds

TABLE 19.2. **How Programs Formed**			
Program	Who Identified the Need	Work Done to Decide What Kind of Program to Create	Initial Outside Funder
MNTIEL	University of Minnesota librarians	Two librarians identified need	None
Rochester	Rochester area librarians	Worked with consultants	Government grant funds
Snowbird	Director of Salt Lake City Public Library	Worked with consultants	Private corporation funding
TALL	Texas Library Association	Reviewed 70 other programs, formed a committee, and worked with consultants	None
WLI	Association of College Unions International	Worked with a variety of higher education organizations including ACRL	None
Frye	CLIR and Emory University	Key leaders from CLIR and Emory created program	Mix of foundation and association
HERS	Group of academic women at Brown University	Formed a committee	Foundation

Longevity and Size of the Program

In seeking to understand if there is a threshold, whether longevity or size of the cohort may ensure success of a program, a comparison of these two factors is presented in table 19.3. The five programs (HBCU, Stanford, Rochester, Snowbird, and Frye) currently not offered show a two commonalities: The majority of them were offered only a few times, and the cohort size was large. On the other hand, the programs that are still enduring have a wide variety of cohort sizes, from only five participants to over 100 per year (see CLDMP, LCDP, TALL for small programs and LIAL, WLI, and HERS for larger programs).

TABLE 19.3. **Program Duration and Cohort Size**			
Program	Actual Years Program Ran/Runs	Total Number of Years	Participant Average Size in a Year
LIAL	1999–present	15	100
CLTP	2012–present	2	9
CLDMP	1992–present	22	15
HBCU	2005–2012	7	25
LFP	2002–present	12	5
LCDP	1997–present	17	19
LC	1993–present	21	10
RLLF	2004–present	10	25
Sr. Fellows	1982–present	32	15
Sunshine	2003–present	12	36
Stanford	2000–2003	3	135
MNTIEL	1998–present	16	12
Rochester	2002–2004	2	40
Snowbird	1990–1999	9	32
TALL	1994–present	20	27
WLI	2005–present	9	150
Frye	2000–2012	12	42
HERS	1974–present	40	70

Process to Enroll in a Program

Six programs required either a nomination or invitation by an administrator for applicants. Twelve programs allowed self-identified enrollment, but five programs then had a review of applicants and a selective, competitive process for enrollment. All of the programs had specific criteria that must be met whether gender, underrepresented population, place of employment, job title or position, or expressed interest in career transition exploration. Several programs required specific documents for the application process. Table 19.4 lists these factors for the various programs.

TABLE 19.4. **Enrollment Process and Criteria**			
Program	Nominated	Self-Identified	Specific Criteria for Participants and Application Documentation
LIAL		X	Academic librarian in managerial or leadership position
ATLA		X	Potential theological library directors
CLDMP		X	First-time director in the first year at a college library with the institutional student FTE at or below 3,500
HBCU	X		Employed at an HBCU
LFP		X	Provide a statement outlining goals and professional relevance of the program to those goals
LCDP		X	From a diverse racial or ethnic group, mid-career, application form, letter from direct supervisor and director, institutional commitment of funds
LC	X		Must work in the Library of Congress
RLLF	X		Interested in becoming a head librarian
Sr. Fellows	X		Currently hold a senior-level academic librarian appointment
Sunshine		X	Application form, letter of support from supervisory, dean or director approval form
Stanford		X	Two letters of recommendation, two essays responding to prompts, resume
MNTIEL		X	Five years' experience, from an underrepresented group, participant institution expected to cover costs along with supplemental vendor funding
Rochester		X	Must work in an area institution, essay, letter of support, project description
Snowbird	X		Early career librarian (1–3 years)
TALL		X	Member of the Texas Library Association, mid-career librarian

TABLE 19.4. **Enrollment Process and Criteria**			
Program	Nominated	Self-Identified	Specific Criteria for Participants and Application Documentation
WLI		X	Female, hold a managerial position in higher education
Frye		X	Personal statement, CV, research project proposal
HERS	X		Female, work in higher education

Structure of the Program

The structure of the various programs fell into categories of a one-time workshop, a multi-session workshop, a multifaceted program with a mix of online and face-to-face time, and a multiyear and multifaceted program. Most of the larger cohort style programs fell under the one-time workshop model, a notable exception being HERS with its multiple weekend sessions over a year's time. In examining the structure of the programs, duration was one variable as illustrated in table 19.5. Number of sessions, type of sessions, site visits, mentors, and whether the program required a project were other factors.

TABLE 19.5. **Program Structure Variables**						
Program	Workshop	Program Duration	Type of Sessions	Site Visits (Number Given)	Mentor	Project
LIAL	X	1 week	1 week face-to-face	No	No	No
CLTP		1 year	12 webinars and 1 day face-to-face	No	Yes	No
CLDMP		1 year	3 webinars and 2.5 days face-to-face	Yes (2, one at mentor's location and one at new director's)	Yes	No

TABLE 19.5. **Program Structure Variables**						
Program	Workshop	Program Duration	Type of Sessions	Site Visits (Number Given)	Mentor	Project
HBCU		1 year	Series of workshops	Yes (2-week exchange program)	Yes	No
LFP		1 year	6 bimonthly webinars and 3.5–4 days face-to-face	Yes (2 at mentor's location)	Yes	Yes
LCDP	X	1 year	5 days face-to-face	No	Yes	Yes
LC		1 year	7 orientations, 12 classes, 4-month reassignments, 2 weeks outside LC, 1 week at another institute's leadership program	Yes (3)	Yes	Yes
RLLF		2 years	5 days, three times	Yes (4)	No	Yes
Sr. Fellows	X	3 weeks	3 weeks face-to-face	No	No	Yes
Sunshine		10 months	1 meeting face-to-face or 2 online meetings each month; sometimes combined with whole cohort meeting at state conference	No	Yes	Yes

TABLE 19.5. **Program Structure Variables**

Program	Workshop	Program Duration	Type of Sessions	Site Visits (Number Given)	Mentor	Project
Stanford	X	7 days	7 days face-to-face	No	Yes	No
MNTIEL	X	1 year	1 week face-to-face	No	No	No
Rochester	X	3 ½ days	3.5 days face-to-face	No	No	No
Snowbird	X	5 days	5 days face-to-face	No	Yes	No
TALL	X	3 years	5 days face-to-face with 2–4 follow-up activities	No	Yes	Yes
WLI	X	3 days	3 days face-to-face	No	No	No
Frye	X	1 year	10 days face-to-face	No	No	Yes
HERS		1 academic year	3 days face-to-face four times	No	No	Yes

While 10 of the programs stated mentoring was part of the program structure, it varied widely. For some of the programs the mentoring was only during the face-to-face session and was more like career coaching (Stanford, LCDP, Snowbird), while for other programs it was coaching on a project (TALL, LFP, and LCDP) or some combination of career and project coaching. Programs such as the CLDMP, CLTP, and Sunshine assigned a program-long mentor with multiple interactions.

Site visits was another reported component. CLDMP required two, one to the mentor's location and the other to the participant's location. RLLF participants visit four other sites that host the cohort. HBCU originally had a two-week exchange program in the pilot year with non-HBCU institutions. LFP incorporates two visits for a week at a time to participants' mentors' location. While LC's program may not strictly incorporate site visits, its seven orientations to different internal units, participants' desks relocated to a new office the duration of the program, and requirement to complete two four-month work assignment in other units and a two-week detail at another institution appeared to accomplish much the same value as a site visit in other programs.

While some of the programs only met face-to-face one time, the length of that time varied from a day to a three-week immersive retreat. In their final format, the five defunct programs were all a one-time workshop. Finally, nine programs had a project, with one of the nine making it optional. The projects ranged from creating a personal career plan to a research project to a leadership plan to be implemented on their home campus.

Curriculum Content

An examination of the programs' content reinforced that there was no one approach. While the delivery of the content contained some widely employed commonalities, such as use of speakers, assessments, and discussions (see table 19.6), the content (see table 19.7), even with the some of the same instructors, was not the same (LIAL and TALL, for example, both had Maureen Sullivan as a lead instructor).

TABLE 19.6. **Curriculum Delivery**	
Curriculum	Number of Programs that Employed this Method
Assessment	9
Career or leadership coaching	3
Case study	3
Discussion	11
Frame flipping[1]	2
Mentor	5
Readings	3
Scenarios	2
Speakers	9
Visit or immersive	3

TABLE 19.7. **Curriculum Content**	
Program	Curriculum Methods and Content
LIAL	Frame flipping, case studies, discussion
CLTP	Practical management skills employing emotional intelligence, Kotter's leadership definitions, and the Friedman Family Systems theory of leadership
CLDMP	Rath and Conchie's *Strengths-Based Leadership*, discussion, guest speakers (higher education administrators on the role of the library director), current issues, participants' identified areas of concern
HBCU	Creating strategy focused organizations, alignment of strategy with performance, new leadership, and transforming organizations/leading change; MBTI; scenarios; effective communication exercises
LFP	Leadership theories, implementing change, practical tools, current issues in the field, networking, career guidance, MBTI and FIRO-B, scenarios, case studies, reflective practices, and emotional intelligence
LCDP	Leadership, strategic planning, priority setting, decision-making systems, project development, cross-cultural communication, motivation, fundraising and influencing, career coaching, national project poster presentation
LC	Varied work experiences and assignments, applied practice opportunities, multiple assessments of strengths and weaknesses
RLLF	360 assessment; group projects; mentors; visits to other libraries, foundations, and corporations; immersive site visits; leadership coaching
Sr. Fellows	Immersive workshop, speakers, discussion, readings
Sunshine	Eight core leadership competencies, Kouzes and Posner's *The Leadership Challenge*, Kotter's *Leading Change*, group work, mentoring, projects
Stanford	Inspirational speakers
MNTIEL	Teamwork, problem solving, career development, decision making, discussions, readings
Rochester	Readings, Kouzes and Posner's *Leadership Practices 360 Inventory*, exercises, discussions
Snowbird	Personality type assessment, speakers
TALL	Reading, exercises, lectures, group discussions

TABLE 19.7. **Curriculum Content**	
Program	Curriculum Methods and Content
WLI	Inspirational speakers, StrengthsQuest assessment, frame flipping, leading change
Frye	Speakers, discussion, exercises, small group projects, projects
HERS	Speakers, MBTI, case studies, discussions, assignments to complete on home campus
Note: For more information about the assessments and books listed, see the individual chapters or this chapter's bibliography.	

Admittedly table 19.7 includes not just what was covered, but also how the content was delivered. (The latter was summarized in table 19.6.) Table 19.7 was presented this way because sometimes how content is delivered is an important consideration for learning styles. If the program consists of speakers, and someone is looking for an interactive learning experience, then that program may not be the best for that person.

Leadership Theories

Perhaps the most striking differences among the programs were to be found in the scope of leadership theories and authors cited. There were 25 different theories and authors mentioned. Those most heavily referenced were change management (7), transformative or transformational leadership (6), emotional intelligence (5), and frame flipping (5). Table 19.8 identifies by program which theories or approaches to leadership were mentioned. The theory or approach is listed in order of highest number of times mentioned to least. Some were grouped if only mentioned once by the same program, such as charismatic, adaptive, and assertive leadership.

TABLE 19.8. **Program Leadership Theories**	
Theory or Approach to Leadership	Programs
Change management	CLTP, CLDMP, HBCU, Snowbird, Sunshine, WLI, Frye, HERS
Transformative or transformational leadership	LIAL, CLDMP, RLLF, Stanford, TALL, Frye
Emotional intelligence	CLDMP, HBCU, LFP, Sunshine Snowbird, WLI
Frame flipping	LIAL, HBCU, RLLF, Rochester, WLI

TABLE 19.8. **Program Leadership Theories**	
Theory or Approach to Leadership	Programs
Skills theory	LC, MNTIEL, Rochester
Behavioral	Sunshine, Stanford, TALL
Situational	Stanford, TALL,
Strategic planning	LCDP, LC
Reflective practice	LFP, LC
Applied leadership	RLLF, Sr. Fellows
Charismatic, adaptive, or assertive leadership	Stanford
Facilitative or transactional leadership	TALL
Informational learning	CLTP
Shared leadership	Snowbird, Sunshine
Note: Each of these theories and approaches were discussed in the referenced program's chapter. For a general book providing an overview of many theories, Peter Northouse's *Leadership: Theory and Practice* is useful.	

Some programs referenced the creator of a theory or a proponent of a theory. John P. Kotter's work led the way with eight references, followed by Lee G. Bolman and Terrence E. Deal's five. These were captured in table 19.8 as change management and frame flipping respectively. Snowbird mentioned Warren Bennis, David A. Kolb, and Peter Senge, while Sunshine also referenced Bennis, but included Tom Peters and Stephen R. Covey. CLTP cited Daniel Goleman (captured as emotional intelligence in table 19.8) and Edwin H. Friedman.[2] Rochester and Sunshine relied heavily on James M. Kouzes and Barry Z. Posner.[3]

Supplied Evidence of Leadership Development

Recognizing that each chapter author was working in isolation describing his or her program, he or she provided many commonalities of "evidence" as support of leadership development. Nine categories were identified: self-report; increased self-awareness; publications; career movement; networking; project funded and/or completed; strategic visions, planning, or change management; teamwork or collaboration; and increased perspective of role on campus. The majority (94 percent) utilized self-reports to document leadership awareness. Publications was used the least as evidence (.05 percent). Table 19.9 provides the overview.

TABLE 19.9. Percentage of Evidence of Leadership Development by Categories

Category	% of Authors Using as Evidence
Self-report	94
Increased self-awareness	67
Publications	.05
Career movement	53
Networking	17
Project funded and/or completed	12
Strategic visions, planning, or change management	47
Teamwork or collaboration	28
Increased perspective of role on campus	17

Fourteen methods to capture evidence for the future were suggested. Some were very concrete and applied like comparing competencies of the program to other programs and groups, while others were open to interpretation such as "collect evidence of accomplishments related to the program"—evidence, accomplishments, and the meaning of related is undefined. Table 19.10 lists the methods and percentage of chapter authors recommending the method as a way to gather evidence of leadership development.

TABLE 19.10. Suggested Methods to Gather Evidence of Leadership Development

Method	% of Chapters Suggesting this Method
Case study	17
Information culled from self-reported end-of-program reports	11
Program evaluations	11
Look at actual change by examining how others used or applied program materials	24
Survey	39

TABLE 19.10. **Suggested Methods to Gather Evidence of Leadership Development**	
Method	% of Chapters Suggesting this Method
Collect evidence of accomplishments related to program	53
Journaling	.05
Dialogue and discussions (focus groups and interviews)	.05
Pre- and post-tests	.05
Career progression: Compare existing national data to program population	.24
Assess value to sponsoring organization to determine continued priority or funding	.05
Run program with same content but different length of time	.05
Study longevity of retention and application of content	33
Compare with other groups using same competencies	18

Discussion of evidence used to support leadership development and how to determine the value of a leadership development program, design a model leadership program, and take the next steps for research are discussed in the next chapter.

Notes

1. Refers to the concept of approaching an issue from different perspectives (human resources, planning, politically, and symbolically), from Bolman and Deal, *Reframing Organizations*.
2. Friedman, *A Failure of Nerve*.
3. Kouzes and Posner, *The Leadership Challenge*.

Bibliography

Bolman, Lee G., and Terrence E. Deal. *Reframing Organizations: Artistry, Choice, and Leadership*. 4th ed. San Francisco: Jossey-Bass, 2008.

Covey, Stephen R. *Principle-Centered Leadership: Strategies for Personal and Professional Effectiveness*. New York: RosettaBooks, 2009.

Friedman, Edwin H. *A Failure of Nerve: Leadership in the Age of the Quick Fix*. New York: Seabury Books, 2007.

Gallup Organization. *StrengthsQuest*. Princeton, NJ: The Gallup Organization, 2000.

Goleman, Daniel. *Emotional Intelligence: Why It Can Matter More than IQ*. New York: Bantam Books, 1995.

High Performing Systems. *The FIRO Community*. http://www.hpsys.com/firo.htm.

Kotter, John P. *Leading Change*. Boston: Harvard Business School Press, 1996.

Kouzes, James M., and Barry Z. Posner. *The Leadership Challenge*. San Francisco: Jossey-Bass, 2012.

———. *The Leadership Practices Inventory: Participants Workbook*. Revised 2nd ed. San Francisco: Jossey Bass Wiley, 2001.

Myers & Briggs Foundation. The Myers & Briggs Foundation homepage. http://myersbriggs.org/.

Northouse, Peter G. *Leadership Theory and Practice*. 6th ed. Thousand Oaks, CA: Sage Publications, 2012.

Peters, Thomas J. *Thriving on Chaos: Handbook for a Management Revolution*. New York: Knopf, 1998.

Rath, Tom, and Barry Conchie. *Strengths Based Leadership: Great Leaders, Teams, and Why People Follow*. New York: Gallup Press, 2008.

CHAPTER 20

Creating Leaders:
Lessons Learned

Irene M.H. Herold

> Changes that occur in the thinking and behavior of students in a leadership institute may be dramatic enough that they fully realize they are going home a changed person. In my case, the changes from my week at LIAL seem to have been subtle and organic, so that they went unnoticed by me initially.[1]

WHETHER LEADERSHIP DEVELOPMENT programs have helped librarians become leaders has been the focus of this book.[2] What is the purpose of a leadership development program? The response may appear obvious, but after examining 18 programs, the outcome may be subtle as noted by Anne Marie Casey above. On the surface why librarians attend leadership development programs may also seem straightforward: to develop their leadership knowledge, skills, and abilities. However, this was not always in evidence for participants due to personal factors, program goals, self-established goals, and curriculum content.

The text descriptions of the various programs' curriculum of the various programs, presented in Chapter 19 (see table 19.7) create a Wordle (figure 20.1) that highlights what was most present in the leadership development programs considered in this book. This included the method of delivery and the content, the former being an important consideration when constructing a new program.

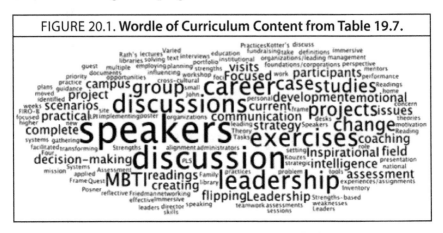

FIGURE 20.1. Wordle of Curriculum Content from Table 19.7.

Excluding the methods of delivery, figure 20.2 provides an image of the emphasis of the program's content. Leadership, change, career, and the name of a particular assessment tool now leap to the forefront of curriculum content. Although these elements were present in programs, it did not guarantee leadership development in the participants.

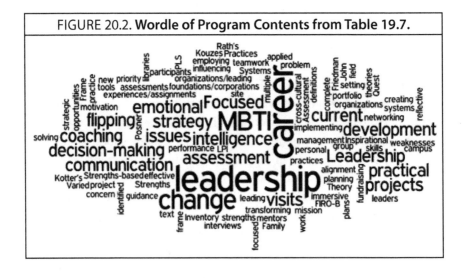

FIGURE 20.2. Wordle of Program Contents from Table 19.7.

Searching For Evidence

> The informal survey of the MNTIEL alumni suggests that
> the program is perceived as a success… This survey, howev-
> er, fails to draw any direct correlation between participating
> in the program and career movement. Nor does it demon-
> strate in any tangible ways in which the skills learned have
> helped the participants be more effective in their positions.[3]

In reviewing the authors' perceptions of evidence for leadership development, while anecdotally compelling, there was no systematically created body of evidence-based results leading to a conclusion that leadership
development programs develop leadership in participants. The authors
discussed awareness, networking, increased knowledge, career transitions,
and self-reported changes in behavior or practices applied from exposure
to program concepts. This does not mean there was no leadership development, just that only hints of evidence were presented. Even among the
authors' own perceptions and their studies of other participants some cast
doubt as to whether it was the program participation or just their own native intelligence that advanced them on their leadership pathway.

The diversity and purpose of the leadership development programs
included in this study did not always accurately reflect each program's stated outcomes. For example, one could argue that including a segment on
assessing one's leadership strengths and weaknesses when the program's
focus is retaining diverse populations in the profession is more about career coaching than leadership development. The College Library Directors' Mentor Program (CLDMP), for example, does not purport to be a
leadership development program, but as the name implies, for the past 22
years it has facilitated a mentoring relationship between a new director and
an experienced director, a network of past participants and mentors via
a listserv, and a face-to-face seminar that includes leadership assessment
content. In short, it is focused on the managerial aspects of running a small
college library. Does this lead to leadership development? The perception
from participants is yes, but there is no documented evidence to support
their claim. This begs the question then, What is the value of attending a
leadership development program?

Determining the Value of a Leadership Development Program

> The fact that the perceptions and perspectives of former fellows have remained stable over time lends substantial credibility to the program. Members... surveyed... noted that the most important aspects of the program were professional networking opportunities, big picture discussions, and dedicated time away from the workplace... Key takeaways included a better understanding of leadership issues and greater personal insight and self-awareness.[4]

With no consistent assessment of whether a leadership development program's approach develops leadership, other considerations must be made to determine the value of participating in a program. On the whole, attendance at a one-day, three-day, or even a week-long leadership development program probably created a greater awareness of leadership in participants. It would be unrealistic, however, to expect enduring change from a one-off experience, unless participants were required to apply such awareness when they returned to their campus.

For the library, having a team member with a greater awareness of leadership and exposure to change management means there is someone who understands what foundational components need to be in place to accomplish dynamic change. Attendees may have learned about tools and resources to help the library through these processes. Whether the program participant leads or serves as a team member working to effect change, the individual will be more understanding of what the process entails and how to help the team move to a desired outcome.

During leadership development programs, participants often assess their leadership strengths and weaknesses. Librarians who have participated in leadership development may return more confident in their abilities due to having undergone an assessment of their strengths. The result of increased confidence may be a willingness to accept further responsibilities, such as chairing a committee instead of simply serving as a member or initiating a program rather than supporting one.

Many participants in library leadership development programs reported feeling supported. This feeling may have been the result of someone encouraging them or nominating them to apply to a program. Just this action was often reported as an indication to the nominees that someone saw their potential or viewed them as a leader in a way they may have not perceived. Those whose programs included a mentor reported feeling their perspectives were validated, giving them confidence as they implemented change at their home institutions.

Participants returned from their experience with a network of other developing leaders and program instructors whom they may consult with. Networking in this instance is not only about a group to bounce ideas off for approaches to issues in common, but also a place to transition from being mentored to mentoring others as the individual grows and learns. Having a cohort who hears and endorses your ideas about how to approach an issue can further an individual's confidence about his or her applied leadership practices.

PARTICIPANT CONSIDERATIONS FOR PROGRAM SELECTION

Lois Merry wrote, "Institutional agendas don't align perfectly with any individual's, and it is imperative for career academics to understand the difference and to know what they can reasonably expect and, even more importantly, what they ought never to expect."[5] Substituting *leadership development programs* for *institutional agendas*, this sentiment could be applied to potential program participants. Knowing what to reasonably expect from a program may make a difference in the effect of the program on the participant.

After reviewing 18 programs, there are a wide variety of approaches. Potential participants need to be clear about their expected outcomes before determining which program will best meet their needs. Do they desire exposure to concepts of leadership? Then a one-time workshop may suffice as an introduction. If they are looking for a network, do they want one with librarians at the same point in their career or a mix of more experienced (mentor or coach) librarians? At the end of the program do they expect to have an action plan? Then a program that includes creation of such a plan for change, such as a scenario, case study, project for their home campus, or blueprint, may be most applicable.

Librarians need to consider their preferred learning style. The review of program structures completed in Chapter 19 pointed out the various learning approaches structured into the programs. If someone learns best passively, then a lecture-based program should be considered. Engaged learning may come from a program that includes exercises, group discussions, and projects. A busy professional who is constantly pulled away from learning may find an immersive program with clearly defined times to not be engaged in work a preferred approach.

How much time participants have to devote to a program is another consideration. While the majority of programs were split between a one-time face-to-face workshop lasting from a few days to a week (27 percent) and approximately a year-long program (72 percent), the amount of activities and commitments, whether presentations, webinars, or site visits, are additional factors that may influence a participant's ability to complete a program and enjoy its benefit. Viewing webinars and site visits as something to be endured and checked off a must-do list rather than opportunities for learning can influence a participant's ability to perceive and implement a program's facets. Participant need to be knowledgeable about the time commitment needed for a program and prepared to embrace it before signing up.

LEADERSHIP THEORY

There is neither one leadership theory that is best for a leadership development program nor one model that should be employed in all situations requiring leadership. In determining what to study, individuals need to be self-aware of their strengths and weaknesses, which is why so many programs include a self-assessment tool. In creating a program, developers need to first consider their theoretical underpinnings, and then what to present. The four most commonly referenced leadership theories or models were change management, transformative or transformational leadership, emotional intelligence, and being able to employ frame flipping.

Change management provides an approach to creating dynamic change in an organization and, for John P. Kotter, includes a multistep iterative process framework that leaders can employ to achieve change. Transformative, or transformational leadership, is about a process that changes or transforms individuals and is concerned with assessing followers' motives and satisfying their needs while treating them as individuals. Emotional intelligence is the ability to be aware of one's own and others' emotions and inspiring them to accomplish more than they thought they could achieve by guiding them through this awareness. Frame flipping is the ability to approach an issue and apply four different lenses: human resource, structural, political, and symbolic. Being aware of a person's dominant frame, but learning how to employ the others, strengthens a leader's repertoire of tactics to achieve solutions.

A few of the programs incorporated multiple leadership approaches and theories. Some used a skills or traits approach, which may be useful if the goal of the program is to increase awareness of what makes one a leader. Other programs incorporated leadership theories that had tools to employ, such as frame flipping. Some of the programs included case studies and scenarios, asking participants to identify what were the leadership actions and how else the leader may have approached the issue based upon the theoretical model previously presented to the group.

Designing a Model Program

The enduring programs did have some components in common. These should be considered if designing a new leadership development program, regardless of the target audience.

FINANCIAL

Enduring programs may have originated using external funding, but virtually all moved to a self-sustaining model. If the program cannot generate enough revenue to pay its bills, it will not be able to function. Some programs have association or institutional support, such as TALL and LFP, but the majority are run on a fee-based business model.

Fees charged for each program also vary. While the RLLF program may cost the participant's institution up to $30,000 over the life of the program, it is multiyear and has a multisite visit schedule. The CLDMP may only charge $750 as the maximum program fee with a sliding scale for institutions with an acquisitions budget lower than $50,000 annually, but then participants or their institutions pay for travel, lodging, and some meals during the seminar. The CLDMP program pays for expenses incurred during the site visits to the participant and mentor libraries. The Sunshine program requires a $250 registration fee, and like CLDMP, other costs incurred during the program are the participant's responsibility.

To be self-sustaining the following costs should be considered:

- transportation of cohort from lodging to meeting location or other sites during the seminar;

- honorarium and expenses (travel, meals, parking, etc.) for seminar instructors and guest speakers;
- paid staff or volunteers (and how are volunteers thanked—a gift, an honorarium, etc.);
- meals (including breaks during the program day);
- materials (books, photocopying, online access to materials and assessments);
- evaluation (internally or externally compiled and analyzed);
- reports;
- grants and grant management;
- planning; and
- promotion and marketing of the program.

While not all programs may need to expend funds on these costs, and this list is by no means all inclusive, it should give a starting point for program planning.

COHORT SIZE

While some of the longest running programs have large cohort sizes, they also are supported by national networks of multiple higher education organizations (WLI and HERS) or have strong brand recognition coupled with a national academic librarian association (LIAL). Programs with very small cohorts (CLTP, LFP, LC, and MNTIEL) have strong institutional financial support. The ARL programs (RLLF and LCDP) and HERS required the participants' institutions to subsidize the participants' funding. The still running, self-sustaining, fee-based programs (LIAL, CLDMP, Sr. Fellows, Sunshine, TALL, and WLI) have an average cohort size of 57 participants, but removing the two largest cohort size programs (LIAL and WLI), 24 is the average cohort size for the remaining four. Whatever the cohort size, instructional pedagogy needs to be taken into account and able to be effective with the group.

LOCATION

Locations of face-to-face components fell into three categories: a retreat location, an institutional site, or a conference center at a hotel. Some programs were held at a consistent location, while others moved around. Programs with a fixed annual location have an advantage of a consistent travel and local arrangement organizational structure for program planners. For participants, costs are easier to estimate with a fixed location, although distance if located on one coast or the other may have led to more regional participation than diverse, national attendance. This did not seem to hamper broad national and international attendance at LIAL, but brand recognition may have factored into this success. Those attached to a conference were held at the conference venue or nearby. Retreat locations at resorts had the benefit of being away from business, but were sometimes thought of as an excuse for a vacation and therefore perceived more frivolous than programs held elsewhere. If a retreat location is perceived to be of value for the program, then the program marketing literature must clearly define what that benefit is. Shellie Jeffries succinctly did so for Snowbird when discussing the Wasatch Mountain location, she said, "Taking advantage of the stunning location, the program also balanced the intellectual content with recreational activities."[6] Since the program included content on emotional intelligence and resonant leadership, taking time to renew oneself was part the program.

VALUE OF THE NETWORK

Satisfaction with programs and feelings of enduring value appeared to be more common with programs that provided an on-going connection for past participants. Whether through reunions at conferences, a listserv, or virtual space on the Internet, individuals with such a connection tended to discuss the enduring value of the program. They also helped market the program through word-of-mouth, and the value was renewed for those individuals.

VARIED CURRICULUM STRUCTURE

While the structure of curriculum delivery varied, a majority of programs utilized the following delivery methods:

- Face-to-face seminar
- Webinar
- Site visits
- Listserv
- Internet-based social communication platform

PROGRAM CONTENT

Desiring to create a leadership development program did not always actually develop such a program. The CLDMP was a case in point. The CLDMP was established by the College Library Section (CLS) to develop new directors. Except for being considered to be part of CLS leadership development activities in section reports, it was actually a managerial-based program, which only recently explicitly added leadership development content.

Leadership development programs were established for a wide variety of reasons, such as to create association leaders, help early and mid-career librarians explore career directions, support exploration of positions above participants' current position in where they work or beyond, and broaden knowledge and skills of existing leaders. Knowing the purpose for the program should then lead to the establishment of clear learning outcomes. The outcomes then must have goals and actions for achieving the goals. A goal could be increase awareness of leadership approaches to problem solving with the action being the teaching about frame flipping during the program. A pre- and post-program evaluation could then be made to evaluate whether participants increased their knowledge of leadership approaches to problem solving. Determining if this results in changed practice and therefore leadership development directly tied to a program is something to be considered under further research.

Taking the Next Steps

Many programs used the immediate post-program evaluation as evidence that they met their learning outcomes for leadership development. Other programs surveyed participants during and after participation, with a few programs engaging in longitudinal surveys several years after participants had gone through the program. This type of information collection only speaks to participants' perception of their leadership development. Of course, no one wants to waste time or money attending a program that does not develop leadership, so the value of this type of information collection is the reassurance that others found the program to be of value. However, it does not provide evidence that leadership was developed as a result of attending a particular program.

Creating a tool to demonstrate leadership development across all academic library leadership programs is highly unlikely. Just as each program has different goals, they might need different ways to capture evidence.

Early and mid-career librarian targeted programs might want to focus on career change but in ways beyond the fact of a position move. Those in leadership positions who desire to expand their leadership knowledge and skills will need to look at other factors.

Programs that are for early and mid-career librarians to explore their potential move into leadership positions need to do more than just track what positions former participants now hold and if they are different. A system needs to be put in place that demonstrates a positive correlation between participation in a leadership development and career movement. Such a system could be a former participant informing the program when he or she changes jobs and giving permission for a questionnaire or interview to be completed by the hiring supervisor and the former participant. The questionnaire or interview could include questions to the hiring supervisor about whether the presence of attending the leadership development program on the individual's resume contributed positively or negatively or was a neutral factor in him or her being hired. Questions about knowledge and skills thought to be developed during the leadership development program could also be asked of the hiring supervisor as to their importance to the position and the hiring of this individual. The same questions would also need to be asked of the former participant, but couched in terms of were these skills and leadership knowledge discussed during the recruitment process and did the former participant emphasize any of them in his or her cover letter or resume when applying for the position.

For research documenting evidence of leadership development in a participant who already holds a leadership position, perhaps the most meaningful approach would be to track changes in participant's behavior. If the participant's supervisor, leadership team members, campus peers, and employees notice positive changes, these changes would support the positive outcome perception commonly held by program alumni. Besides observation, participants could keep a brief log or journal of what they learned during the program. Then for a year after participation note when an action was taken or a procedure or policy was completed and how they applied their increased leadership awareness, knowledge, and skills to that instance. During the next performance review a discussion of the year's leadership development activities could be substantiated and noted, reinforcing the value and leadership development outcome of program participation. A researcher could then request case studies of applied, documented leadership actions from program alumni, which would be based upon more than self and others' perceptions of the participant seeming to be more confident.

Conclusion

The 18 programs studied in this book provide a diverse template for those contemplating attending a leadership development program or creating one. There is much room for study of leadership development and whether programs actually develop leadership in their participants. Many of the programs reviewed have strong adherents who truly feel they would not be the leaders they are today without having attended their programs. That is a strong testimonial to the perceived effectiveness of academic library leadership development programs.

Notes

1. Casey, Chapter 1, 17.
2. Some portions of this chapter were originally published in an article for *Library Issues* and have been adapted and revised for use in this chapter: Herold, "How to Develop Leadership Skills."
3. Dawes, Chapter 13, 196.
4. Ryan, DeLong, and Garrison, Chapter 10, 149.
5. Merry, Chapter 18, 315.
6. Jeffries, Chapter 14, 222.

Bibliography

Herold, Irene M.H. "How to Develop Leadership Skills: Selecting the Right Program for You." *Library Issues* 35, no. 2 (2014): 1–4.

Contributors

Neal Baker is the library director at Earlham College in Richmond, Indiana. His publications span SF/fantasy scholarship, librarianship, and information services. He is a senior bibliographer for the MLA International Bibliography.

Miranda Bennett is the head of liaison services for collections and research support at the University of Houston. She received her MLS from Indiana University and her PhD in religious studies from the University of Virginia.

Rachel Besara is the director of STEM libraries and research initiatives at Florida State University.

Vicki D. Bloom is the dean of library services at Indiana University South Bend. Previously, Vicki held positions at University of California, Riverside; Alzheimer's Association; and Loyola University Chicago. Her most recent publication is a reading guide to auto racing (https://sites.google.com/site/raceintoreading/).

Carolyn Carpan is head of collection development at Central University Libraries, Southern Methodist University. She is the author of the books Rocked by Romance: A Guide to Teen Romance Fiction; Jane Yolen, part of the Who Wrote That? series; and Sisters, Schoolgirls, and Sleuths: Girls' Series Books in America.

Anne Marie Casey is dean of retention and student success at Embry-Riddle Aeronautical University. She holds an AMLS degree from the University of Michigan and a PhD in managerial leadership in the information professions from Simmons College.

Jon E. Cawthorne is the dean of libraries and university librarian at West Virginia University in Morgantown, West Virginia. He graduated from the College of Information Studies at the University of Maryland, College Park, and holds a PhD in managerial leadership in the information professions from Simmons College.

Trevor A. Dawes, associate university librarian at Washington University in St. Louis, earned his MLS from Rutgers University and has two MA degrees from Teachers College, Columbia University. He is an active member of ALA and a past president of ACRL.

Leland R. Deeds is the head of systems and an information systems librarian at the University of Miami Libraries.

Kathleen DeLong is the senior human resources officer for learning services at the University of Alberta in Edmonton, Alberta, Canada. She earned her PhD in managerial leadership in the information professions from Simmons College.

Catherine Dixon is the library director at St. John's College in Annapolis, MD.

Julie Garrison is the associate dean of research and instructional services at Grand Valley State University Libraries in Grand Rapids, Michigan. Julie also held positions as director of off-campus library services at Central Michigan University and associate director of public services at Duke University Medical Center Library. She received her MLIS from UCLA.

Irene M.H. Herold is the university librarian for library services at the University of Hawai'i at Mānoa. Her PhD is in managerial leadership in the information professions from Simmons College. In addition to attending three leadership development programs, she was the program director of the College Library Directors' Mentor Program from 2012–2013. Irene is the 2016-2017 ACRL President.

Melissa Jadlos is the library director at St. John Fisher College in Rochester, New York. She is also codirector of the College Library Directors' Mentor Program since 2013.

Shellie Jeffries is the codirector of the Grace Hauenstein Library at Aquinas College in Grand Rapids, Michigan. Shellie previously worked at the University of Illinois at Urbana-Champaign and Wayne State University. She received her ML from the University of Washington.

Vivian Lewis is the university librarian at McMaster University in Hamilton, Ontario, Canada. Vivian is a frequent speaker and writer on topics related to strategic planning, library assessment, professional development, and workforce transformation.

Adriene Lim serves as dean of libraries and Philip H. Knight Chair at the University of Oregon. Adriene's prior positions were dean of libraries at Oakland University and other leadership roles at Portland State University and Wayne State University. Adriene's PhD is in managerial leadership in the information professions from Simmons College.

Jennifer McKinnell is the director of the Health Sciences Library at McMaster University in Hamilton, Ontario, Canada. Previously, Jennifer served as the head of public services and the education coordinator. Jennifer participated in the 2011–2012 cohort of the National Library of Medicine/Association of Academic Health Sciences Libraries Leadership Fellows Program.

Lois K. Merry retired in June of 2014 as a professor providing reference and instruction at the Mason Library at Keene State College in Keene, New Hampshire. She is the author of the 2011 book *Women Pilots of World War II: A History with Biographies of American, British, Russian, and German Aviators.*

Teresa Y. Neely, PhD, is associate professor and director of learning space initiatives at the University of New Mexico's College of the University Libraries and Learning Sciences.

Monika Rhue is the director of library services at the James B. Duke Memorial Library, Johnson C. Smith University in Charlotte, North Carolina. Monika received the ACRL Harvard Leadership Institute Scholarship, attended the HBCU Library Alliance Leadership Institute, and authored *Organizing and Preserving Family and Religious Records: A Step-by-Step Guide.*

Ann Campion Riley is the associate director of libraries for access, collections, and technical services at the University of Missouri, Columbia. She is the 2015–2016 ACRL president.

Martha Rinn, associate professor and university librarian, Texas Lutheran University in Seguin, Texas, holds the Luther W. and Ruth E. Sappenfield Chair in Library Science. She has participated in the College Library Directors' Mentor Program and the TALL Texans Leadership Institute. She received her MLIS from the University of Texas.

Marianne Ryan is the associate university librarian for public services at Northwestern University. Previously she held positions at Purdue University and the University of Maryland libraries. She received both her MA in library and information science and PhD in higher education policy from the University of Iowa.

Karen B. Walfall is a digital reference specialist at the Library of Congress.

Jeff Williams is the associate director of research, education, and clinical support for the Health Sciences Library, New York University Langone Medical Center. He received his MLIS from UCLA.

Index